T0323483

The New World of Work

Arguing that a functional approach to Human Resource Management is fast becoming obsolete, this book explores the many areas of accelerated change in the workplace and how business leaders must evolve their thinking to meet the needs of their workers and managers alike.

With a clear focus on the accelerations caused by Covid-19 and how technological platforms have enabled working practices and business continuity, the book effectively lays the groundwork for a changed but well-functioning people management system. The authors present the new model of Strategic Human Asset Lifecycle Management that incorporates the drastic changes in how jobs are designed, how human talent is acquired, how work is performed, how work is rewarded and conditions set, and crucially, how labor laws must change – all to meet the fast-moving requirements of a digitized world.

Enriched with cases that illustrate both well-adapted and badly adapted organizations, as well as helpful summaries and thought-provoking challenges, this book is an essential resource for all those who aspire to great people leadership in their organizations, including HR professionals, instructors, and upper-level students.

Bashker "Bob" Biswas, Ph.D., is a senior professor at DeVry University/Keller Graduate School of Management.

William Garrison, M.Ed., MBA, is a professor and an online faculty chair at DeVry University and Keller Graduate School of Management.

Robert L. Ramirez, DBA, is an award-winning professor of International Business and faculty chair at DeVry University and Keller Graduate School of Management.

"A must read for current and future Leaders! The authors take readers to new depths as they challenge the reader to re-think 'old' HR concepts by creating, embracing, and adjusting to processes necessary for a digitalized workplace and a 'New World'!"

Charlotte Phillips, Department of Defense (Retired)

"Given how much – and how rapidly – the world has changed, no one can afford to be left behind. From philosophy to practice, this book helps leaders to ensure that their organizations stay at the forefront of HR innovation."

Mark Stackpole, MA, EdD, Director of the Office of Academic Success and Instructional Support (University of the Pacific)

"As changes in daily life and business have accelerated based on technological advances, the growth of 'applications', and regulatory and legal changes followed by Covid-19, we've had to rethink how and where we work, hire, get work done, etc. With that context, *The New World of Work* is the perfect resource for HR practitioners and business leaders to use to lead the reengineering of the HR function on the changing nature of work. I applaud the authors for so capably handling this critical topic that has thoroughly dominated my profession's focus for the last 2 years!"

David Fay, Chief People Officer (Countsy)

"In an ever-changing world and digital age, continuous formulation and modifications of total structure are unavoidable."

Ibiyomi Ogunbiyi, Director of Compensation, Benefits, and Operations (Green Africa Airways)

"A timely, informative, and strategic approach to human resource management and how the function needs realignment due to the changing work environment."

Dr. Robert Abel, Jr., Chief Academic Officer (Abraham Lincoln University)

"Insightful content based on actual HR experience and evolution that would enable today's HR professionals towards the ongoing journey of change."

Nour Chbaro, Former CHRO, HR, & Change Management Consultant

"Dr. Biswas is the most skilled and knowledgeable teacher of Best Human Resource practices in general and Employee Compensation in particular. His books would be my first choice!"

William Young, 40-year veteran of corporate and private Human Resource practice

The New World of Work

People Leadership in The Digital Age

Bashker "Bob" Biswas,
William Garrison,
and Robert L. Ramirez

 Routledge
Taylor & Francis Group

LONDON AND NEW YORK

Cover image: Getty

First published 2023
by Routledge
4 Park Square, Milton Park, Abingdon, Oxon OX14 4RN

and by Routledge
605 Third Avenue, New York, NY 10158

Routledge is an imprint of the Taylor & Francis Group, an informa business

© 2023 Bashker Biswas, William Garrison and Robert L. Ramirez

The right of Bashker Biswas, William Garrison and Robert L. Ramirez to be identified as authors of this work has been asserted in accordance with sections 77 and 78 of the Copyright, Designs and Patents Act 1988.

British Library Cataloguing-in-Publication Data
A catalogue record for this book is available from the British Library

Library of Congress Cataloging-in-Publication Data
Names: Biswas, Bashker, 1944– author. | Garrison, William, author. | Ramirez, Robert L., author.
Title: The new world of work : people leadership in the digital age / Bashker Biswas, William Garrison and Robert L. Ramirez.
Description: 1 Edition. | New York, NY : Routledge, 2023. | Includes bibliographical references and index.
Identifiers: LCCN 2022023962 (print) | LCCN 2022023963 (ebook) | ISBN 9780367641290 (hardback) | ISBN 9780367641283 (paperback) | ISBN 9781003122272 (ebook)
Subjects: LCSH: Personnel management—Technological innovations. | Management information systems. | Leadership. | Organizational change.
Classification: LCC HF5549.5.T33 B57 2023 (print) | LCC HF5549.5.T33 (ebook) | DDC 658.300285—dc23/eng/20220725
LC record available at https://lccn.loc.gov/2022023962
LC ebook record available at https://lccn.loc.gov/2022023963

ISBN: 978-0-367-64129-0 (hbk)
ISBN: 978-0-367-64128-3 (pbk)
ISBN: 978-1-003-12227-2 (ebk)

DOI: 10.4324/9781003122272

Typeset in Bembo
by Apex CoVantage, LLC

I dedicate this book to my granddaughter, Mayah.

Dr. Bashker Biswas

To my mom, Susan Garrison. Oh, the Places You Have Inspired Me to Go!

Professor William Garrison

To my amazing wife, Patricia, and talented children Bryan, Michael, Melissa, Shawn, Matthew, and Megan. Keep living your dreams, challenge yourself, love abundantly, and enjoy each day.

Dr. Robert L. Ramirez

Contents

14   The Obsolete Labor Laws

BASHKER BISWAS

15   People Analytics and Measurements

BASHKER BISWAS

Foreword

In a sign of the times, three authors, Professor William Garrison, Dr. Robert L. Ramirez, and Dr. Bashker "Bob" Biswas, all members of the faculty at DeVry University and its Keller Graduate School of Management, collaborated remotely on a venture that heralds the changing landscape of the world of Human Resources. They are all professors in its College of Business and colleagues who work together on various academic matters regularly. Professor Garrison and Professor Ramirez are also faculty chairs. They have never met in person and are geographically dispersed across the length of California, with Professor Garrison in Bakersfield in the Central Valley, Dr. Ramirez in Santa Clarita in Southern California, and Dr. Biswas in Lincoln in Northern California. Despite their physical distances, they teamed up on all elements of this project including concept development, outlining, writing, editing, proofreading, and engaging with the publisher on preproduction and postproduction activities.

Ventures such as this would have been nearly unthinkable not long ago. The last couple of years have witnessed tectonic shifts in the way work gets done, hastened by the global pandemic, causing a new workforce landscape to emerge and evolve. This new world order is characterized by virtual and remote work, digital and artificial intelligence (AI)-enabled transformation of traditional work processes, Gig Workers, and new generations in the workforce that demand a focus on environment, social, and governance (ESG) themes that extend well beyond traditional profit-motives. Consequently, Human Resource professionals will have to consider the short- and long-term impacts on organization culture and employee relations, even as they navigate through archaic global employment laws, transition to appropriate compensation mechanisms, redefine the nature of supervision and management, adapt to more effective modes of employee communication, and find ways to analyze and predict behaviors that support or derail the missions of the organizations they serve.

Organizations increasingly are also being called upon to build a culture of inclusion – one where all employees feel comfortable to share their views and perspectives and offer up their skills. Those which fully leverage diversity of thought, background, and experiences will reap the benefits of innovation and enhanced performance. In this era of scarce talent, going beyond traditional hiring sources in the quest for diverse talent will not only broaden the pool, discourage biases, and question stereotypes but will also allow us to create a society that is just and more equitable.

HR professionals can no longer be mere bystanders, watching from the sidelines as the World of Work changes and evolves. HR, which was once viewed as a "back-end" function, will have to lead from the front. How the function deploys can be a gamechanger in winning the war on talent and achieving a competitive advantage for the business.

The changes described above have enveloped us all, as employers or employees – in corporations, government, or other institutions. The academic world has also been upended, and the authors have also been deep participants in this change. It is no wonder they have combined their collective experiences and intellect to write this paradigm-shifting book.

There is a vacuum in organized thought, scholarship, and know-how, which documents the issues that may be holding us back while exploring potential solutions. This new book seeks to do just that and is a timely attempt to fill this gap. It is a collection of the most significant changes as they exist today and is a pivotal asset for anyone who leads, supervises, manages, or advises in the field of people management. The book is a road map for the changing nature of Human Capital Management, work relationships, and digital structures. It discusses and analyzes the various dimensions and facets of the changing Nature of Work in a systematic manner. The book comes out at the right time, because decision makers are now working diligently to adjust to all the different ways work is being done in a postpandemic, digitized, remote, and technologically intensified world.

Given the role of the HR function is also rapidly changing, this book will serve as a guide for astute HR professionals to reengineer the profession and their roles so they can quickly adapt and successfully operate within this new paradigm and also lead their organizations to success.

This book discusses a myriad of elements within the Human Capital Management process and presents a renewed model for conceptually and practically looking at the Human Capital Management life cycle.

Beyond Human Capital professionals, this book will also help other business and organizational leaders to evaluate and redesign the people management function. Every organization is unique and impacted by the pace of change differently; therefore, standardizing best practices may not always be appropriate. This book will enable the reader to critically examine the nature of changes and their implications on the workforce and business and provide thought-provoking insights into how best to customize and redesign processes that will be a "best fit" as opposed to a "best practice". It is THE book you will want to guide you right now as you navigate the new and uncharted waters of Human Capital Management.

Sandra Mahadwar
Senior Vice President of Talent Management
and Chief Inclusion & Diversity Officer, KLA Corporation

Preface

A recent IBM advertisement asked us all to rethink how the world works and that changing isn't for tomorrow, it's imperative for today. The advertisement goes on to say that the way we work is being reimagined at every level, not just where we do it, but what we do, and, most important, how we do it.

The World of Work is transforming rapidly. The devastating economic effects of Covid-19, technological advances, environmental challenges, and shifting demographic patterns have all dramatically altered the employment landscape. The World of Work is transforming. Artificial intelligence, robotics, and automation will make this transition as significant as the mechanization movement in the prior generations of manufacturing and agriculture. On the one hand, some jobs will be lost, while on the other hand, many jobs will be created. Almost all will change.

If this is the case, as more prognosticators say it is, it is indeed the New Normal, or even the new abnormal, or a significant pivot. Then, how we manage Human Resources and/or Human Capital also has to be reimagined. How we acquire, motivate, maintain, develop, and redeploy human assets need to be reimagined. This book is all about this reimagination.

Currently, one can say that there are Four Forces of change that seem to be ushering in seismic change to the future of work and thus human relations and Human Capital Management in the workplace. These Four Forces are digitization, new public health crises, environmental sustainability, and demographic changes leading to creative talent management.

A young financial analyst in the early 1970s whose primary job was to tabulate a lot of data had to use a slide ruler to do all the calculations. That took a lot of time. That analyst, fresh out of college, to create job security for himself, had to spend many hours to complete the tasks given to him. Many of those hours were after the workday ended. He burnt the midnight oil completing all his required work with a trusted slide ruler.

A few years later came the large-sized desktop adding machines made by Sharp, Burroughs, and Olivetti. That made the computational tasks a little easier for the young man. Then started the march of calculator innovation. Over the past five decades, the calculator has moved from slide rulers to Anita machines, to Friden calculators, to Texas Instruments and HP calculators, and now on to applications on handheld cell phones, and finally to voice-activated calculating applications. Now, look where we are with the required computations in the workplace. This is one example that shows how technology affects how work gets done in the current workplace. And there is more technology to come.

David Susskind, in his book, *A World Without Work*, starts by talking about the "Great Manure Crisis". He dramatically discusses the fact that the invention of the combustion engine made the "horse" completely obsolete. In his book, he suggests that, according to the Noble Prize–winning economic scientist, Wassily Leontief, a new technology, the combustion engine, ultimately took the existing central factor of economic life – manual labor – and banished it to the periphery (Susskind, 2020).

"Thinking machines" and exponential advancements in artificial intelligence are yet central factors that the concept that "humans do jobs" will be banished to the periphery. This is one of the two primary forces compelling us to take a look at the New World of Work and the role of traditional Human Capital and Resources.

During the past three decades, technological advancements have dramatically changed how organizations perform work with exponential speed. With the rapid development and encroachment of robotic technologies into various aspects of existing human endeavors, more significant changes are expected with how humans will perform the required work.

In just a few months, the world experienced the most significant pandemic in the past 100 years to accelerate these change paradigms further. The Covid-19 Pandemic crisis that began in early 2020 forced and continues to force further accelerated change upon us humans in ways that were not faced in a very long time. How we live our lives is undergoing forced alterations.

Also, environmental sustainability concerns and challenges are gaining more traction in many companies. This is because of the ever-growing implications of catastrophic incidents that Climate Change has brought upon us and continues to threaten us into the future throughout the world. In organizations and businesses, there is no doubt that to maintain economic viability and mitigate the effects of the projected increase in the earth's temperature by 1.5 centigrade, strategic and operational actions need to be implemented by the end of the current century. Senior Management proactively has to facilitate driving the execution of the organization's efforts in sustainability management (Susskind, 2020).

A case can be made, which this book plans to do, that the Human Resource function and its leaders are uniquely positioned to tackle these existential challenges. This is mainly because the Human Resource function is responsible for people initiatives within organizations. And environmental sustainability management can be regarded as primarily a "people" issue within organizations. This would involve broadening HR functional responsibilities to include sustainability management by making their Human Resource policies and programs "green" emphasizing practices that lead to "sustainability".

Due to Climate Change, governmental pressure, and societal demands, "sustainability" has become a critical strategic concern in several organizations resulting in increased demand for greater environmental and social responsibility.

In many businesses, this change in focus is leading to a different way of managing. In addition to financial objectives of growth and profit, organizations should set goals centered around being held accountable for the impact their actions have on society and the environment. Assessing social and environmental risks and opportunities needs to become an operational requirement. This approach is often called "the triple bottom line", the simultaneous delivery of positive results for the planet, people, and profit. Sustainability issues, such as environmental stewardship, workplace responsibility, human rights protection, and good corporate citizenship, are becoming an extremely important component of an organization's social duties. The HR department can make or break a company's success. The HR function can be important to attaining success in a sustainability-driven firm.

Sustainability practice permeates every aspect of performing business and needs to be embedded at all levels across an organization, becoming an ongoing change process. HR professionals should lead and implement sustainability strategies since their prime focus and skills include organizational process, change management, and culture stewardship.

Social and demographic changes are also a significant impetus for change in Human Resource and Human Capital Management as we move into the future.

Family structures are changing in many places around the world. The one-parent family is becoming more and more common. Parents have to manage work, parenting, household chores, and childcare. We are witnessing an aging population worldwide, and this factor is putting more and more pressure on health and welfare services. There are continuous pressures on positive aging and gradual retirement opportunities. Then there are current and continuing pressures emanating from more positive and proactive participation of women in all levels of the corporate hierarchy.

Furthermore, organizations now have substantial external pressures to improve ethnic and religious diversity in the workplace. Then there are pressures arising out of accommodations needed for people with disabilities. Also, one must not forget the current health and stress issues arising from workplace stressors.

Finally, continual talent management issues and challenges are being faced. This category includes the dilemma that the number of people in the active labor force is dwindling despite the burgeoning population. This is because of the seismic skills and knowledge shift that the New World of Work is undergoing. This presents employers with challenges in finding the right people at the right time and place. Thus, the continuing and increasing challenges of talent and skills management. In addition, the New World of Work is fast moving to an organization that will need only a very skilled and selective workforce. These demographic changes will have profound and transformative implications for employers and organizational leaders.

So, these quadruple forces of accelerating technological advancements, unprecedented health risks, environmental sustainability, and social and demographic changes have ushered in not just New "Normals" but also new "abnormals".

New thinking needs to be implemented on how we humans will perform economically productive work, leading to possible new definitions of jobs, Employment Contracts, and employment conditions. New ideas have to be developed on how to work, and our related employment livelihoods will need to be organized. New light has to be thrown into how employer–employee relationships must be arranged. New skill profiles need to be hired, compensated, trained, and motivated in our workplaces. In essence, organizations need to rethink the entire concepts, structures, and principles of how Human Capital and Resources are utilized and managed in organizations, leading to significant pivots. After all, the forces of change stated above might require that we revisit the basic rules of employment, and we really cannot carry on just thinking business in the way it was.

The impact of the Four Forces on how work will be performed and how Human Resources and Human Capital must be managed in organizations will need a drastic rethink. There is much talk now that companies will need to change their operational mindsets under the pressure of the Four Forces.

Technology-based transitions were already in the works, and now people think it will be accelerated because of the pandemic.

There is a lot of chatter in books, journals, magazines, and the internet about the impending changes.

Let us discuss some examples.

The prestigious *Economist* magazine almost every week now has something or the other about these changes. In their June 2020 issue, the magazine talked about an analysis produced by the chief economist of Upwork (Upwork is a website where one goes to find a "Gig"). We will be discussing how "Gig Work" will be one of the major factors that will require a major rethink about how Human Resources are currently managed in organizations. Also, the impact and lessons learned from the Covid-19 Pandemic will require a massive change in future work patterns. In a survey conducted by Upwork, 62 percent of hiring managers said that their workforce would be more remote than before the Covid-19 Pandemic. Traditionally, the practice of having employees working remotely was not popular but has now been on the upswing for about a decade. And today, as we are dealing with the impact of the Covid-19 Pandemic and shutdowns, it is becoming an organizational reality. This will require a major rethink and redo of Human Resource policies and practices.

Another editorial in the *Economist* on June 27, 2020, talked about the boss of a big company, who, while talking to his staff via Zoom, was heard praising his employees about the remarkable increase in productivity at his company now that many employees were working from home. The boss continued to say in the same breath that, of course, one can say that the remarkable increase in productivity was because of a keyboarding software that was installed in all company computers when employees started to work from home. The boss then says that in his company, all parties are regarded as family, but he should be considered the Big Brother. This was meant to be tongue in cheek, but in the future, Human Resource policies may need to address the use of keyboarding, tracking, and monitoring software to prevent the concept of employee loafing while working from home and instead place a larger emphasis on the value of employees and the human element of work.

Other operational changes that are inevitable are the ways corporate communications take place, the fact that collaboration in the workplace or teamwork has to be reconfigured, and that new Human Resource systems, equitable policies, and procedures have to be established for the Insiders (the regular full-time employees) and the Outsiders (freelancers and "Gig Workers").

Another trend that will be very significant is the changing nature of the employment relationship. Therefore, this might require a major rethink of the principles that form the foundation of the current Employment Contract. In other words, there might need to be a major paradigm shift in the principles that currently govern boss-subordinate relationships. For example, the Insiders (the regular full-time employees) will receive protections insured by employers, but the Outsiders (freelancers and "Gig Workers") will not. This certainly will impact Human Resources policies and programs.

The cost of labor for Insiders is expensive because they receive benefits and other perks, naturally making the cost of labor for the Outsiders less expensive. So, will this very fact prompt employers to further reduce the ranks of the Insiders and increase the numbers of Outsiders? These factors will need significant rethinking to affect Human Resource policies and programs.

The World of Work has been changing over the past 40 years. But now, the Four Forces are now operating all over the World of Work. Some of these forces are increasing in intensity and are on their way to creating seismic change that we as humans have never encountered before.

Are we prepared to face these changes?

Are we prepared to ask ourselves these tough questions?

As a global human society, are we prepared to make the tough choices we are facing now and will be facing with greater intensity as all the countervailing forces surround us with ever-increasing velocity?

We do not think so!!

So, this book will present the challenging issues and ask the forbidden questions with the goal to stimulate thought and create discussion to harness the potential and the power of the changing Nature of Work and the changing nature of the workforce. This book is built around the premise of the carpenter's rule – "measure twice, cut once".

In addition, artificial intelligence (AI) poses a new challenge. With the rapid deployment of automation and robotics, how will employee roles and responsibilities change? What changes will be required in strategic Human Resource Management to accommodate workplace automation? Will these Four Forces usher in an era of constant downsizing? If this becomes the New Normal, then how should the Human Resource function be positioned within organizations?

We will look at all these possible change paradigms that will affect current Human Resource policies, programs, and practices. Finally, we will be presenting a new, or some might say, a renewed view of strategic Human Resource and Human Capital Management ushered in by the Four Forces.

This is a book on the required changes on how Human Resource Management should be strategically and operationally structured in the modern organization. We will address how to effectively manage the Human Resources in any entity within the context of an ever-changing work environment. These changes are being rapidly introduced because of the Four Forces of change.

Significant changes are being observed in the changing Nature of Work is currently being done and how jobs, skills, work roles, and working conditions are evolving. Changes are being designed and organized to sync with the required digital reengineering of work and, therefore, jobs. Thus, this book focuses on laying out a renewed conceptual structure and related practical applications, programs, and systems for a changed but effective operation of Human Resource Management function.

We will begin by taking a look at the principles and assumptions that currently guide Human Resource Management in most organizations. Then, the book will make a case for why these assumptions and principles need to be revisited. Next, an analysis of the efficacy of these assumptions and guiding principles in The Digital Age will be presented. Finally, a case will be made for the need to change these principles and assumptions along with a presentation of renewed structures, formulations, and programs for digitized work environments.

The book's main purpose is to present strategic Human Resource models and structures for the efficient management of an organization's Human Capital investments in the modern work environment, which is affected by the Four Forces of change.

To do so, we will discuss the historical path for the evolution of modern Human Resource Management. Our goal here will be to discuss the evolution of the "as is" processes of Human Resource Management. We will do this to set the stage for shifting the paradigm and proposing new concepts and models that arise out of the Four Forces described above. To understand the "new" Human Resource Management model, we need first to absorb where we came from. Chapter 1 is devoted to this look back.

In the rest of the book, the chapters are dedicated to the Human Resource program, policy, and system changes that will be necessary to respond to the Four Forces of change. First, we will discuss and then propose Human Resource strategic changes in programs and policies emanating from the Four Forces of change. In all the following chapters, we will introduce a new Human Resource or Human Capital dimension and the resulting implications and changes that will need to be made to existing models and structures of Human Resource and capital management.

Therefore, the main themes of the book are:

1 A critical review of the principles and assumptions of the current formulations and structures of Human Resource Management
2 A case for the need to change and focus on the obsolescence of the functional approach to Human Resource Management
3 A presentation of a renewed model for a strategic Human Resource Management system
4 A chapter-by-chapter discussion of the key required change areas within Human Resource Management

Therefore, the road map for the book is:

Chapter 1 is devoted to looking at the history of Human Capital Management as we take a look back at where the current Human Resource Management came from.

In Chapter 2, we will discuss the external and internal forces that are changing the World of Work. We will look at how the current workplace has been impacted by technological advances leading to automation and how the workforce has been impacted by globalization. We will also lay out the issue of our current skills gap and how to help fill it along with discussing how temporary work and remote work are growing.

Chapter 3 will discuss the evolution and composition of the current Employment Contract. A case will be made as to why the current macro employment model needs to be changed. This will include an in-depth view of the current four generations in the workforce. Finally, we will present a proposed conceptual structure and formulation of a changed Employment Contract that would be appropriate for the digital workplace.

In Chapter 4, we will provide evidence of how the very Nature of Work is changing and impacting how work is effectively performed in digitized workplaces. Evidence will also be provided that many of the traditional employment categories are becoming obsolete. There will be a discussion that Blue-Collar and White-Collar work designations are blending and may not be appropriate anymore. Various new concepts of work categories, such as contingent work, flexible work, and "Gig Work", will be presented and discussed. The changing nature of employment structures will also be addressed.

Chapter 5 will discuss the external and internal forces that are changing the very Nature of Work, and so are the specifics on how people work. We will look back at the motivation theories of the past and discuss how the way employers or managers relate to workers might need to be revisited also. The boss-subordinate relationship is changing. This is all the more evident as we see organizations reducing levels of management. Technology, in many cases, might take over many of the administrative activities of managers. Closely associated with these changes, we see changes in working conditions such as remote work and telecommuting. We will also look at some of the impacts of the Covid-19 Pandemic and how companies are making adjustments. This chapter will study and analyze these trends and changes.

In Chapter 6, we will focus on freelance workers. This category is becoming a significant component of many modern work environments. This is called the "Gig Economy". The leading proponents are Uber and Airbnb. The workers are neither guaranteed steady work nor regular compensation and benefits, yet they are an integral part of modern workforces. So, in this chapter, we will tackle questions such as, what does the future of such types of work look like? And how does an effective Human Resource Management process integrate such workers into the integrated culture of organizations?

Chapter 7 is devoted to managing the remote employee. This category of employee has come into extreme focus as we deal with the impacts of the Covid-19 Pandemic. It is most likely that this type of work will become more prevalent in modern work environments. In this chapter, we will emphasize the working conditions of remote workers. In addition, we will consider unique elements of the Human Resource processes as it applies to this unique category of the modern digital work environment.

In Chapter 8, we will observe the whole subject of digital communities and collaboration and how to cultivate a great corporate culture. The chapter will analyze the challenge for Human Resource professionals attempting to build high-performing work teams in digital environments. Since strong corporate cultures improve revenue, the challenge for Human Resources lies in building a culture of social cohesion in a diverse and global workforce. Various challenges that lie ahead in building powerful corporate cultures will be discussed. We will study the required levels of group intelligence, speed, problem-solving, and learning that only a culture supported by technology can deliver. This chapter also provides valuable concepts to help explain the relationship between Cultural Intelligence or C.Q. and the working generational cohorts of organizations, managers, and leaders. This leads to assessing human behavior and targeted C.Q. training, which can give companies tremendous success in culturally diverse markets.

Chapter 9 is devoted to the dimensions of organizational behavior. Organizational behavior is an examination of individual and team behavior in the workplace or an organization. This leads to assessing human behavior and its impact on work performance. Organizational behavior examines subject areas, such as motivation, leadership, communication, and teamwork. This chapter will study these concepts in the light of digitization of work and the required changes in organizational behavior. Digital leadership empowering employees to lead and create self-organized teams that optimize their day-to-day operations will be discussed.

In Chapter 10, we will propose that the Human Resource department should be the "Home of Green". With Green Human Resource Management, the people experts can lead in improving the environment and the society in which they operate. This will lead to a more positive relationship with customers and other stakeholders alike. This chapter will look at the history of The Green Movement and how it can be modified to attract more adherents. This chapter will also review how companies can adjust their Corporate Social Responsibility efforts into making real change. Finally, we offer a Green HR Framework on how to implement Green Practices into every aspect of the Human Resource processes in any company.

Chapter 11 looks at the concept of employees as owners. In this chapter, we will consider the proposition that organizations that look upon employees as owners will enhance the organization's value to other key stakeholders such as customers and shareholders in turn. There will be a discussion of the programs that can be implemented by Human Resource departments to extend the concept of Employee Ownership from both the extrinsic and intrinsic dimensions. The idea that the perception of Employee Ownership can be enhanced with appropriate human programs will be presented in this chapter.

In Chapter 12, a new formulation and structure of total rewards will be presented. We will first trace the evolution of current reward systems. Then, we will discuss the shortcomings of traditional reward systems in The Digital Age. We will also introduce and talk in detail about the new concept of paying the person or person-based pay. Finally, we will present arguments and justifications for why person pay versus job-based rewards is more appropriate in The Digital Age.

In Chapter 13, another innovation will be discussed and presented. The Human Cloud is an emergent set of work systems and structures that enable work arrangements and work completions to be established and executed through a digital/online platform. Management and control of work can be enabled through digital media. Crowdsourcing, online work services, and online staffing and onboarding platforms can be utilized in the Human Cloud. This exciting new work delivery system will be explored in this chapter.

In Chapter 14, a case will be made about the non-applicability of current labor laws to the changing digital workplace. First, the evolution and environmental factors governing the passing of current laws will be described. Then, an explanation will be provided why the assumptions about the work environment that brought about the current laws are, in many cases, no longer applicable. Thus, a discussion will be presented as to what legal protections might be more appropriate in the digital workplace.

In Chapter 15, an extensive discussion of the whole area of people data analytics and measurements will be presented. A case will be made, and an explanation will be provided about the inadequacies of current accounting rules and regulations regarding the proper accounting of Human Capital monetary outlays. Human Resource accounting concepts will be introduced. A discussion of effective Human Resource measurements will be presented. The research will describe how new sensors and "big data" can help organizations understand how people work. Explanations will be presented on how new technologies can be deployed to optimize work in various organizational units, such as call centers. Examples will also be provided on how people analytics can improve the effectiveness of various Human Resource policies.

In Chapter 16, the last chapter, we will tie everything together by proposing a new strategic approach to Human Resource Management that will be more appropriate for digitized work and connected environments. This model uses a Human Asset Lifecycle approach instead of a Human Resource approach to managing Human Resources in a technology-infused workplace.

This book's core message presents a strategic Human Resource model and structure to efficiently manage an organization's Human Capital investments in the modern digitized work environment.

Let's begin the journey!

Bashker Biswas

References

Coyle, D. (2018). *The culture code: The secrets of highly successful groups.* New York: Bantam.
Susskind, D. (2020). *A world without work: Technology, automation, and how we should respond.* New York: Metropolitan Books.

Acknowledgments

We three authors wish to acknowledge the extraordinary individuals who supported us in completing our adventure into the exploration of the New World of Work.

There were many who were instrumental in contributing to our outlooks represented in this book, and this book would not have been possible without the support of our colleagues at DeVry University and its Keller Graduate School of Management.

A special word of thanks goes to our University Deans of Teaching and Learning, Dr. Mack Modifi and Dr. Moe Saouli, for their continuous encouragement and support.

We are also grateful and would not have been able to complete the symbiosis of the content of this book without the assistance of Bhawna Tripathy who helped us in the early stages of the project remotely and as a member of the "Gig Economy".

Our appreciation also goes to Terry Clague, Amy Laurens, Meredith Norwich, Alexandra de Brauw, and Helena Parkinson from our publisher Routledge, Taylor & Francis Publishing Group, for so ably guiding this book to completion. Here also we want to acknowledge the assistance we received from Project Editor Sathyasri K and Copy Editor Sanchari Banerjee. They were calm, collected, competent, clear, concise, coherent, and cogent.

We also want to thank our many students who have helped us in various ways to improve the clarity of our thinking as we proceeded with this project. Also, their eager yearn for learning and understanding provided us continued motivation as we journeyed through understanding the new vistas of the changing Nature of Work.

All three of us, most important, want to recognize our families' patience and support, which was a constant source of motivation for the fortitude and tenacity that drove us to the fruition of this timely book.

Finally, we three authors are proof of the "Gig Economy" in The Digital Age, where we bonded as brothers, never having met in-person, but over remote technologies and sometimes in slippers and embarrassingly casual attire during the Covid-19 Pandemic, our current times of rapid change, and the evident changing Nature of Work we collaborated in while completing this project. Our learning has not yet ended, nor will it.

Chapter 1

History of Human Capital Management

Bashker Biswas

Consider the human element in companies as a capital cost rather than an operational cost.

This is the first major paradigm change in the structure and positioning of the Human Resource Management function that has been witnessed in recent years and is predicted to gain traction in the future. Human Capital Management is a step up from Human Resource Management. According to the Human Capital concept, employees should be viewed as business people and economic firm value enhancers, not just expendable resources.

It is essential to analyze the history of the human element in the workplace to comprehend this fundamental paradigm change. Taking the human factor into account in an organizational setting has been and continues to be a long and winding road. The adventure continues. The voyage of the human element has not yet arrived at its destination. This book attempts to describe a structure for this journey's culmination, the destination.

Before we delve into the future of Human Resource Management, it is worth looking back at the historical journey.

Before the advent of the Industrial Revolution, with few exceptions, people spent their whole lives working, the great majority as farmers. In the pre–Industrial Revolution era, industries such as the cotton trade were particularly hard for workers because they had to endure long hours of labor. Because of the nature of the task, the workplace was extremely hot with steam engines adding to the mix. Since machinery was not always walled off, workers were exposed to the moving parts of the machines as they worked. Because children were tiny enough to fit between tightly packed machinery, they frequently were asked to navigate between them. As a result, they were put in danger, and factory mortality (death rates) was relatively high.

Working hours were extraordinarily lengthy and debilitating, adding to the industry's risks. In the hot and physically demanding work environments, it was usual for laborers to work 14 hours or more every day. Exhaustion automatically led to the worker becoming sluggish, making the workplace more dangerous. Workers were not protected in their jobs by any laws; they were subject to being fired at any moment by their employer, who instructed them

DOI: 10.4324/9781003122272-1

what to do. They then paid them what they believed they were worth unless a labor shortage forced them to pay more. When a worker's ability to accomplish obligations to his employer's satisfaction deteriorated, he ran the risk of losing his job.

The next phase of the journey was ushered in by the Industrial Revolution. However, these changes did not lead to better working circumstances. The working class, who accounted for 80 percent of the population, had little or no bargaining power with their new employers. To find work, people from the countryside rushed to the factories in the cities in high numbers. Since substantially more unskilled laborers with minimal abilities would take any job, the new factory owners were able to set the terms of employment. This resulted in an exceptionally high unemployment rate for employees. And, because the textile industries were so new at the turn of the century, there were no regulations to protect the workers.

Migrants, desperate for work in the new industrial cities, had no bargaining leverage to demand higher wages, more equitable work hours, or better working conditions either. Most of the other unemployed or underemployed were skilled professionals, such as handweavers whose talents and experience were rendered obsolete by the efficiency of modern textile machines. Working conditions for the initial generation of laborers were harsh, even disastrous at times. Most laborers worked 10–14 hours a day, six days a week, with no paid vacation or holidays.

In addition, each industry had safety hazards. Accidents in the workplace were common under such hazardous settings. For the first generation of Industrial Revolution employees who remembered a slower and more relaxed pace in the countryside, living in the factory was particularly difficult. Factory bosses expected a complete departure from village life in pace and discipline. Workers couldn't talk to their neighbors or family like they could when they worked in the country. They couldn't go back to the village to support their relatives during harvest season unless they were willing to risk losing their jobs. Instead of being their bosses, foremen and overseers oversaw a new working culture to guarantee focused and efficient workers.

Then, on March 9, 1776, *An Inquiry into the Nature and Causes of the Wealth of Nations* (commonly referred to as simply *The Wealth of Nations*) was published. Adam Smith, a Scottish philosopher by trade, wrote the book that shifted the paradigm of the mercantilist system. He ushered in a theoretical discussion of the factors of production, along with other classical economists. Smith believed that when each individual is acting within their own self-interest, all outcomes would increase. In relation to productivity, this meant that when the employees were acting in their own self-interest, not just the employers, both the employee and the employer would benefit.

Factors of production, resources, and inputs are utilized in the production process to produce output or finished goods and services. According to a relationship known as the production function, the amounts of various inputs are used to determine the quantity of output. Land, labor, and capital are the three essential resources or components of production.

Classic Factors of Production (Adam Smith)

- Land
- Labor
- Capital

These variables are frequently referred to as "producer goods" to distinguish them from "consumer goods", which are items or services purchased by consumers. To produce a product, all three of these must be present simultaneously.

Entrepreneurship is sometimes seen as a production factor. The condition of technology as a whole is sometimes referred to as a factor of production. The number and definition of components depend on the theoretical objective, empirical emphasis, or school of economics. The structure of the discussion of the production factors depends on the particular School of Economics. Therefore, under this structure, the factors of production were land, labor, capital, and entrepreneurship.

- Land
- Labor
- Capital
- Entrepreneurship

Under the classical economics structure of Adam Smith and David Ricardo mentioned earlier, the focus was on physical resources. These economic philosophers referred to the "components parts of price". These were (1) the cost of using land or natural resources, (2) the payment for use and the received income for the landlord as rent, and (3) the wages and the revenue resulting from one's labor. Labor is the human effort employed in production, the payment for someone else's labor, and all income derived seeded from one's labor. Labor can also be defined as an employee's physical and mental contribution to the production of commodities, the capital stock, which consists of human-made goods utilized to make other goods. Machinery, tools, and structures are examples of them. Classical economists also used the term "capital" to describe money. But money was not considered a factor of production because it was not used directly to produce any good.

Another structure that evolved was Marxism, which considered the "elementary factors of the labor process" or "productive forces" to be (1) labor, (2) the subject of labor or objects transformed by labor, and (3) the instruments of labor. In addition, Marx distinguished between labor performed and an individual's "labor power", or potential to work. Labor, not labor powers, is the critical factor of production for Marx and the basis for Marx's labor theory of value.

Marxism Factors of Production

- Labor
- Subject of Labor (or Objects Transformed by Labor)
- Instruments of Labor

Neoclassical economists started with the classical factors of production of land, labor, and capital. However, it developed an alternative theory of values and distribution. Neoclassical economists added various aspects of production such as (1) capital, (2) fixed capital, (3) working capital, (4) financial capital, and (5) technological progress.

Neoclassical Factors of Production

- Capital
- Fixed Capital
- Working Capital
- Financial Capital
- Technological Progress

Labor was the human element during these early periods as it was then categorized. Although not conceived in that fashion, labor during the early times was the ability, effort, skills, time, and knowledge needed from humans to make the economic entity successful, operating, and meeting its financial objectives.

The Industrial Revolution and the History of Labor Management

Before and immediately after the Industrial Revolution, labor was considered a necessary input factor in the production process because of the brawn and the muscle required to make the organization function. As we have mentioned, masses of people moved from rural areas to work in factories and sweatshops in the urban cities during this period. And this human capacity provided the brawn and muscle needed to keep machines and factories functioning. As long as the brawn and the muscle were provided, the organization's owner employed this Human Resource. But as soon as there was a diminution in the brawn, the "labor" was discarded and replaced. And during the period of employment, wages were provided mainly at the subsistence level. Most often, labor survived but barely above dire poverty levels. But they continued to serve their company masters. This "brawn" or labor capacity was considered input into the financial value creation process but not the primary value creator. The human factor was considered a necessary but a secondary input that was not considered a value-adding factor. Human Capital was necessary to input the production process, but the owners were the real value enhancers. Thus, the owners' treatment meted out to "labor" was mainly command and control.

Personnel Management

The usage of the term "personnel" dates back to after World War II. So, before the advent of World War II, the human element in the organizational context was a mere afterthought. And the management of this function was left to the mercies of the manager and the owner. But, based on the incidence of some disruptions to the work process by employee protest actions, some enlightened owners realized that attention needed to be paid to the human element. Thus, these pioneering owners and managers ushered into a specialization called Personnel Management (PM) or employee relations. Before this specialization evolved into an organized function, certain managers were appointed as employee welfare officers, whose job was to ensure employees' welfare but addressed the lower-level needs of adequate wages and working conditions. These dedicated employee welfare officers were chartered to take care of the welfare of employees.

As indicated earlier, this formal recognition of the employee side of the production process started seeing widespread acceptance after World War II. But there is evidence of sporadic recognition of the contribution of the human as early as the 1920s. Mass production processes were the catalyst for this focus. In 1920, labor managers and employee relations managers came into being. But, after the Great Depression, large corporations began realizing the increasing need and values of hiring specialized professionals who would be in charge of recruiting, retaining, and motivating employees to achieve higher productivity levels.

In the aftermath of a problematic strike and lockout in 1901, the National Cash Register (NCR) Company established the first PM department to consider grievances, safety, dismissals, court cases, record-keeping, and salary administration. Many other factories quickly followed suit, establishing similar personnel departments. The role of such labor divisions in factories was to maintain their earlier commitment to oversee pay, safety, working hours, and other related concerns. However, this reform still meant that there were now established personnel departments to ensure that the law was followed.

Increased competition and the pressure to meet orders forced factory owners to pay attention to productivity, and concerns like employee absenteeism and excessive turnover became more prominent. Employees accepted strict standards and worked faster if given training and pay, which was prevailing. Frederick W. Taylor developed a Scientific Management Theory based on time and motion studies to determine the most efficient finish a process.

During this time, the personnel department was a tool in the employer's hands to achieve an optimal output. It disrupted strikes by blacklisting union members and compelling workers to sign "yellow-dog" contracts or agreements not to join unions. In the light of all these worker-related issues, the Personnel Administration (PA) or PM evolved into being to support the workers.

Human Resource Management

After the PM era came the human relations era from the early 1930s until the late 1950s. Within organizations, this era was marked by a growing appreciation for the importance of worker attitudes and motivation. The Hawthorne Studies of the 1930s was a catalyst for highlighting the critical nature of worker attitudes. Workers' psychological states were becoming increasingly important to industry leaders.

At the same time, the supervisor's role was changing. PM's advent and growing popularity shifted much responsibility for hiring and replacing workers away from supervisors. In addition, jobs were becoming increasingly complex, and supervisors were no longer expected to know everything about their subordinates' jobs. As a result, training programs for supervisors were implemented.

The effect of these training programs on the leader's behavior and attitudes was evaluated after the training program when the supervisors returned to their plants. The results showed that a positive impact might be obtained immediately after training. Still, these effects are significantly influenced by the "leadership climate" in the plants the supervisors returned.

The supervisor's changing role and the emerging professionalism of the personnel function characterized the beginning of human relations or the Human Resources era. It was accentuated by the new theories of the multidimensional roles of management. These changes had major implications on how organizational leaders viewed the human dimension.

Training became an essential function, and new training content was widespread. Also, training specialists were being recognized and employed. Management thinkers and luminaries such as B. F. Skinner, Chris Argyris, Douglas McGregor, and Herbert Simon dramatically influenced management thinking. They encouraged the changing role of people specialists from mere personnel officers to Human Resource managers.

Then we moved onto the Participative Management Era (1960–1990). The 1960s saw the growing application of Peter Drucker's Management by Objectives (MBO), in which managers and subordinates negotiate performance objectives for subordinates.

This somewhat distributed the formal power of leaders and ushered in a greater emphasis on employee empowerment and upward communication. Several participatory management strategies popular in Japan, such as quality circles, self-directed work teams, comprehensive quality management, and continuous process improvement, were widely adopted in the 1970s and 1980s.

In the 1960s, as Japan started flexing its industrial muscle, it recognized the need for people management systems. In addition, businesses entered the global expansion phase, and along with this trend, organizations understood the need to hire skilled and knowledgeable personnel. And PM professionals were trained to handle the human side of the enterprise.

In actuality, the term "Human Resources" is not old at all. This term evolved in the United States out of PM in the early 1960s. And by the 1980s, the term "Human Resources" started appearing, and it quickly replaced the term "personnel" or "labor".

Human Capital Management

But now, we move into the era of Human Capital Management. We started moving into this era about two decades ago. Academic literature saw publications appearing from authors such as David Ulrich and others. Born was the concept of Human Capital and the Human Resource function as a strategic business partner. Financial concepts of Human Resource metrics were introduced by seminal authors like Jaq Fitz Enz and Mark Huselid. Strategic Human Capital Management started coming to the forefront. We suggest that the foundation of the new Human Resource Management function will indeed be the concept of Human Capital Management.

What follows is the justification of the reasons for this conceptual paradigm shift.

A Company's Most Valuable Asset – The Intangibles

Let's start with the following. As an example, in a recent year, Google's (now Alphabet) stockholder's equity value was approximately $22.7 billion in their financial books. At the same time, the market value was around $179 billion. The market values Google more than Google's accountants value their equity. Why the $156 billion difference? The stock market sees $156 billion of additional value. What accounts for this additional value?

There is a shift from tangible capital assets to intangible capital assets now more than ever from an economy where factories and office buildings were key to an economy where software, ideas, brands, and general know-how matter most. The way intangible capital is accounted for (or not accounted for) distorts earnings and book value measures.

In service-led economies, a company's value is increasingly based on intangible assets, which cannot be touched, seen, or counted. It might be software; think of Google's search algorithm or Microsoft's Windows, or it might be a consumer brand like Nike.

Intangibles are also the skills of a company's workforce. In other cases, the most valuable asset is a company's culture: a set of routines, priorities, and commitments that the workforce has internalized. It may not be possible to write down culture, and it will be challenging to enter numbers on culture into a spreadsheet. Nonetheless, it may be really valuable.

Accounting for Intangibles – From Human Resource to Human Capital

Accounting for intangibles is tricky. Thus, the accounting profession has been hesitant to account for Human Resource expenditures as capital outlays. They claim that the more flexibility in converting operating costs into capital assets, the more room it has to tamper with reported results.

Today, only 15 percent of our resources are tangible, represented by easily quantifiable equipment, products, and plants. A whopping 85 percent of our assets are intangible: knowledge capital and people (Lev, 2001). So Google's $156 billion difference can be accounted for as the value of their intangibles – knowledge capital and people or their Human Capital, structural capital, customer capital or brand value, and organizational capital. All these are intangibles and, as such, are not accounted for by current accounting thinking.

If we go back 50 years, we'll find that the figure is almost the exact opposite. However, we have seen no change in our accounting practices developed for tangible asset accounting over these years. Therefore, we must look for better ways to account for intangible assets, emphasizing the entire people side of the business.

Vast Improvements in Productivity Due to the People

And when we look back, we realize that the vast improvements in productivity have been on the people side. Of course, technological advancements provided the workforce with efficient tools, but it was the people who had the knowledge, did the planning, participated in collaborations, executed those plans, supported each other, and exceeded their competitors' outputs (Gueutal & Stone, 2005).

While executives understand a cost focus, it does not account for the dynamics of people. Human Capital is the critical strategic factor that drives the return on all tangible capital investments.

Fleeting Intangible Assets and the Need for Retention

People will continue to become an increasingly critical part of an organization's intangible assets. Therefore, HR must adapt its financial practices to the unprecedented: accounting for intangibles. Future employees will stay with an employer for only about three years. Unless HR can retain a worker, that person becomes a fleeting intangible asset. The successful HR practitioner will become highly skilled at identifying true talent and increasing the time those particular people want to stay with the company. This has extensive monetary implications due to the high cost of hiring top performers. An updated financial system will account for the fact that the practice of retaining the best workers and turning over nonperformers does have bottom-line implications.

We have looked at the tremendous power of technology to propel us forward. Yet, however advanced technology becomes, it is and will be limited in its ability to accommodate the ambiguity inherent in organizations driven by the unpredictable: human beings.

Our good news/dire news predictions for the future underscore the necessity of embracing the realities of intangibles. The good news is that we have much better technology at our fingertips than we did 25 years ago. And the bad news is that technology is changing so quickly; we have difficulty keeping up with it. HR must be smarter than technology when it comes to the variability of the intangible. But variability promotes longevity, and too much specialization leaves organizations vulnerable to destruction. Standardization must happen with caution because the greater the human component, the greater the need for flexibility. Rigid strategies must be abandoned instead of strategizing, scenario planning, and incorporating flexible processes.

References

Gueutal, H. G., & Stone, D. L. (2005). *The brave new world of eHR: Human resources management in the digital age.* San Francisco, CA: Jossey-Bass.

Lev, B. (2001). *Intangibles: Management, measurement, and reporting.* Washington, DC: Brookings Institution Press.

Chapter 2

The Changing Nature of Work

Bashker Biswas

Change is the only constant. This was the reality even before the current pandemic. But now, in the year 2022, we are faced with change that is coming at us with breathtaking speed. Suddenly, companies, employers, and employees have to adjust to new ways of working. But as we move forward, there is no doubt that more change will be forthcoming.

All the technologies that have been imagined during the last decade will become a reality with even more rapidity. Robotics, artificial intelligence (AI), augmented reality, and machine learning will impact our working lives. And then there is the change we all will have to encounter from the other three forces we have talked about – environmental sustainability, demographic changes, and global health security. This is the current reality. These Four Forces will usher in a significant paradigm shift or require a significant pivot on how the Work and Talent Management concept is viewed in the changing work environment.

The Changing Nature of Work

The Nature of Work refers to one or more of the four dimensions of how gainful employment is currently regarded in society. The first of these dimensions is what we do for a living. The second is the occupations or professions we occupy in our quest for gainful employment. The third are the processes, methods, and skills we use to complete the required tasks, responsibilities, and duties. And the fourth is the structural context society has set up for engaging in gainful employment. This includes the existing organizational and institutional frameworks through which gainful employment occurs.

The Nature of Work also covers the ways our work lives affect our daily lives. This covers how we take care of ourselves and our families. It also affects our self-worth and self-esteem. It affects how we connect with the communities we live in. So, it is easy to see how gainful employment can affect all aspects of our daily lives.

DOI: 10.4324/9781003122272-2

Technology and the Changing Nature of Work

One of the recognized forces shaping how work gets done today is technology. Technology currently appears to be affecting the Nature of Work in the same manner as it did in the First Industrial Revolution in the late 1700s and early 1800s and the Second Industrial Revolution at the end of the nineteenth century. At the beginning of the twentieth century, technological innovations such as electric power, the electric motor, the telephone, machine tools, the internal combustion engine, and several new office technologies (including the typewriter and then the personal computer) all accelerated the transformation of the Nature of Work and affected all four senses described earlier (Houndshell, 1984; Yates, 1989). Existing vocations such as clerical work became increasingly mechanized and diversified into subspecialties such as typewriter and filing clerk, while new occupations such as vehicle mechanics and electricians arose. The rise of major corporations and urbanization, which created the conditions for unionization, also irreversibly altered the work environment.

The Third Industrial Revolution, or The Information Age, provided easier access to information and collaboration. This Age was marked by a democratization of energy, information, manufacturing, marketing, and logistics empowering more entrepreneurs that now had access to more factors of production than ever before. This began in the late 1960s but really exploded during the 1990s during the Dot-Com Boom.

The Fourth Industrial Revolution – Automation and Workforce Diversity

Several authors (Bell, 1973; Dertouzos & Moses, 1979; Nora & Minc, 1980; Perrole, 1987; Negroponte, 1995; Stewart, 1999) contend that present changes, like work driven by digital technology, are evidence of a Fourth Industrial Revolution known as The Digital Age. They claim that advances in microelectronics, robotics, and computer-integrated manufacturing, as well as AI, electronic data exchange experimentation, and the explosion of digital telecommunications evidenced by the unprecedented growth of the World Wide Web and the internet, have all ushered in a transformation akin to the Second Industrial Revolution. Three other external forces are usually cited as factors in the changing character of labor. The workforce demography, market globalization, and rules and regulations governing work and employment interactions are all considered factors. The changing demography of the workforce includes a growing presence of women in the labor market, particularly young mothers; increasing racial and ethnic diversity, including a declining majority of white workers; an increasing number of dual-career families; rising levels of educational attainment; and the aging of the workforce. These demographic trends have been well documented; they not only increase the heterogeneity of the working population, but they also put pressure on employers to expand existing lines of work and create new ones to meet the needs of a labor force that were previously met outside of the paid economy, through family and community.

Globalization

Globalizing product markets provide higher and more uncertain competitive pressures, broader labor markets, and a propensity toward specialization in an international division of labor. As a result, firms in the United States and Europe have embarked on a hunt for greater flexibility to maintain their competitiveness. Lean manufacturing and quality management, downsizing, business service outsourcing, contract labor, and the increased acceptance of strategic alliances, even among competitors, are all examples of this adaptability.

Technology as a Disruptor

Technology has been a significant disruptor and change agent to the Nature of Work. It has harmfully substituted human involvement with digitization in many areas. But it has also had a beneficial complementary effect. It not only has displaced workers but also has augmented human effort.

Rapidly developing digitization is steadily making more work "segmented into modules" and broken up into small stacks of tasks distributed outside and within internal entities by companies. Companies are on the way to becoming clearinghouses that orchestrate, organize, and synthesize the segmented, machine-augmented work needed to make products and services.

In a recent article, Tom Friedman, the famed *New York Times* reporter, quoted the head of the System Integration firm Infosys, Ravi Kumar, saying, "[W]ork will increasingly get disconnected from companies, and jobs and work will increasingly get disconnected from each other" (Friedman, 2020). Some work will be done by machine automation, some will be done in a factory or office, and some will be done remotely. Some will be one-time tasks distributed to "Gig Workers".

As more work is organized into stacks and modules and augmented with digitization and decoupled from an office or factory, the work can be done by diverse groups of workers. These "work completers" will become diverse and distributed. The work can be done by company "Insiders" and "Outsiders". The workforce composition can also become more diverse; those living in distant locations, those living in rural areas, minorities, those with disabilities, and other underrepresented groups will all be able to compete for the available work.

Friedman recently gave an example of how his employer is an example of the changing Nature of Work. He noted that when he became a columnist in 1995, one had to be an employee of the *New York Times* to be a contributor. In today's *New York Times*, along with their full-time columnists, they have contributors from all over the globe, including some who only make a one-time contribution. He further explained that the moderators of the comments online work remotely, the artists are freelancers, and his own copy editor works from home (Friedman, 2020).

Technology is blurring the firm's boundaries, as indicated earlier, and as evident in the increase in platform marketplaces.

Entrepreneurs develop worldwide platform-based firms using digital technologies, which differ from typical production processes where inputs are entered at one end and output delivered at the other. Platform companies frequently generate value by building a network effect that connects customers, producers, and Suppliers while facilitating interactions in a multisided approach. As a result, digital platforms scale up faster and at a lower cost than traditional businesses.

Second, technological advancements are altering the abilities required for employment. As a result, less advanced abilities that can be replaced by technology are in short supply. Simultaneously, the demand for advanced cognitive skills, behavioral skills, and skill combinations associated with adaptability is rising. Already prevalent in developed countries, this pattern is emerging in some developing countries. These changes show up through new jobs replacing old jobs and the changing skills profiles of existing jobs.

The concept of machines taking over jobs is resonating with people. The threat of technology to jobs, on the other hand, is exaggerated – as history has often demonstrated. These fears are just not supported by facts on global industrial jobs. Industrial jobs have been lost in industrialized economies, but East Asia's business sector has more than compensated. To make full use of the opportunities presented by new technology, organizational structures, and changes in labor force characteristics, images of work and the categories used to discriminate among jobs must be updated to represent better these changes: (1) the workforce's diversity; (2) the service economy's dominance; (3) the growing importance of cognition and analysis, interactions, and connections, and the adoption of digital technology in people's work; and (4) the blurring of conventional labor divisions in the industrial period. For example, the Blue Collar-managerial distinction no longer defines what people do at work. Future research and action should focus on changing or restructuring behaviors, institutions, and public policies that rely on this or other outdated images.

The "Reskilling" Challenge

Friedman also sees that "reskilling" is the new frontier. In some cases, radical reskilling could include taking a front-desk hotel clerk and teaching them to do cybersecurity or convert an airline counter agent into a data consultant (Friedman, 2020).

A lot is being said about "reskilling" these days. The primary reason for this focus is the impact of automation and robotics. The question that is continually asked is whether automation and robotic processes will replace people. Automation historically has only been seen in production and manufacturing processes, but now automation is affecting occupations and professions that were heretofore regarded as beyond the scope of automation. Even the legal and medical professions are directly being influenced by automation and robotics. The question now is whether employees who are capable of being extremely creative and can accomplish anything will be able to adjust to changing work modalities as easily as circumstances will require for organization efficiencies.

It can be said that work transformations can be manifested now in three different ways:

1   "Redeploying" – moving a worker or an employee to another business entity, thus ensuring employment continuity.
2   "Upskilling" – the process of increasing an employee's current job performance by assisting them in gaining advanced skills that will enable them to be more efficient and successful.
3   "Reskilling" – providing training to reengineer the employee's skills. This type of occupational transformational training is getting a lot of attention because experts see these training efforts as having a social purpose and demonstrating Corporate Social Responsibility. And it does touch on employer obligations and the rights of employees.

But these work transformation efforts have not been as successful as hoped for. Research shows that companies are struggling to train people to do something completely different.

Predicting Reskilling Needs

Therefore, a careful analysis needs to be conducted as to what an employee is doing today and what that employee can be good at in the future. As an example, take auto insurance claims. Today, a computer can do almost everything a claims adjuster can do. First, the computer can take a picture of the auto accident. Then computer algorithms and AI can review the damage to the car, the driving record of the car owner, and other details about the policyholder and can then crunch the number and accurately determine how much it would cost to repair the car. The computer can then determine how much should be paid on the claim. Therefore, the claims adjuster's job can soon be replaced by automation. So, what could insurance adjusters do in the future? They can become sales representatives. During their time as an adjuster, they will have seen many accidents giving them a lot of knowledge about damage patterns resulting from those accidents. This knowledge will allow them to advise prospective clients on what type of policies would best fit a specific client's needs, thus making them highly skilled sales advisors. They can say to a prospective client, "Hey, I know you don't want that coverage. But let me tell you, I have seen when the tree hits the windshield. And your current coverage does not protect that. You really should have it".

So, before implementing a specific employment transformational plan, Human Resource professionals must see the skill connections between different jobs, professions, and occupations. This analytical effort should be made before any major organizational "reskilling" program is undertaken.

Today's Skills Gap

Some companies are experiencing a shortage now. But companies cannot just worry about today's skill shortages; they also have to look to the future. For example, Futuro Health is a partnership between SEIU-UHW and Kaiser Permanente to train healthcare workers in California. In proactively looking at changes in the medical profession, Futuro Health has noticed that the more basic elements of medical care delivery can be automated with successful results. But they have concluded that their care providers still need to possess superior interpersonal skills. So, in designing their training programs, they are focusing on the development of interpersonal skills, and thus, they are keeping the future skill gap in mind.

Research has indicated that 30 percent of the workforce would have two-thirds of their jobs automated. But the research also shows that when the jobs were analyzed and broken down into tasks suddenly, it was evident that something like 75 percent of jobs could have up to a third of their tasks automated. This left companies wondering whether jobs first need to be decomposed and then recomposed into "new" jobs with a different set of skills. This is the "reskilling" challenge that needs to be tackled by Human Resource professionals.

Take a data analyst role who mostly manually collects and does data entry into a spreadsheet and does a little bit of analysis and maybe presentations of the data. If the basics are automated, just possessing Excel expertise will not be sufficient. That data analyst now has to learn how to analyze the data and then present it. This requires cognitive enhancement into critical thinking.

Often, we think of "reskilling" only in terms of digital skills. But it is also about the human skills that remain once things are automated. In most White-Collar jobs, the routine, repetitive tasks will be automated, but higher-level cognitive tasks will increase. This human element is where much of this "reskilling" and "upskilling" focus needs to be.

Can the Humans Do It?

The human element in the Nature of Work is critical when jobs are decomposed into their parts. In doing this decomposition, it is discovered that the human element is often an essential ingredient of job success. Then, we find ourselves asking questions about whether humans can handle these critical tasks instead of other technological innovations. The capability question swiftly follows. We also ask ourselves whether humans can indeed be trained to enhance productivity in these critical tasks further. This is when we are faced with a conundrum in that we are forced to ask ourselves whether humans are the most suitable to complete the decomposed tasks and activities. This question becomes critical irrespective of how effective humans have been in completing those tasks and activities in the past. Then inevitably follows the question of social responsibility or moral obligations. In essence, we are confronted with the fundamental question of human employability.

Assessing Human Capital

Thus, organizations must take critical stock of the realities of the current workforce. Human Capital audits become a crucial responsibility of Human Resource executives. Organizations need to conduct an audit of their existing talent. Then they need to look ahead in the light of automation and technological innovations of where that talent will be in five to ten years. Organizations need to develop formal Human Resource plans to "reskill" and redeploy their Human Capital.

Companies like Walmart have already started doing just such an exercise. They are proactive by determining their Human Capital needs in the future. They are "reskilling" their workforce with requisite skills-oriented training programs. These companies are therefore investing appropriately in their Human Capital. They are allowing their employees to learn. Companies should develop perspectives on the realities of their workforce related to technological advancements and need to develop plans to "reskill" their workforces to meet future needs.

In the past, the arguments against such "reskilling" efforts have been that if investments are made, then when the "reskilled" employees leave, the return on investment suffers. However, despite this potential loss, employers have an obligation to ensure that their current Human Capital investments are preserved for future requirements.

When an organization is suffering from high levels of turnover, should not an employer be more diligent in analyzing the high turnover and reengineer those jobs maintaining the interest factor of those jobs. Investing in Human Capital in this manner has demonstrated chiefly positive results.

Currently, it has been observed that the most significant skills gaps are in digital skills. Following this are shortages of English-language customer service skills. Companies in the United States have been observed tackling this difficulty by developing talents in limited supply but will be required in the future.

Recently there has been a significant move toward virtual business. There has been much fascination with lowering capital costs, on-time inventory management, fewer physical locations, and thus fewer people. But these trends have now gravitated to a middle point. Many older Buyers still want to touch before they buy, younger Buyers wish for an interplay of digital and mobile experiences, and then there is a vast group in the middle who want the online buying experience as their main buying platform. But, despite these trends, brick-and-mortar shopping mall buying has not seen declines. Shopping malls still attract a lot of people.

High Touch in a High-Tech World

This mixture of customer needs has made customer service even more complicated and affects business sectors in all categories and not just consumer industries. For example, healthcare is now much more customer-service-centric than it has been in the past. Healthcare customer service has morphed into loyal patient care, which involves care coordination. And this requires enhanced interpersonal skills. When hospitals realized that they needed more customer relations skills, they started recruiting from other customer-service-oriented industries such as hotels and entertainment services. This is because these employees were experienced in providing customer services. Instead of customers, these people could be trained to provide patient X-ray and pharmacy services.

In recent times, the medical services role has gone from services provided by a medical doctor to medical technicians and medical assistants. The required certifications for these professions can easily be secured from a local community college. The actual tasks are similar, involving working with machines in providing services, but to do these tasks, one no longer needs to be a Board-Certified medical doctor. As soon as the knowledge and skill requirements are realistically lowered, or the skills requirements are broken down, and the cost and barrier to entry are removed, the pool of qualified candidates to do the tasks increases. Thus, when you analyze and break down jobs into charges, duties, and activities, you find more opportunities for "reskilling".

Governmental customer service is also seeing a lot of growth. According to the various government-sector IT officers in the many US states, the Governor's top priority is mainly improving the customer experience. So, there is a clear-cut need to develop customer service representatives who can respond to customer needs. This customer service orientation goes beyond retail and is becoming key to organizational success in healthcare and government services. But, unfortunately, this growing need is creating a huge customer service skill gap.

Decomposing Jobs and Skills Inventories

Organizations have started to decompose jobs via structured job analysis to understand these current internal skills gaps. In these efforts, internal job databases were inadequate in capturing the skill inventories of the current workforces. It has been found that external automated social platform sites like LinkedIn were doing a better job of collecting what members have done, where they have worked, and what credentials and certifications they possess. Internal Human Resource systems usually contain job titles but do not do an excellent job aggregating specific skills and acquired knowledge. This shortcoming has hindered progress with specific "reskilling" efforts.

Thus, internal operational deficiency organizations have started projects where internal job data is integrated with internally sourced skills data using AI to handle the organization's skills supply. This leads to a strategic initiative in Human Resource departments to develop aggregated Interoperable Learning Records. It is believed that Interoperable Learning Record databases will give organizations a much better view of their skills gap, leading to better reskilling programs as organizations move into the future.

Interoperable Learning Record

An Interoperable Learning Record is like an educational transcript, but it adds and gives weight to earlier work experiences. For example, take the job of a grocery worker to bag groceries and assist customers by carrying their groceries to the customer's car. The job title for such a job can be customer service clerk, but this job also requires additional duties such as cleaning up areas of the store and lifting boxes and other supplies. Many people who do these jobs learn various people skills such as empathy and responsiveness. These individuals know a lot about human relations while doing their assigned tasks. Now aggregating information about skills learned as a customer service clerk and high school and college transcripts will give an employer a deeper understanding of job candidates' real skills, such as empathy and conscientiousness.

Hard job-related skills are required, but knowing who employees are and then understanding what the employee learned from specific work experiences give an employer information about an employee's skills, attitudes, and behaviors. Therefore, employers need to know who employees are and what they can expect from that employee in an all-around whole person profile.

Suppose an employer can gather employees through external sources like LinkedIn and tools like AI through Interoperable Learning Records. Then they can better understand the employee's soft skill profile like attitude, diligence, and commitment.

Job descriptions are not always written with the whole person structure in mind and thus are inadequate to understand the skills needed for future jobs. There are efforts underway, like the U.S. Chamber of Commerce Foundation's Job Data Exchange project, developing skills-based job descriptions. But on the whole, most job descriptions today are inadequate in defining and describing jobs using a complete job structure.

So, the essence of a successful "reskilling" effort is the ability to break down jobs into tasks, duties, and responsibilities. This breakdown then gives an employer a detailed understanding of the organization's skill gaps as it moves toward the future.

Validating the contention stated earlier, it has been found that those who decompose their jobs into skills, tasks, and responsibilities are twice as likely to have a successful program among companies that have undertaken "reskilling" programs. To derive the hard work of breaking down a job into specific tasks and then connecting those tasks with tasks employees currently possess is critical to ensure that the program is successful.

For example, telecommunication workers who have worked with older networks and then asked to work with IP-based voice-over networks must learn different skills. Like IT companies that moved from device-based computing to cloud computing, this situation has found that a different skill set is now required.

Therefore, "reskilling" starts with organizations asking some critical questions. What skills will become vital as the organization strategically plans for the future? What skills does the organization currently have? What skills will be in short supply? How does the organization "reskill" most of its employees so that they can retain them going forward? Organizations need to realize that not all employees are going to be successfully "reskilled" in reality. So, there will be a need to plan for some off-boarding strategies.

Temporary Work

Temporary labor has always been a key element of an organization's talent management strategies. This has included the acquisition and management of a pool of IT, clerical, manufacturing, and supply chain workers who were hired during periods of planned and unplanned peak activities. In manufacturing companies, temporary workers have been vital to meeting short-term manufacturing targets.

Before the Covid-19 Pandemic, companies had already established processes and procedures to hire temporary workers when managers opened requisitions that needed to be filled, often with very few lead times. These policies were designed to have a sufficient pool of temporary on-call workers to meet flexible capacity needs as and when required. During the year 2020, many companies were faced with unprecedented challenges. Many organizations had to rethink many aspects of their organizations and operational processes. Organizations like grocery chains, online retail outlets, and delivery services rushed to manage the high demand to satisfy the increased and changed consumer demand. All of these unexpected changes created massively new operational challenges.

Many companies had to shift their operations overnight to a remote work environment. All these challenges directly affected the temporary labor force. Companies have had to adapt to changing demands for specific skills. Companies have had to undergo a significant pivot to their hiring, onboarding, and the management of temporary remote workers. Companies that take advantage of the changing environment by optimizing their temporary workforce and related management strategies can come out of recent disruptions with greater flexibility and added efficiencies to tackle future challenges.

Usually, when companies cannot fill a permanent position expeditiously, they might use temporary workers in the short term. However, in recent times because of the labor market disruptions caused by the Covid-19 Pandemic, the temporary labor market has seen unprecedented declines. But because of the changing Nature of Work, companies are indicating optimism about prospects of temporary work. Initial trends in employee hiring indicate that the temporary labor market is posed to see unprecedented growth in the future. In addition, employers have recently been noticed altering temporary worker contracts to include work from home opportunities.

So, because of recent labor market disruptions, it is evident that employers are planning to increase the portion of temporary and remote workers in their overall workforces. Upwork, one of the largest current job search sites, "estimates that 1 in 4 Americans over 26% of the American workforce will be working remotely through 2021. They also estimate that 22% of the workforce (36.2 Million Americans) will work remotely by 2025" (Apollo Technical, 2022). With this transition to temporary work, many organizations are indeed experiencing improved productivity along with collaborative and operational flexibility.

Another employment trend that also affects temporary employment is the hybrid employment model. The Nature of Work is fast moving toward a combination of regular workers and temporary workers working either remotely or in the employer's physical location. So, both regular employees and temporary workers will have to collaborate, which will require acclimatization that can be achieved with targeted training programs. Because of the advent of this hybrid employment model, companies will be forced to adopt customized approaches to their workforce profiles, which will depend on their industry and the jobs they are trying to fill.

The demand for temporary workers varies significantly by industry. Healthcare, drug manufacturers, e-commerce, and food processing have all experienced significant increases in the demand for temporary workers. Because of the pandemic, the need for temporary workers has declined dramatically in the hospitality and food and beverage industries. The IT industry saw initial declines when major disruptions first started appearing. But the current conditions have accelerated the importance of digital technologies and e-commerce. Demand has skyrocketed for temporary traveling nurses and also in food-delivery services. These developments occur because of the pandemic and major adjustments in consumer wants and preferences.

According to research, substantial changes in work will have a long-term impact because customers are currently experiencing buying behavior paradigm shifts that will be recognized as part of the New Normal. Thus, the main advantage of temporary and contract workers is that they can provide greater flexibility in times of economic uncertainty. Automakers, for example, employ many temporary contract workers because they are somewhat a shock absorber to fluctuations in productivity while also lowering labor costs (Tong, 2018).

In industries where employment has tremendous variability, more workforce policies are pursued. Temporary employment can be a leading variable in an economic recovery. During recessions, temporary labor sees major job losses, but temporary labor shows greater rebounds as an economy shows a rebound.

Companies must acquire, retain, and motivate temporary workers due to the changing Nature of Work and the increasing relevance of temporary labor. To ensure companies take full advantage of this vital resource, there need to be five focus areas.

1   Renegotiate Temporary Contracts

Based on all the factors discussed so far, the prospective pool of temporary workers will increase significantly. So, it will benefit organizations greatly if current temporary labor sourcing contacts with agencies are renegotiated.

2   Move Sourcing Strategy to a Vendor Management Model

Companies should attempt to use the current opportunities to modify their sourcing strategies and then move from the temporary agency model to vendor management.

3   Keep Track of Temporary Workers' Tenure Time

Companies could also keep track of their temporary workers' present tenure, set more stringent limitations, and negotiate tenure discounts. It's crucial to focus on temp-to-perm conversions when critical responsibilities need to be filled. These steps can help cut costs while also utilizing the increased skill on hand.

4   Improve Temporary Worker Onboarding and Training

Companies can no longer rely on in-person onboarding to perform administrative responsibilities for new workers, so they must update their processes. This initiative will include training and change management expenses to prepare staff to undertake remote requisition and onboarding. Several apps have been developed to engage remote workers and manage a variety of transactional duties, allowing procurement and HR to focus on higher-value work. Employers are less inclined to hire directly into permanent roles when future demand is uncertain. As a result, they may rely on and require more temporary workers to meet current labor needs.

5   Investigate Risk Mitigation Strategies for Temporary Workers

Companies will need to investigate and adopt short-term risk mitigation strategies for temporary workers who must work in person soon. Increased perks and safeguards for temporary workers are also being advocated, which might drive up prices. All these variables will have to be considered in new talent-seeking tactics.

Remote Work

The shift from office to kitchen tables among White-Collar workers in 2020 seemed unprecedented and was only possible with videoconferencing software developments like Slack and Zoom. But it's nothing new. Moreover, the history of home working suggests some parallels with today.

Around the birth of capitalism from 1600 to the mid-nineteenth century, work did not just occur primarily in factories and people's houses. In many European countries, around a third of the workforce is working from home. According to one estimate on remote work in America, in the early 1800s, more than 40 percent of the total workforce labored from home.

More recently, before the world health crisis of 2020, remote work was quite prevalent in the technology sector. Open-source software development that created over $1 trillion in value was mainly developed by distributed teams of programmers who did their work in distributed teams from across the world. These distributed teams communicated, collaborated, and contributed to developing valuable products in locations around the world. The work was primarily done in a distributed, asynchronous online modality.

The global health crisis of 2020 has made this way of working normal for everyone. For many, this change in the Nature of Work was disruptive. But after initial hitches, many organizations accepted this changing Nature of Work. Many organizations now realize the long-term value of the remote work concept. Employees express satisfaction with the flexibility, the lack of commute, and the inability to work without disturbance and interruptions. Organizations realize that they can hire the best talent from anywhere in the world with distributed remote work. The search for the best talent is not constrained by office locations or the need for travel.

But remote work will not do away with offices, but how offices are used will change. Employees will come to work in an office with flexible arrangements. Concepts like "hot-desking" and "hoteling" will become popular. This will result in a reduction in office footprints. Companies will be able to reduce their commercial space obligations. Employees will go to the office to engage with their coworkers, not because company policies dictate office attendance.

All this will change how work gets done and how corporate cultures evolve. There will be more of a need to collaborate and build cohesiveness virtually. These will raise challenges, mainly because teamwork must be fostered across time zones and work environments using technology that might necessarily be new but must be repurposed. In addition, whole new work practices will have to be fostered. Work processes like videoconferencing, virtual meetups, and instant messaging will be critical. These new practices will become the new tenets of the changing work culture. All these changes, like work, will require deliberate changes in the way people work.

This might also usher in changes in leadership behaviors. Managers tasked to build a culture of collaboration in the remote work environment will discover that new leadership styles might need to be adopted. Recent studies have found that the skills and traits of successful leaders in an in-person work environment differ from those required to lead distributed remote teams.

In this changing Nature of Work, companies will stop seeing remote work as an inconvenience and will be required to embrace it as a chance to create interconnected, asynchronous, global workforces that are more flexible and dynamic than they have ever been.

Automation and the Changing Nature of Work

Automation, which includes AI, is changing the nature of businesses and will contribute to economic growth by increasing productivity. At the same time, new technologies are changing the nature of employment and the workplace itself. Machines will carry out more current human tasks and complement the work that humans will only be able to do. Machines will also perform some tasks that go beyond what humans usually do. This will result in some occupations declining and others growing, while most will change in some manner or form.

Automation and AI are not new phenomena, but recent technological trends in technological advancements are pushing what machines can do. A McKinsey research suggests that society needs these improvements to provide value for businesses, contribute to economic growth, and make significant progress on some of the most challenging societal concerns. Furthermore, McKinsey estimates that the most advanced deep learning approaches using artificial neural networks could generate $3.5 trillion to $5.8 trillion in yearly value, accounting for 40 percent of the total value created by all analytics techniques (McKinsey Global Institute, 2018).

It has been suggested that AI and automation technologies will do a lot to lift the global economy and increase global prosperity when aging and declining birth rates are slowing economic growth. This will be happening while labor productivity, a key driver of economic growth, has dropped over the past few decades. The decline accelerated in the aftermath of the 2008 global financial crisis.

AI and automation can reverse that decline. It is estimated that growth can be 2 percent per year moving forward. This can be achieved with the use of AI and related automation. Nevertheless, even though AI and automation benefit businesses and society, there will be associated disruptions to work.

It has been shown that in over 2,000 work activities across more than 800 occupations, specific categories of activities can be easily automated. Examples are physical tasks in highly predictable and structured contexts and data collecting and processing. These activities are roughly half of humans' activities across many industrial sectors (McKinsey Global Institute, 2018).

It has also been shown that automation will affect most occupations in some way or form. But it is interesting to note that only about 5 percent of occupations can be automated with existing technologies. Furthermore, many occupations will only have portions of their activities automated. It has been suggested that only about 30 percent of activities in 60 percent of all occupations can be affected by automation. Therefore, it has been estimated that between 2015 and 2030, roughly 15 percent of the global workforce, or around 400 million workers, will be displaced by automation. As workers are displaced in specific industrial sectors, there will be growth in demand for work and an increase in jobs. With continuing economic growth and productivity growth, both old and new jobs will be created. Many new occupations will be created and account for about 10 percent of jobs created by 2030 (McKinsey Global Institute, 2018).

In many cases, automation will only partially affect jobs, and in these cases, the machines will complement human effort. However, some aspects of the work, like repetitive troubleshooting, can be automated with certain systems in other occupations. For example, in Amazon, employees who previously lifted and stacked goods are now being asked to operate the robots that now do lifting and stacking. These operators now monitor automated arms and troubleshoot operational problems with the robots as and when the issues arise.

There will be enough work to ensure single-digit unemployment levels by 2030. But during the transformation of the Nature of Work because of automation and AI adoption, there will be significant changes in the mix of occupations. There will also be changes in skill and educational requirements. As a result, the occupational mix will need to be reengineered to ensure that humans work alongside machines in a complementary manner.

As discussed before, automation will accelerate the shift in required worker skills. Advanced technical abilities such as programming and coding will be in high demand. In addition, higher cognitive capabilities such as creativity, critical thinking, complex information processing, and social, emotional, and higher cognitive skills will be in great demand. The demand for basic digital abilities has been rising, and this trend is expected to continue and accelerate. Physical and manual talents will become less in demand.

Workflows and workspaces will continue to adapt as intelligent devices and software become more fully integrated into the workplace, allowing humans and robots to collaborate. For example, cashiers can become checkout assistance helpers as self-checkout machines are introduced into establishments, answering queries and troubleshooting the machines. More system-level solutions will prompt a reengineering of the entire workflow. Warehouse designs may change significantly as some portions accommodate robots and others primarily to facilitate safe human-machine interaction. More system-level solutions will force a reassessment of the workflow and workspace as a whole. The layout of a warehouse may alter substantially as some areas accommodate robots, and others are designed to allow for safe human-machine interaction.

All forms of jobs will continue to be in high demand. However, that work will be different, requiring new talents and a far greater level of workforce adaptability than we've seen before. It will be critical to teach and retrain mid-career professionals and younger generations for future problems. Governments, business leaders, and innovators must collaborate to coordinate public and private activities better, including providing the correct incentives for additional Human Capital investment. With automation and AI, the future will be challenging but will have micro benefits to societies as long as we deal with the adverse effects strategically.

References

Apollo Technical (2022, January 16). Statistics on remote workers that will surprise you. Retrieved January 21, 2022 from www.apollotechnical.com/statistics-on-remote-workers/

Bell, D. (1973). *The coming of Post-Industrial society, a venture in social forecasting*. New York: Basic Books.

Dertouzos, M. & Moses, J. (1979). *The computer age: A twenty year view. MIT Bi-centennial Studies*. Cambridge: An MIT Press Classic.

Friedman, T. (2020, October 20). After the pandemic, a revolution in education and work awaits. Retrieved December 29, 2021 from www.nytimes.com/2020/10/20/opinion/covid-education-work.html

Houndshell, D. (1984). *From the American system to mass production – 1800–1932, The development of manufacturing technology in the United States (Studies in industry and society)*. Baltimore, MD: John Hopkins University Press

McKinsey Global Institute (2018, April 17). Discussion papers and briefings. Retrieved July 15, 2022 from https://www.mckinsey.com/mgi/our-research/discussion-papers-and-briefings

Negroponte, N. (1995). *Being digital*. New York: Alfred A. Knopf.

Nora, S. & Minc, A. (1980). *The computerization of society*. Cambridge, MA: MIT Press.

Perrole, J. (1987). *Computer and social change*. Belmont, CA: Wadsworth Publishing

Stewart, T. A. (1999). *Intellectual capital: The new wealth of organizations. Doubleday*. New York: A Currency Book.

Tong, S. (2018, November 15). How temp workers became the norm in America. Retrieved December 30, 2021 from www.marketplace.org/2018/11/15/how-great-recession-helped-normalize-use-temp-workers/

Yates, J. (1989). *Control through communication, the rise of system in American management*. Baltimore, MD: The John Hopkins University Press.

Chapter 3

The Changing Nature of the Employment Contract

William Garrison

The Current Employment Contract

Business owners often contemplate the changing needs of their customers and constantly are tinkering with the Business Plan they either set initially up or have recently revised. The Business Mindset is always thinking about creating a well-oiled machine that can run on its own to produce the desired results. Disruptions to the setup create additional work and effort. Then, as employees are added into the equation, there are both positive and negative emotions of this "most valuable asset".

Employees have their own set of hopes and dreams, and they have families and relationships. They have hobbies and vacations to occupy their time. They even have that ever-growing queue of Netflix shows to binge. And, although they spend a majority of their lives at work, they don't always see their company's mission as their highest priority.

The current Employment Contract has been around since the Industrial Revolution, in which farmers left their farms and their families to work for the factory owner. The factory jobs were stable compared to the highs and lows of running your own farm. The contract included the owner needing labor and the wages to exchange for that person's time. The money was the motivation, and since many farmers were not good at farming or were frustrated with the elements and volatility of the crops, they signed the factory worker's contract.

Although this example seems archaic, it paints the picture of the typical Employment Contract of today. The business owner has a task to complete, and the employee has the skill to complete that task. Money is exchanged, the company achieves its objectives, and the employee shares in its success through promotions and bonuses.

The current Employment Contract takes differing forms still today. As an employer begins to divide the work that needs to be completed in an organization, it becomes apparent that employees are required to do that work. Some of the work is rudimentary and requires low-skilled labor, but lots of it. Some of it requires expertise and the need to retain high-performing talent. These forms

DOI: 10.4324/9781003122272-3

of labor include an exchange of money (and benefits) to the employee to compensate for their loss of freedom and time. Some may say they love their job so much that it feels strange that they get paid to do it. Still, nearly all work involves giving up an individual's freedom to a level that the work would not be done if that compensation were not there.

- **Hourly Wage (Part-Time and Full Time)** – some work needs to be done at differing frequencies and may not be constant enough to justify a long-term agreement of hours worked. Hourly wage is widely used in all industries and can be both part-time and full-time. Typically, the supervising manager decides the hours scheduled for the coming period and has the employee track that time to submit on a timecard for later compensation.
- **Annual Salary (May Include Bonuses)** – some work needs to be done on a prolonged, consistent schedule and often requires additional skills and education. This work is budgeted by the year, and the workers are hired with this in mind. Bonuses can also be budgeted for work accomplished at a higher rate than expected to provide additional motivation.
- **Contract** – some work is inconsistent and/or short-term. This work is budgeted for the short term or embedded into a project. The work is done by contractors separate from the company, so they are not technically employees. Some liability and safety concerns are applied, but the worker is not part of the company. When the work is completed, the contractor does not have any obligation until a new contract is negotiated.
- **Stock Options** – some work is very complicated and would require a huge allocation of funds to retain that set of skills as an employee of the company. Sometimes that arrangement includes being paid in company stock rather than a salary. This means that the person gets a small stake in the company in exchange for their expertise while still having the freedom to seek employment with other companies simultaneously.
- **Partnerships** – some work is highly complicated and requires a level of commitment far beyond the norm. This work involves a sense of ownership so high that the individual would consider starting their own company. Instead, the owner creates an agreement in which the individual becomes part-owner at a predetermined percentage (typically less than 50 percent) to indicate the expected contribution level. It may even require a financial contribution to "buy into" the company, but it also arranges for benefits usually reserved for the ownership.

Employee Engagement – Time for Change

This Employment Contract has done well for the past 100 years as more and more newcomers to the workforce have understood that working for someone else was the way to achieve their American Dream. Of course, the American

Dream used to be the idea of starting and running your own business and not having a boss, but most workers are risk-averse and have bought into the path laid out before them. As a teenager, you ask friends and family for opportunities to earn money and end up mowing lawns or babysitting, or you may work in the fast-food or retail industry for a minimum wage. You may be given a raise or promotion as your skills improve. Some choose to go to school and learn a skill or earn a degree, which sets them up for higher pay and perhaps a stable salaried position with great benefits. They work their entire lives to help their company make the owners rich while living a pretty good life between shifts (Kruse, 2012).

The Baby Boomer management mindset believes that since the company pays its employees, they should be engaged. If needed, they may add additional off-task activities to enhance their employees' enjoyment, such as parties, allowing jeans to be worn on Fridays, and perhaps even an off-site activity. Of course, there are incentives for working harder and longer, there are promotions to entice employees to go the extra mile, and there are pensions and retirement packages to build up.

As Gen Xers and Millennials began to want more, they felt they needed to seek employment elsewhere. As the internet boomed, there were plenty of incognito ways to view the workplace culture of other companies via chat groups, company websites, social media, and even LinkedIn. Employees began using their time at work to find their next job.

For many of these employees, the reason they are looking to leave is dissatisfaction with their manager, not their employer. As companies began to see their employee retention rates drop, they investigated the reasons why. Employment surveys, such as the Employee Engagement Survey, began to ask probing questions to discover the areas of dissatisfaction and management blind spots to address these concerns before the employees left. These surveys led to preventative measures to proactively implement programs and other incentives to retain employees even after disengagement.

Baby Boomer Loyalty and the Promise of a Pension

As they learned from the generation before them, workers from the Baby Boomer generation (those born between 1946 and 1964) tended to be loyal to the company, nonetheless. They would work to become a valuable member of the company, and, in exchange, the company stayed loyal to them. The Management Team devised opportunities to measure and encourage longevity with the company, including training, career paths, and awards to retain their employees as it is much cheaper to retain an employee than to rehire.

The Employment Contract for the Baby Boomer generation reflected the society of the time in which there was an emphasis on cooperation and building a better future. These workers grew up in an era with massive parades, traditional celebrations, and community investment. There were also ample opportunities to make an impact outside of work in several social movements, including the Hippie Movement, Women's Liberation, the Sexual Revolution, and anti-war political activities. This generation was able to have quite a fulfilling life outside of work and maintaining a separation of the two. They did not expect that their workplace would be the place to expect social justice initiatives but rather a place to contribute to their company's goals. Baby Boomers also saw that they could accomplish quite a bit outside of work. Thus, they had healthy self-esteem from the workplace to overcome the struggle of repeated tasks and office politics.

However, as companies began looking at their quarterly earnings more and more, the most significant expense on their balance sheets was their wages. So, to survive, and in some cases, to continue to grow, companies began compromising on their loyalty to their employees. Then their employees started not to pledge their allegiance back (Mulvanity, 2001).

Gen X – The Individual Who Cannot Be Defined but Still Wants Paradise

Then came along Generation X (those born between 1965 and 1980). These kids were raised in a time when the Sexual Revolution was burning. The freedoms from the conventional perspectives were being fought daily. During this time, divorce laws became more relaxed, while simultaneously both the mothers and the fathers of Gen Xers believed in the concept of self-actualization and found ways to both express themselves and find meaning in their lives. This led to many Gen Xers becoming latchkey kids competing for their parents' attention and not winning. At the same time, Gen Xers found meaning with their freedom to associate with their friend groups and enjoyed the explosion of technological advances. There were a lot of entertaining options as the TV channels and programs directed toward them increased.

Gen Xers saw the world as a place of endless opportunities to explore. They tried on many different identities to figure out what their peer group accepted since there weren't many adults around or interested in their development.

As they entered the workplace, they found a three-tiered hierarchical structure. The older generation held the top management positions, the Baby Boomers held the middle management positions, and their peers were the frontline workers. They came to the workplace with a need for higher compensation either from their commercialized desires to own the latest and greatest tech or to pay off their massive educational loans due to the meteoric rise in college tuition.

They also came prepared. Gen X workers brought with them their social skills and technological skills without fear of technological advancements. They saw technology as a tool to work smarter rather than harder and had no concept of the Luddite fear of their superiors seeing their value threatened as their knowledge became more and more obsolete.

However, their opportunities to grow were also stifled by the older generations' increased health and financial insecurity. The Boomers and the generation before them held the positions longer. They showed no plans to retire and vacate those positions for the aspiring Gen Xer. In addition, the wave of downsizing prevalent in the 80s and early 90s eliminated many of the middle management positions that Gen Xers aspired to. It also provoked a deeply engrained insecurity due to their employer's apparent lack of loyalty to the Baby Boomers that had put their time in and went the extra mile.

This led Gen Xers to be more entrepreneurial than their previous generations. As a result, many Gen Xers started their own companies. They enjoyed their autonomy to work their schedules on their terms, while those that stayed employed flipped an internal switch to be entrepreneurial in their current position while bolstering up their skills to make themselves more marketable if the opportunity to move ever became available or if they were inevitably downsized.

Today's Gen Xers are now 40- to 60-year-olds with older kids and grandkids. Many of them have been through divorces and have had to reinvent themselves through their two to three careers, let alone the number of jobs they have held. Unfortunately, what has remained constant is the number of Baby Boomers in positions over them that still don't show the prospect of retiring and the monthly student loan bills that seem never to end. In addition, they have taken advantage of the Tech Boom in the 90s and survived the Housing Bubble while also leveraging their debt to afford all the amenities, vacations, and oversized homes their credit score allows. As a result, they are highly positioned to be significant contributors in their roles but are still waiting for those opportunities.

Gen Xers thrive in a workplace that offers ongoing training opportunities and allows employees to be part of short-term projects. They value regular feedback sessions and career conversations with their managers and be provided the flexibility of their work schedule and production expectations. They also love working for organizations that value their verbal and monetary contributions. And, they feel most appreciated when they can be involved in conversations at the highest levels of the organization where their input can lead to the organization moving in the direction of purpose that sets out to fix some of the societal ills they also perceive (Mulvanity, 2001).

Interestingly enough, the Gen X generation took the global pandemic in stride. They are very resilient since they spent a lot of time on their own afterschool and had to entertain themselves (Dabney, 2020). As latchkey kids, Gen Xers had the opportunity to create their own reality in the face of a bad situation.

The Millennial Experience!

But for the Millennials (those born between 1981 and 2000), their willingness to hop jobs quickly means that Employee Engagement Surveys can be too little, too late. According to Amy Adkins in an article for Gallup in 2019,

- 21 percent of Millennials have changed jobs within the past year
- Millennial turnover costs the U.S. economy $30.5 billion annually

- Only half believe they will be still working at their company a year from now
- 60 percent are open to a different opportunity
- 36 percent are looking
- Only 29 percent of Millennials are engaged at work
- 16 percent are disengaged
- The majority of Millennials (55 percent) are not engaged (Adkins, 2019)

This apparent lack of commitment can be viewed by Baby Boomers in upper management that Millennials are lazy and that they don't have a good work ethic. Baby Boomers began work at a time where a secure career was the goal. The Employment Contract leaned heavily toward the employer's direction. In the early stages of their careers, their supervisors were quite heavy-handed. However, longevity in a company was one of the best ways to progress toward the Boomer's secure career. Boomers were loyal and hardworking and believed their work ethic would pay off with receiving training and for security such as retirement or pension (Ladders, 2019). Boomers believed that if they worked hard and did tasks beneficial to the company, they would be more valuable employees. When layoffs or downsizing occurred, those with seniority and value would be the employees they would retain. Millennials, on the other hand, have figured out that this "deal" no longer exists. They've seen too many companies go under; make massive, indiscriminate layoffs; suffer under bad economies; and even open themselves up to be shut down entirely by regulators. Millennials have come to terms with this and have instead turned it into a benefit for themselves.

They want a job that is directly in line with their career equity because they believe the employer will not be loyal or value long-term employment. They will put a lot of effort into activities that are in line with their long-term goals, and they are willing to go above and beyond for the company's benefit if they see it as a way to gain an advantage for themselves indirectly. The result is that companies get some tremendous outcomes on projects that wouldn't have existed otherwise. In these tasks, the company receives a highly engaged employee.

Millennial Mindset and the Happiness Formula

The Millennial Mindset is the product of their parents' wisdom and advice and the unparalleled economic success in the latter half of the twentieth century. The Baby Boomers grew up in the postwar era in which career opportunities were vast, and, with enough blood, sweat, and tears, a Baby Boomer could gradually create a very secure career. They put their time in and were loyal to their employers (Lipman, 2016).

For Baby Boomers, the careers they worked for and put their time in actually turned out to be better than their expectations. Thus, their happiness with

Happiness = Reality - Expectations

Figure 3.1 The Happiness Formula (Urban, 2013)

their secure career was high, and they were very willing to recommend that path to those younger than them.

Using this same formula, Millennials are experiencing low happiness levels because their expectations are so much greater than the reality of a 25- to 35-year-old. Millennials believe they are special because their parents told them that they were. As a result, they have a very optimistic view of their future. They believe they can have a secure career and a fulfilling one. In their pursuit of happiness, they have added purpose to the above equation.

Millennials have a "strong resistance to accepting negative feedback" and "an inflated view of oneself", which leads to "a great source of frustration for people with a strong sense of entitlement . . . to a level of respect and rewards that aren't in line with their actual ability and effort levels". Also, they've grown up in the age of social media, something prior generations were spared from.

Millennials see the world in three ways:

A)   What everyone else is doing is very public,

B)   Most people give an exaggerated version of their existence, and

C)   Those who chime in the most about their careers (or relationships) are usually those whose jobs (or relationships) are going well. At the same time, those that are struggling are less likely to advertise their situation. (Urban, 2013)

The reality for an average career of a 25- to 35-year-old is progressing just fine, but when compared to this inflated image, Millennials can feel "frustrated and inadequate".

Urban (2013) suggests that Millennials "1) Stay wildly ambitious, 2) Stop thinking that you're special, 3) Ignore everyone else". "The reality is, everyone else is just as indecisive, self-doubting, and frustrated as you are, and if you simply do your thing, you'll never have anything to envy".

For employers, it is crucial not to dismiss Millennials based on a generational bias. Their strengths are much more valuable than their shortcomings, and their innate desire to infuse passion into a company's operations can help catapult an organization to greatness. What organization wouldn't want to be passion-driven where the workforce finds fulfillment in serving their customers? Especially since Employee Engagement is defined as an employee's emotional commitment to the company and to its mission (Kruse, 2012).

Gen Z and the Quest for Stability and Relationships

Behind the Millennials is a dynamic workforce that will chart the new Employment Contract as long as the Millennials allow. These workers were born into a world where the internet has always existed, smartphones and tablets were plentiful, and connectivity was never an issue. They were raised on iPhones and understand how the Internet of Things helps make their lives easier, including turning on the lights in a room. And, they will be quite a force once they realize it.

Right now, they are the largest generation. They will soon become one-third of the workforce accounting for 40 percent of the consumer base. Although many of them do not work, they are still driving a lot of household spending (DeFelice, 2019).

Gen Z workers were born between 2001 and 2020. They are beginning to show up in the workplace and are distinct from the Millennials. They desire stability.

One of the leading factors to this desire is that they came of age during difficult economic times. They watched the adults in their lives suffer the effects of the Housing Bubble burst and the slow economic recovery after that. They began to enter the labor market amid the economic recovery in the late 2010s, only to have it all vanish by 2020 owing to the Covid-19 Pandemic. And, they are fed a constant diet of looming catastrophes such as Climate Change and unstable governments worldwide. Although they see Elon Musk as a real-world Avenger superhero, they realize even his ultimate desire is to leave this volatile planet.

Ironically, they also crave human connection. Although they are very tech-savvy, they use their internet-connected devices to interact with their friends and family whenever they are away from each other. They also watch their digitally connected parents always working and don't want that lifestyle.

However, they see these devices as ways to socialize when they're apart but not necessarily when they are together. They don't have as many stories of going camping and playing out in the streets as their Gen X parents, so when they get these opportunities, they love them! This craving also is exhibited in their relationships with their managers. They enjoy genuine, in-person conversations and desire authentic feedback.

Unlike their Millennial counterparts, they are not as keen on flex work as it comes to having a flexible schedule but instead crave flexibility and ownership over how they do their jobs (DeFelice, 2019).

They enjoy having a sense of ownership because they think in that way.

They will also be the most diverse workforce ever and value concepts such as sustainability and inclusion.

It's essential to understand the need to motivate Gen Z workers.

- They enjoy working in teams and crave positive relationships
- They need a work-life balance

- They want frequent touchpoints and check-ins with tangible metrics
- They see failure as a chance to learn and progress (Stahl, 2019)

Attracting and Retaining Talent in a Diverse World of Work

With so many different views from each generation, companies have the challenge of managing the diverse desires of each of these generations. An organization's culture will be covered in greater detail later in this book. Still, it's important to note that organizations that do not feel addressing these desires will continue to see increased levels of turnover. And, for those workers who are not engaged at work, one view would be that employers should become more accepting of higher levels of turnover than before. However, smart organizations understand that attracting and keeping talent is worth the effort.

Great Places to Work for Millennials

And, from what the research shows, it doesn't take much of an investment to be a place where Millennials and Gen Z workers become as loyal as their Baby Boomer and Gen X colleagues.

Companies detailed by "Great Places to Work" for Millennials before the Covid-19 Pandemic were these companies and the reasons they state about why they like them:

1 **Cisco** – belief in leadership and direction
2 **Edward Jones** – teamwork approach where I matter
3 **UKG (formerly Ultimate Software)** – empowered to do the right thing; transparent leadership creates a sense of unity and ownership
4 **Pinnacle Financial Partners** – integrity, care, concern, and compassion for our clients, flows to us for both our professional and personal needs
5 **Kimley-Horn and Associates, Inc.** – given the resources and support needed to succeed, anyone can start a thriving practice based on their desire and initiative
6 **Hilton** – part of a family; lots of opportunity for growth, hard work is appreciated, feels good knowing that our guests are happy
7 **Progressive Insurance** – so much focus on our culture; encouraged to bring their whole selves to work; devoted to diversity and inclusion; gives me pride that we are encouraged to give back to our community
8 **Power Home Remodeling Group** – encouraged to dream and innovate, regardless of age, race, gender, tenure; feel safe expressing my opinion; they have my back

9 **Slalom Consulting** – hire great people who care and want to make a positive impact; solid core values; put in the investment and effort to operate by them; provide opportunities for its people to live by them

10 **Target Corporation** – teams that are engaged; set up for success in terms of resources; responsibility and decision rights pushed down that empower all levels; great learning and development opportunities and team-building events

These businesses have in common that they all recognize the significance of culture. These companies have spent time and resources stating their mission, vision, and values and back them up with learning opportunities, investments in their local communities, and organizational structures that empower employees at all levels. Employees at these companies feel supported in both their professional and personal lives and feel like they are part of a family. They are also encouraged to dream, develop, and innovate regardless of "age, race, gender, or tenure", and they feel safe expressing their opinions and creating initiatives. They love serving their customers' and clients' needs (Fortune, 2020).

Top Industries for Gen Z

Gen Z workers and aspiring workers express many of the same concepts. Although Gen Z is the most tech-savvy generation ever, investing in technology and dashboards is not what attracts them and keeps them. Instead, they are seeking out employers that deal well with the human element of the workplace.

Companies such as Google, Amazon, and Apple are always near the top of companies that Gen Z wants to work for. Still, it's because of their perception of those companies' culture and positive impact on society they cite as the reason. They are also looking for careers in the healthcare and hospitality industries because they help people. Many expressed interest in being "Gig Workers" in the beauty industry, daycare, and book sales. What these industries all have in common is that they are driven by serving others with their products. Gen Z is very interested in impacting the world in that matter (Beckman, 2019).

Structure and Formulation of New Employment Contract

So what should employers do to meet the objectives of their organizational goals with a workforce that seems to be less engaged than ever before? There appear to be three different types of Employment Contracts to choose from.

Option 1: Traditional Approach

Traditionally, the Employment Contract is entered into when an employer needs labor and can create value and/or return on investment into opening a new position. First, that position is crafted using a job description, and the Human Resources department decides which skills and qualifications a person would need to do that task well. Then, there are job postings, resumes exchanged, interviews performed, and offers made. The employer analyzes each candidate during this process to see if they are the "right fit" for the position. Meanwhile, each candidate has researched the company, reviewed and updated their resume, compared this position with others, and attended different types of interviews.

Once the Human Resources team has made their ideal candidate selection, they send out the offer, negotiate salaries and benefits, and hope to hire that candidate. If they have done so already, the candidate can decide if the employer is the "right fit" for them. There are terms laid out in the offer to outline this Employment Contract that focuses on whether or not the position is part-time or full-time, paid hourly or salary, and what sort of additional benefits they may be able to earn. This process rarely focuses on promotional opportunities, professional development, manager-employee relationships, social justice stances, or other cause-related activities.

When the employee begins, they go through varied onboarding activities that start to unpeel the layers of the organization back to get a sense of where they belong and how their daily routine will look. The employee begins to sense and experience the corporate culture. By interacting with other employees, they learn more about the employer's expectations and guidelines than they did in the job posting or the interview process.

The employee then has a period of time in which they feel out the organization and decide whether or not they have made the right choice. Their manager is going through a very similar process.

As the weeks and months pass, there appears to be an unspoken agreement on the Employment Contract conditions that both parties agreed to on the day of their hire. Even still, the employee's memory of the incident lasts considerably longer because they are only thinking about themselves, their organization, and possibly their immediate supervisor. On the other hand, the employer tends not to focus on the terms of that hiring date for long. At best, the Human Resources department may have an established set of policies or performance standards they lay out on an annual basis that defines that initial contract. However, as the annual review of those policies occurs, they make subtle changes to them to amend that contract. And, these changes apply to much more than the single employee; they affect every employee in the organization. It's easy to see how Millennials have become jaded on this approach and have chosen not to participate.

Those who share the Millennial Mindset's traits find this Employment Contract to be obsolete. For a time, they will play along because they have heard the criticism from their parents, grandparents, and society regarding their apparent lack of work ethic. But the issue is not that they don't want to work hard; they feel powerless to amend the Employment Contract as often as the organization seems to. Organizations that choose to stick with this traditional contract will see increases in employee turnover, decreases in Employee Engagement, and even worse, an organization full of employees that are more passive in nature that feels they are on the losing side of the contract.

Option 2: Contractor Approach

One apparent solution to this Employment Contract imbalance that has been used for decades now is hiring contract employees to do the tasks. This is a win–win for both the employer and the contractor.

This Employment Contract is fairly similar to the Traditional Approach, but it specifies the length of time and the salary much more flexibly.

In the Contractor Approach, the employer recognizes a need for labor and wants to have that labor add value and return on investment, too, but is either not sure of how long that need will exist or knows that it will not be a need for long. This strategy has also been hailed as a fantastic way to avoid union pressures, increased benefit expenses, and the need for additional liability. Unfortunately, labor is the largest or at least one of the most significant expenses an organization takes on. When an organization adds a multiyear or non-expiring traditional Employment Contract for full-time or part-time employees, they lock themselves into maintaining that labor expense or make it difficult emotionally and financially to end those relationships.

However, for the Contract Employment, the terms of the relationship are mutually agreed upon by both parties. The contractor can choose to enter into that contract and has both the clarity and the power to amend it as needed. Contractors are willing to do the work, shoulder the liability, and focus on completing the tasks. There is very little time spent on organizational objectives, mission statements, and Employee Engagement concerns. They notice and participate in the corporate culture as they know how to operate within the organization as a means to an end. Still, they rarely can influence that culture.

The negative aspect of this type of Employment Contract is the lack of Employee Engagement as there tends to be very little, if any, emotional ties to the organizational goals. Contractors are there to perform their tasks and get paid.

When contractors are kept on or recontracted, they begin to form good working relationships and sometimes even personal relationships with other employees and management as they feel the need to belong. And, if these relationships coupled with their performance are value-added, they sometimes can be converted into full-time Insiders with a traditional contract.

This does not solve the issues brought up in this book thus far, though. Contract workers, by definition, are separated from the organization and often perform more like machines rather than a vibrant workforce. Their focus is on completing the tasks, not building its culture. For this type of Employment Contract to work, they are often employed by a contractor agency that can move contractors in and out of jobs as needed. The employer also has to add a layer within the Management Team or Human Resources team to manage these relationships and supervise these contractors to ensure organizational goals are exceeded, safety standards are met, and corporate cultural norms are maintained. It takes additional effort to build and oversee this workforce that will not add long-term value or create a sustainable environment. If an organization is willing to put in this extra effort, the results would be more sustainable and growth-oriented for both the organization and the workforce.

Option 3: Purpose-Driven Approach

One of the best options for reaching organizational goals and creating an engaged workforce is developing a Purpose-Driven Approach to the organization's Employment Contract. This approach combines the best of all the elements of the Traditional Approach, the Contractor Approach, and the Millennial Mindset.

As mentioned previously in this book, since the Industrial Revolution, most organizations have placed revenue generation and profits as the top priority. With this in mind, the organization would hire workers if they were needed and only if they could provide a return on investment. However, the drive toward automation demonstrated that the employer viewed labor by people as a necessity only as so far as they couldn't find a way for a machine to do it instead. In the early days of production, factory owners invested in the ideas brought forth by Fredrick Winslow Taylor and those who believed in the Scientific Management Theory. Taylor believed that employers could measure how long a task would take a worker and then replicate that over time.

And although there has been a lot of research and improvements since that time, the concepts outlined by Daniel Pink in his book *Drive: The Surprising Truth About What Motivates Us* provide the best foundation for motivating our workforces. In *Drive*, Pink says that money is not a good motivator for tasks above the rudimentary level but that autonomy, mastery, and purpose are the key. When workers are given the flexibility to get the job done, are given opportunities to "reskill", improve their existing skills, and rally around a purpose, they thrive (Pink, 2011).

One of the simplest of those three is purpose. Simon Sinek, the author of *Start With Why*, says that great companies have a purpose at their core and then expand on how they do what they do and eventually what they do. When companies start with "why", the "how" and "what" becomes meaningful (Sinek, 2011).

When the company's purpose is laid out clearly, the Employment Contract can be built onto it. For example, instead of employers exchanging work for money, workers can contribute toward the purpose in meaningful ways. Perhaps they are salaried, long-term workers who regularly shape and steer the work toward achieving that purpose. Or, they are hourly workers who seek ways to improve their skills or "reskill" independently to contribute toward that purpose. Alternatively, they may be entirely disassociated from the firm and seek ways to contribute to its mission by completing a task in exchange for payment or donating their time and abilities. The Employment Contract then becomes a living, breathing document.

Millennials and Gen Z Are the Future of the Workforce

The future for organizations is bright as many of these desires of the Millennial and Gen Z workforces also happen to be what is best for the sustainability of organizations. Therefore, companies should embrace the emerging workforces and do all they can to provide a welcome environment. With more proof of their demonstrating self-imposed responsibility for "reskilling", desiring remote work, embracing freelance roles, and implementing individual future-proofing strategies, companies will see quite a return on their investment into these workforces (Gilchrist, 2019).

This provides organizations with the freedom to either offer short-term "Gig" opportunities with little long-term engagement or refocus and build a sustainable, purpose-driven organization that inspires them to stay, or even both! Companies should give equal attention to attracting and retaining these valuable workers but need to evolve to do so (Robison, 2021).

Final Thoughts on Managing Millennials and Gen Z Workers

As Millennials and Gen Z workers become more and more a part of organizations, it's important to know how managers can positively impact productivity by achieving the organizational goals while treating their workers right. With the right mindset, both can be accomplished by doing the following:

- Don't expect that they will stay in the long term.
- If the tasks are related to their career goals, they will go above and beyond. They like autonomy and the ability to hone their skills independently.
- They want to be asked about their aspirations and are blunt about their expectations.
- They don't mind taking on responsibility quickly.
- They will stay longer if they feel they are needed and valued.
- They need to be part of a purpose.

References

Adkins, A. (2019, December 16). Millennials: The job-hopping generation. Retrieved December 29, 2021 from www.gallup.com/workplace/231587/millennials-job-hopping-generation.aspx

Beckman, K. (2019, May 03). The top industries and companies where Gen Z wants to work, according to all the reports and studies. (n.d.). Retrieved December 29, 2021 from https://ripplematch.com/journal/article/the-top-industries-and-companies-where-gen-z-wants-to-work-according-to-all-the-reports-and-studies-0b1b2cc8/

Dabney, C. (2020, April 01). It took a global pandemic, but Generation X is finally getting love. Retrieved December 29, 2021 from www.papercitymag.com/culture/generation-x-earns-respect-conronavirus-pandemic-stay-home/

DeFelice, M. (2019, October 31). What gen Z wants at work will blow your mind. Retrieved December 29, 2021 from www.forbes.com/sites/manondefelice/2019/10/31/what-gen-z-wants-at-work-will-blow-your-mind/?sh=5c60f759b8e7

Fortune. Best Workplaces for Millennials™ 2020. (2020). Retrieved December 29, 2021 from www.greatplacetowork.com/best-workplaces/Millennials/2020

Gilchrist, K. (2019, March 5). How millennials and gen Z are reshaping the future of the workforce. Retrieved December 29, 2021 from www.cnbc.com/2019/03/05/how-millennials-and-gen-z-are-reshaping-the-future-of-the-workforce.html

Kruse, K. (2012, June 22). What is employee engagement. Retrieved December 29, 2021 from www.forbes.com/sites/kevinkruse/2012/06/22/employee-engagement-what-and-why/?sh=3557f5b7f372

Ladders Contributor. (2019, March 14). The disconnect between Baby Boomers and Millennials when it comes to work ethic. Retrieved December 29, 2021 from www.theladders.com/career-advice/the-work-ethic-disconnect-between-baby-boomers-and-millennials

Lipman, V. (2016, June 25). Understanding the millennial mindset is increasingly important to management. Retrieved December 29, 2021 from www.forbes.com/sites/victorlipman/2016/06/20/understanding-the-millennial-mindset-is-increasingly-important-to-management/?sh=18ef14fe250f

Mulvanity, E. W. (2001). Generation X in the workplace: Age diversity issues in project teams. Paper presented at Project Management Institute Annual Seminars & Symposium, Nashville, TN. Newtown Square, PA: Project Management Institute.

Pink, D. H. (2011). *Drive*. Edinburgh: Canongate Books.

Robison, J. (2021, September 20). Why millennials are job hopping. Retrieved December 29, 2021 from www.gallup.com/workplace/267743/why-millennials-job-hopping.aspx

Sinek, S. (2011). *Start with why*. London: Penguin Books.

Stahl, A. (2019, September 10). How generation-Z will revolutionize the workplace. Retrieved December 29, 2021 from www.forbes.com/sites/ashleystahl/2019/09/10/how-generation-z-will-revolutionize-the-workplace/?sh=3c91b4a24f53

Urban, T. (2013, September 9). Why generation Y yuppies are unhappy. Retrieved December 29, 2021 from https://waitbutwhy.com/2013/09/why-generation-y-yuppies-are-unhappy.html

Chapter 4

The Changing Nature of Workforces and Employment Categories

William Garrison

The concept of a "workforce" is a way to define the collective group of those who work in a given society. Societies track and study "workforces" to help guide the potential and effectiveness of that society. In the United States, the Bureau of Labor Statistics (BLS) defines, delineates, tracks, and studies the workforce compared to the population. BLS uses "labor force" to define those in the population that are working.

Workforce Definitions

Here are some of the concepts and definitions from the BLS website:

- **Civilian Noninstitutional Population** – number of people living in the country, age 16 or older, who are not active-duty members of the U.S. Armed Forces, confined to or living in an institution or facility (such as prisons or nursing homes).
- **Civilian Labor Force**, or **Labor Force** – all people, age 16 or older, employed or actively looking for work.
- **Not in the Labor Force** – anyone above the age of 16 who is unemployed and not actively searching for a job. Those who choose not to work (such as stay-at-home parents), those who haven't sought for work in over a year, and those who are "Marginally Attached to the Labor Force" are all included (looked for a job in the past year, but not in the past four weeks).
- **Employed** – all people, age 16 or older, who meet any of the following criteria:
    - Wage and Salary Workers – worked at least 1 hour as a paid employee.
    - Self-employed – worked at least 1 hour in their own business, profession, trade, or farm.
    - With a Job, Not at Work – were temporarily absent from their job, business, or farm, whether or not they were paid for the time off.
    - Unpaid Family Workers – worked for a minimum of 15 hours without compensation in a business or farm owned by a family member.

DOI: 10.4324/9781003122272-4

- **Unemployed** – all people, age 16 or older, that meet all of the following criteria:
  - Not employed during the survey week.
  - Available for work.
  - Made at least one effort to find a job during the 4-week survey period.
- **Labor Force Participation Rate** – number of people in the labor force as a percentage of the civilian noninstitutional population.
- **Employment-Population Ratio** – number of employed people in the labor force as a percentage of the civilian noninstitutional population.

Part of the reason the BLS tracks and studies the labor force is to use it as a dashboard or scoreboard so governmental adjustments can improve the nation's productivity. Economists study the Production Possibility Curve to see how effectively we utilize the current labor force to increase the gross domestic product (GDP). And, one of the primary measures of the effectiveness of an American presidential term is the unemployment rate.

Unemployment Categories

It helps to understand what constitutes employed versus unemployed when discussing the future of workforces, so the new workforces are captured in these statistics and studies. The BLS further divides up the unemployed to find an even more distinct picture of any given period's unemployment issues. These are measured using the following six measures:

- U-1 – people unemployed for 15 weeks or longer
- U-2 – people unemployed due to losing a job, including people who completed a temporary job
- U-3 (Official Unemployment Rate) – total number of people as defined as unemployed (not employed, available to work, and have made an effort to find work)
- U-4 – Unemployed (U-3) plus Discouraged Workers
- U-5 – Unemployed (U-3) plus Marginally Attached to the Labor Force
- U-6 – Unemployed (U-3) plus Marginally Attached to the Labor Force plus People at Work Part-Time for Economic Reasons

Current Workforce Terms and What's Missing

The BLS in the United States also defines Class of Workers to "identify general categories of employment arrangements". Wage and salary workers, self-employed workers, and unpaid family workers are among them.

Employees

Workers who get wages, salaries, commissions, tips, or payment in kind from a private-sector employer or a state, a local, or federal government agency or institution are classified as wage and salary workers. In addition, employees of charities, nonprofits, religious, and civic groups are included.

Self-Employed

Self-employed people run their own business, profession, trade, or farm for profit or fees.

Unpaid Family Employees

Unpaid family employees are those who worked for a minimum of 15 hours without pay in a family member's business or farm during the survey reference week. The unpaid family worker must be related to the business or farm owner by marriage, birth, or adoption and must live in the same household (BLS, 2021).

"Gig Workers"

What's missing from this group is the "Gig Economy Workers". "Gig Workers" are those individuals who provide a service in exchange for something without being self-employed. Although it could be argued that "Gig Workers" are undocumented business owners, the aforementioned BLS definitions do not fully describe their work.

When the word "Gig" is mentioned, many conjure images of a garage band playing a set at a local bar. The band was formed as a side hobby by several friends, and they met together and practiced in their parents' garage for some time. Then they get the chance to perform in front of an audience one day. Eventually, if they are good enough, they can get paid for doing so. The "Gig" often is a nonverbal contract that promises a small monetary amount for the band to entertain the bar patrons and may even include side perks like free beers while they play. The band then is left to divvy up the stipend as they see fit. The bar owner is under no obligation to book the band for future evenings, nor is the band obligated to continue playing at that bar for that previously arranged amount. Each evening is negotiated separately.

The "Gig Economy" is growing and includes much more than just garage bands. The most recognizable recent high-growth "Gig" is being an Uber driver. As an Uber driver, an individual offers up their vehicle, their gas, and their time to drive other individuals to wherever they request in exchange for a fare. Uber, as the company, does help with the technology infrastructure and, in turn, takes a fee for doing so. Uber drivers are under no obligation ever to drive a passenger, but they can also work for longer than most hourly jobs. Thus, Uber drivers can control their schedule, work intermittently, and earn decent money in fares and tips.

Other "Gig Workers" include different roles that would traditionally be seen as off the books. Still, with the ability to connect globally using the internet and the tech-savvy skills of today's workers, "Gig" work can also include one-time tasks such as paralegal services, computer programming, and management consultations from anywhere in the world.

Labor Force by Age

In addition, the number of older workers in the labor force in the United States is increasing. This is due to various causes, including increased access to healthcare, improved nutritional knowledge and utilization, and a culture that values healthy practices. As seen in Figure 4.1, workers aged 55 and up continue to expand as a share of the total labor force and is projected to reach nearly a quarter of the labor force by 2050, with an adverse effect on the younger 16- to 24-year-old labor force and little to no effect on the 25- to 54-year-old labor force. Those 55 and older in 2050 would have been born before 1995, and (if considering those under the age of 80) as far back as 1970, this would constitute all of the Millennials and the remaining Gen X population.

Current Employment Categories

As companies set organizational goals and five-year plans, the tasks are divided, the organizational structure is outlined, and the number of employees is decided and budgeted. These include four types of employment categories traditionally used:

Percent of labor force by age, 2000, 2010, and projected 2050

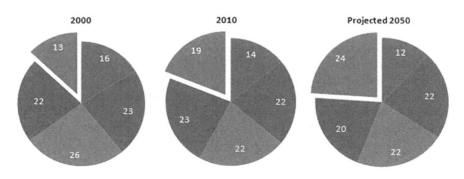

Source: U.S. Bureau of Labor Statistics.

Figure 4.1 Percent of Labor Force by Age (BLS, 2012)

Full-Time Salaried – these positions are used to complete long-term and repeated tasks that typically require some level of education or advanced training. Workers sign an open-ended contract for a definitive amount for the year and are paid out in segments determined by the organization. They should be the most loyal workers and the most engaged as they see the workplace as their second home. These include most, if not all, management and some frontline technical workers. Typically, these workers also receive additional benefits such as health insurance, bonuses, retirement plans, profit-sharing, and stock options.

Full-Time Hourly – these positions are used to complete long-term and repeated tasks but may not require any educational background. These workers typically are doing more technical work that is not consistent at the operational level. Most weeks, these workers will work 40 hours, but those hours can fluctuate based on the organization's current needs. Most overtime pay is used with this category of worker. As the tasks become more regular and the overtime pay becomes a normal procedure, most employers will convert this position to Full-Time Salaried to predict the costs annually better. These workers may also receive additional benefits as well.

Part-Time Hourly – these positions are used to complete short-term operational tasks that require very little training and may even be considered unskilled labor. These workers are typically paid near the minimum wage as it may be difficult to quantify their contribution to the bottom line financially. Both the manager and the employee may have some flexibility in deciding which shifts or hours are worked each week in these positions. This category typically does not include any benefits paid and has a very high turnover rate. However, some Part-Time Hourly workers can be very engaged with the organization's mission, vision, and values as they enjoy a sense of belonging among the staff and management.

Contract – these positions are used to complete short-term tasks that are not necessarily routine tasks for the organization. When a company starts on a new project, hiring a contract worker makes more sense because they are paid to fulfill a set of tasks in a set amount of time. Contract workers are compensated for doing the activities outlined in the agreement. Contract worker costs are relatively straightforward to estimate because they are close-ended, unlike low-cost hourly workers, and may be difficult to define in an annual budget. Contract workers are usually not subject to withholdings or get any supplementary perks. Despite having extensive technical training, abilities, and knowledge, contract workers are rarely involved with the company's mission or culture.

Why They Are Becoming Obsolete

Human Resources departments are finding that these classifications are insufficient to characterize their developing positions. For example, more automation is introduced into firms, and more individuals adopt a "Gig"-type arrangement or prefer a purpose-driven role. Also, the labor force itself is changing and sees some of these labels as psychologically damaging.

Gray-Collar Work: Why Blue-Collar and White-Collar Labels Are No Longer Appropriate

One of those labels is "Blue-Collar". As the factory model became the norm in American society, the lines between Blue-Collar work and White-Collar work were well defined. Blue-Collar workers wore blue dress shirts, performed manual labor, and had their name on their shirts. Meanwhile, White-Collar workers wore white dress shirts, did no manual labor, and had their name on their desk. Blue-Collar workers tend to be either unskilled or low-skilled, while White-Collar workers tend to be educated and highly dependent on their thought processes and decision-making.

Although these distinctions were easy to see and made it easier for organizations to divide up the labor, they also led to discrimination, classism, and even psychological damage. Young adults growing up in America were faced with educational paths as early as junior high school and were asked to choose that path they would travel the remainder of their lives. Apparently, White-Collar careers were much more preferable to Blue-Collar jobs, and both parents and school counselors encouraged their kids to pursue them. White-Collar professions promised ideal working conditions in air-conditioned, corner offices. They included long-term contracts with excellent salaries and benefits, including company cars, country club memberships, and stock options. Meanwhile, Blue-Collar jobs were performed in filthy, unhealthy working conditions that necessitated the formation of labor unions, the use of time clocks that had to be punched in and out to the minute to avoid earning more money than one was working for, and an hourly wage with few to no benefits.

As more young adults chose the well-traveled path of economic growth, which resulted in more significant salaries, property ownership, and a lack of basic handyman skills, these professionals began to have an increased need for Blue-Collar work to be done, and they had the money to pay for it. As fewer and fewer young adults chose the Blue-Collar route and the demand for those services increased, the Blue-Collar workers began to charge more. Then, as the internet and other technologies evolved, Blue-Collar work became much more than unskilled labor. Many so-called Blue-Collar jobs today include high-tech tools and sophisticated computer systems (Parietti, 2021).

As seen in the following table, some Blue-Collar jobs now outpace White-Collar jobs in salaries from November 2016 to November 2018:

Furthermore, with so many more young adults pursuing a college education, they find it difficult to find work straight after graduation. In contrast, those who didn't go to college have four to five years of experience in their field and are earning higher pay.

Job Title	Approximate Median Pay
Air traffic controller	$90 K
Boilermaker	$72 K
Electrical supervisor	$66 K
Elevator mechanic	$88 K
HVAC controls technician	$65 K
HVAC service manager	$68 K
Instrument and electrical technician	$68 K
Journeyman lineman	$75 K
Lineman	$71 K
Locomotive engineer	$81 K
Operating engineer	$67 K
Police sergeant	$68 K
Refrigeration mechanic	$69 K
Senior piping designer	$92 K
Stationary engineer or boiler operator	$66 K

Source: Wilkie (2019)

Mason Bishop of WorkED Consulting has noted that the label "Blue-Collar worker" comes with a stigma of being a "dirty job". He has seen that the label "Gray-Collar work" or "technical careerist" is much more fitting as many of today's manufacturing jobs require more understanding of technology and the skills to use it (Wilkie, 2019).

Furthermore, employers created a Skills Training Gap that needed "Blue-Collar workers" and "Gray-Collar workers" but found there were not enough prepared applicants. As a result, instead of increasing their own training programs, hiring immigrants and moving jobs overseas became easier instead. However, with the Covid-19 Pandemic of 2020, U.S.-based businesses found that decreased manufacturing capabilities domestically led to a significant interruption in the supply chain and limited productivity significantly.

With the growing demand for "Gray-Collar" jobs and rising salaries, there has been increased pressure on high school districts to expand their Career Technical Education Paths to more students and de-emphasize President George W. Bush and Senator Ted Kennedy's "No Child Left Behind" policies, which encouraged all students to attend college.

In Janesville, Wisconsin, Superintendent Steve Pophal feels that the traditional educational approach doesn't give his students the skills they will need as they enter into the New World of Work. So, he has sent several of his teachers to pursue degrees in "mechatronics", a developing subject that mixes mechanical engineering and electronics, so that they may educate their kids about it (Wilkie, 2019).

Businesses are beginning to respond to these coming trends by adding paid apprenticeship programs to high school and community college students. Still, there is a massive gap in skills training in the United States that needs to be filled. Jessica Culo, an Express franchise owner, noticed that companies that are looking for specific skills from their new hires need to also consider their "soft skills" abilities, but that is increasingly difficult to find. In addition, companies are going to need employees who can expertly perform the tasks that automation cannot duplicate. Shane DeCoste, also an Express franchise owner, suggests that applicants need to be eager to learn how to use their employer's software programs, peripheral devices, and other electronic devices in jobs where this was not previously common. There is now a higher expectation of technology skills than ever before (Express Employment Professionals, 2020).

As stated by Bill Stoller, CEO of Express, one thing is for sure is that employees and employers need to be always changing and learning how to leverage new technologies, regardless of job classification. Companies can ease the concerns of artificial intelligence and automation by maximizing the effectiveness of Gray-Collar jobs (Express Employment Professionals, 2020).

New Employment Categories

With all of this in mind, new employment categories are emerging.

Contingent Worker

Much like a contract worker, contingent workers are not employed directly with the company but are instead paid to do a set of tasks. However, while contract workers are provided a specific contract in which the time frames, tasks, and pay are laid out, contingent workers are not given specifics about how or sometimes even when the work will be completed. These could include freelance writers, consultants, editors, and even salespeople (Chron, 2020).

Flexible Worker

A flexible worker often is an employee of the company but doesn't have to be. As the emphasis on work-life balance increases and the workforce because more diverse, workers are looking for more flexible options than the traditional categories mentioned earlier.

By providing work flexibility, companies are experiencing lower employee turnover, increased morale, and lower fixed costs. In surveys administered by FlexJobs, over three-fourths of respondents claimed they would be more loyal to their company if they had flex work options (FlexJobs, 2021).

Flex work comes in many different forms:

- **Remote Workers** – workers who are not required to work at a physical office location; can work while traveling as well (Writers, Online Professors, Customer Service)

- **Freelance Workers** – typically are self-employed and work for a contracted period of time such as a project (Consultants, Graphic Designers, IT Technician)
- **Part-Time Workers** – work less than 40 hours per week, paid by the hour, and typically not provided other benefits (Food Service Worker, Social Media Contributor, Photographer)
- **Alternative Schedule Workers** – workers who do their tasks outside the normal business hours such as nights and weekends (Lyft Driver, After-Hours Adult Care)
- **Flex Workers** – schedule is determined by employee and agreed upon by employer (Medical Billing and Coding Specialist, Accountant, Groundskeeper)
- **Short-Term/Temp Workers** – substitute workers who are covering a full-time worker's role for a specified period of time while on leave (Substitute Teacher, IT Technician, Project Manager)
- **Seasonal Workers** – workers who do their work during a particular season (Lifeguard, Wedding Planner, Christmas Tree Salesman) (FlexJobs, 2021)

Additionally, according to the U.S. Department of Labor (n.d.), the Fair Labor Standards Act (FLSA) does not address flexible work schedules. Therefore, alternative work arrangements such as flexible work schedules are a matter of agreement between the employer and the employee.

Employees view the opportunity for flex work as highly beneficial to fit their lifestyles and changing needs as they can continue to build solid careers and financial stability and security.

"Gig Worker"

Finally, as defined earlier, "Gig" work has become increasingly more popular as HR departments are aligning their labor needs to be filled with the desire of workers to perform these tasks. "Gig" work is a single task that is completed for a predetermined reward, typically monetary. As mentioned earlier, the best "Gig" work example is a garage band playing a set for a local bar. Neither the bar nor the band is contractually obligated beyond that "Gig". Uber drivers choose to work a "Gig" by turning on their availability and picking up and dropping off a passenger. After that ride is completed, the Uber driver is under no obligation ever to drive again.

Other examples of "Gig" work could include website builder, dog walker, software coder, babysitter, video editor, lawnmower, and logo designer. Some examples are traditionally seen as "Gigs" you would pay a teenager to do, while others are highly paid salaried positions. In our New World of Work, these highly skilled workers seek the ability to perform the one "Gig" and then be freed from further contractual agreements. As we will see in Chapter 6, some of this work is even performed without any promise of pay but rather a chance to win a huge reward!

Opportunities and Benefits of New Employment Structure

Even though reimagining these new categories into the traditional HR organizational mindset can be quite challenging, there are numerous opportunities and benefits to moving toward this new employment structure.

1   Employees can shift between roles as desired to fit their work-life balance
2   Instead of assigning additional tasks to existing roles, those tasks can be completed by "Gig Workers"
3   Time can be spent on cultivating a purpose-driven organization
4   Employee Engagement by all workers will increase
5   Turnover will not be costly but offers a new opportunity
6   Internal promotions will increase
7   Non-skilled workers will be encouraged to learn new skills
8   Employees will feel empowered to contribute meaningfully toward organizational goals

References

BLS. (2021, October 21). Retrieved December 29, 2021 from www.bls.gov/cps/definitions. htm#marginallyattached

BLS. (2012, December 3). Overview of the labor force from 1950–2010 and projections to 2050. Retrieved December 29, 2021 from www.bls.gov/opub/ted/2012/ted_20121203. htm

Chron. (2020, June 16). Contingent vs. contract employees. Retrieved December 29, 2021 from https://work.chron.com/contingent-vs-contract-employees-8965.html

Department of Labor. Flexible schedules. (n.d.). Retrieved December 29, 2021 from www. dol.gov/general/topic/workhours/flexibleschedules

Express Employment Professionals. (2020, January 22). The emerging grey collar workforce. Retrieved December 29, 2021 from www.globenewswire.com/news-release/2020/ 01/22/1973745/0/en/The-Emerging-Grey-Collar-Workforce.html

FlexJobs. (2021, July 8). What is a flexible job? FlexJobs. Retrieved December 29, 2021 from www.flexjobs.com/blog/post/kinds-jobs-are-flexible-jobs

Parietti, M. (2021, September 13). Blue-collar vs. white-collar: What's the difference? Retrieved December 29, 2021 from www.investopedia.com/articles/wealth-management/120215/blue-collar-vs-white-collar-different-social-classes.asp

Wilkie, D. (2019, February 6). The blue-collar drought. Retrieved December 29, 2021 from www.shrm.org/hr-today/news/all-things-work/pages/the-blue-collar-drought.aspx

Chapter 5

The Changing Nature of Employee Relations and Working Conditions

William Garrison

Current Employee Relations

The employer has traditionally initiated the Employment Contract with terms that seek to fulfill the organizational goals. Human Resource departments write job descriptions and post jobs on websites to attract the types of workers who will fulfill the job's roles and fit with the organization. The employee has the burden to filter out these opportunities and commit to whichever job works best. However, the current Employment Contract includes rigid categories and still tilts toward the organization's benefit. Therefore, HR departments have studied and implemented many motivation theories of management to help attract and retain these highly skilled, highly qualified, and valuable workers. By implementing the theories that work best for the organization, Employee Engagement increases, thus leading to higher productivity toward organizational goals.

Motivation Theories

The role of management is to create a balance between accomplishing the organizational objectives while also advocating for the employees. As mentioned before, this hasn't always been the case, but through decades of research and acknowledgment of worker exploitation, employee relations have improved. With the emergence of the Millennial and Gen Z workforce, the need to improve upon motivational strategies and tactics is more crucial than ever in order to increase employee retention and productivity. Several motivational theories have been formed over the years, and companies have chosen to base many of their compensation packages and corporate cultures on them.

Each motivational theory is based on how employers view their employees. Two of the most prominent views are extrinsic versus intrinsic and Theory X versus Theory Y.

DOI: 10.4324/9781003122272-5

Employees come to the workplace with the ability to be motivated either extrinsically or intrinsically.

- Extrinsically motivated employees require some sort of external stimulus to create action. They are motivated to perform because they will get something for it from someone else.
- Intrinsically motivated workers find their motivation within themselves. They work harder or longer because it makes them feel better inside. They feel their extra work will increase their self-esteem. These types of workers even come to work motivated because they are driven internally.

Other management researchers have looked at the managers and how they view their employees. This viewpoint is summed up with the label Theory X or Theory Y.

- The Theory X management viewpoint is that employees only work to receive money. This means that money is the primary motivator, and the employee's view of how much money they receive will determine how hard they will work for it.
- In Theory Y, managers believe that workers are highly self-motivated. They think that money is a good base for compensation, but many other factors come into play and that you can get more work out of an employee when you tap into their self-motivations.

Both concepts are seen in many of the following motivation theories. Each of these theories should be viewed in isolation from the others. They are not meant to build upon each other but should be thoroughly understood and then used as the basis of organizational charts, employee compensation packages, job descriptions, performance evaluation systems, and even manifested in the company's culture.

Maslow's Hierarchy of Needs (1943)

One of the most extensively used motivational theories is Maslow's Hierarchy of Needs. In 1943, Abraham Maslow proposed that people are motivated by five levels of needs that build upon each other. He believed that each of the lower levels needed to be met for the next level up to be addressed. From a manager's perspective, this means that managers should assess the needs of their employees and realize that they will not be able to achieve the highest level that leads to significant productivity if lower levels are of concern. Thus, the manager should use empathy to discover and support the employee who is struggling with lower-level needs rather than discipline them.

1   **Physiological Need** – able to obtain food, shelter, and clothing

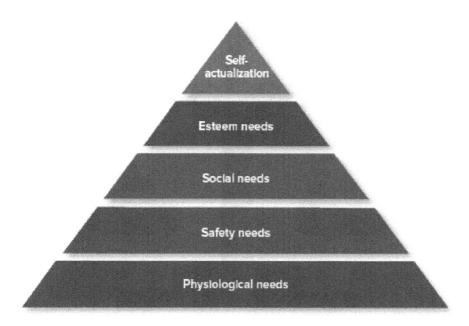

Figure 5.1 Maslow's Hierarchy of Needs

2   **Safety Need** – able to feel safe physically, emotionally, and can avoid violence; can include insurance, job security, safety culture, and retirement plans
3   **Social Need** – able to find love, have friends, and be affectionate; can include employee resource groups, social events outside of work, and off-site retreats
4   **Esteem Need** – feels respected, has a good reputation among coworkers, confident; can include awards and other forms of recognition
5   **Self-actualization Need** – able to operate at the highest level, in the flow; can include outside opportunities beyond the organization including authoring a book or presenting at a conference (Kinicki & Williams, 2020).

Equity Theory (1963)

J. Stacey Adams theorized that motivation was based on the worker's perception of the equity of outcomes between what an employee inputs and what they receive as outputs compared to other workers' inputs and outputs. Inputs

Figure 5.2 Equity Theory

include educational degrees, certifications, previous work experience, and hours worked, while the outputs they receive are in the form of promotions, bonuses, and awards among others. If the workers perceive to be operating in a fair system, they are motivated to increase their time, effort, and other organizational inputs leading to higher productivity (Kinicki & Williams, 2020).

Herzberg's Two-Factor Theory (1964)

After interviewing 203 accountants and engineers, Frederick Herzberg discovered that there were two categories of factors that influenced workers: Motivating Factors and Hygiene Factors. The concept was that workers would be more productive if management increased satisfying Motivating Factors and decreased dissatisfying Hygiene Factors (Kinicki & Williams, 2020).

Expectancy Theory (1964)

Victor Vroom developed the Expectancy Theory to explain that workers will put forth an effort if they believe that effort will lead to the performance of a given task and subsequently lead to the desired outcome. In other words,

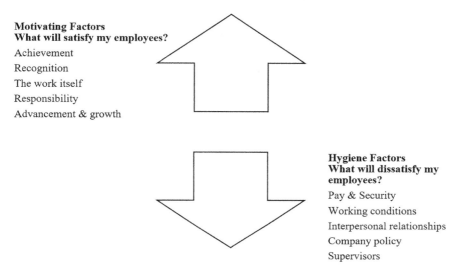

Motivating Factors
What will satisfy my employees?
Achievement
Recognition
The work itself
Responsibility
Advancement & growth

Hygiene Factors
What will dissatisfy my employees?
Pay & Security
Working conditions
Interpersonal relationships
Company policy
Supervisors

Figure 5.3 Herzberg's Two-Factor Theory

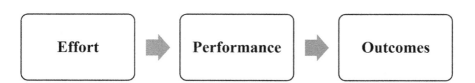

Effort   **Performance**   **Outcomes**

Figure 5.4 Expectancy Theory

workers will be more motivated to increase their effort if they perceive they will do it and get something valuable out of it (Kinicki & Williams, 2020).

Goal-Setting Theory (1968)

Psychologists Edwin Locke and Gary Latham discovered that employees naturally want to set goals and strive to achieve them. They also found that this process works best when the employee understands and accepts these goals. Therefore, they encourage managers to have ongoing conversations with their employees to determine, set, review, and update goals to increase the desired outcomes and create an ongoing performance cycle (Kinicki & Williams, 2020).

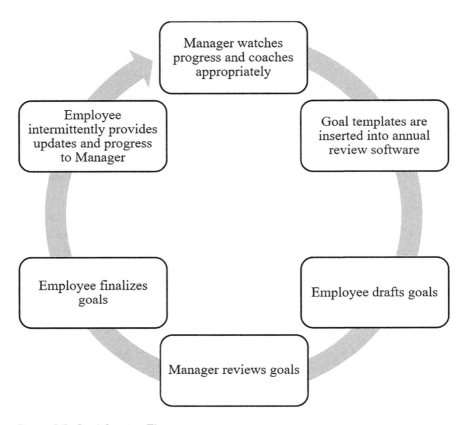

Figure 5.5 Goal-Setting Theory

Self-Determination Theory (1985)

Edward Deci and Richard Ryan, psychologists at the University of Rochester, established the Self-Determination Theory, which assumes that employees desire to advance and are motivated by three needs: autonomy, competence, and relatedness (Ryan and Deci (2017).

In his book *Drive*, Daniel Pink develops this further. He uses autonomy, mastery, and purpose as needs that employees have that could lead to massive improvements in productivity if provided by their manager (Pink, 2011).

Five Sources of Power

John Maxwell, famed leadership author of many leadership books, states, "Leadership is influence. Nothing more, nothing less". In the boss–subordinate relationship, there are five different sources of power:

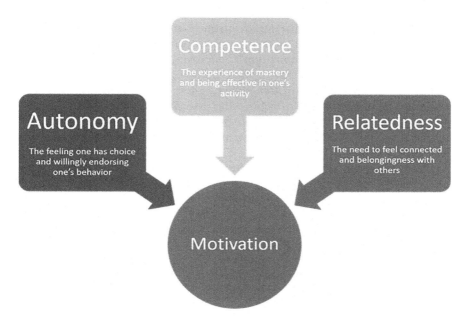

Figure 5.6 Self-Determination Theory (University of Rochester Medical Center, n.d.)

1   **Legitimate Power** – the power a manager has due to position and title
2   **Reward Power** – the power a manager has due to being able to reward their workers
3   **Coercive Power** – the power a manager has due to being able to punish their workers
4   **Expert Power** – the power due to the person having expert knowledge
5   **Referent Power** – the power due to the person having an attractive personality (Kinicki & Williams, 2020)

In Maxwell's book *Five Levels of Leadership*, he sees a common thread with these five powers with a slight twist:

- **Level One Leader: Position** – people follow because they have to
- **Level Two Leader: Permission** – people follow because they want to
- **Level Three Leader: Production** – people follow because of what you have done for the organization
- **Level Four Leader: People Development** – people follow because of what you have done for them
- **Level Five Leader: Pinnacle** – people follow because of who you are and what you represent (Maxwell, 2013)

Boss-Subordinate Relationship

Most of the research shows that improving the boss-subordinate relationship can benefit the organization. As most managers are action-oriented and rewarded for accomplishing organizational goals, improving the boss-subordinate relationship will increase productivity and employee retention. HR departments can be the critical drivers to strengthening these relations through increased management training and implementing research-based motivational programs. In addition, these training programs need to improve the managers' interpersonal skills, leading to more meaningful relationships that empower the employee.

The boss-subordinate relationship can also be a source of conflict. According to Fernando Bartolomé and André Laurent, writing for the *Harvard Business Review*, while managers may feel that personality conflicts drive workplace issues, HR departments should first evaluate the organization's power hierarchy to see any distortions of expectations. They state that the "[u]nevenness of power in the organization subtly influences how managers and subordinates relate to each other" (Bartolome & Laurent, 1986). HR departments and organizations can gain productivity when these power structures and the boss-subordinate trust relationships are optimal.

Hierarchical Structure

To help define this relationship, managers and owners construct organizational charts or simply org charts. As seen next, org charts provide a visual representation of the reporting relationships and hierarchies within the organization (Kinicki & Williams, 2020).

At the top of an org chart is the chief executive. This could be the business owner but is typically the President and/or CEO of a publicly traded company. One tier down from there demonstrates a boss-subordinate relationship to top-level managers. For example, in Figure 5.7, we see that four vice presidents report directly to the President. The President's "authority" over the vice presidents is indicated by them being on the second tier, and a solid

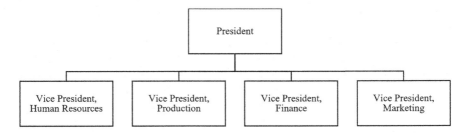

Figure 5.7 Organizational Chart (Org Chart)

line indicates the "responsibility" over those vice presidents. We also see in this org chart that the company has been divided up into four key areas: Human Resources, Production, Finance, and Marketing. If we expanded this org chart further, we would begin to see the number of next line managers that each vice president oversees and the number of additional tiers showing lower-level boss–subordinate relationships.

Top-level managers research, analyze, and modify the organization's production and efficiencies on these charts to represent those changes. For example, as a company increases the number of subordinates reporting to a single manager, they design a "Wide Span of Control". This means that each manager is responsible for more individuals. When they reduce the number of subordinates reporting to a single manager, they design a "Narrow Span of Control". Each has its pros and cons.

Organizational Structures and Efforts toward Improving Employee Relations

Since the Industrial Revolution, employers have hired large numbers of workers to do the tasks laid out for the organization to meet its stated goals. As the work needed to be supervised, managers were added to increase the workers' productivity. Employers found the need to sort out these relationships and divide them up into workable pieces. As mentioned earlier, organizational charts were born as a result of this. Organizational charts include boxes and lines that illustrate formal lines of authority and official positions or division of labor. A row of boxes symbolizes those with an equal position in the organization. For example, the row of boxes immediately under the President would typically include all company vice presidents. A vertical line from each row of boxes would rise into the box representing the President. The row of boxes under that row of boxes would indicate a lower position in the company. This vertical hierarchy of authority helps clarify reporting relationships and, in some sense, the organization's power structure. Each box in a row would represent the "Horizontal Specialization" or the division of labor that would be performed under the position that row of boxes reports to.

Organizations take time and effort to carefully select and create their illustration of the division of labor on their organizational chart. It can be used as a guide for both new employees and employees transitioning into new roles. Those who create and revise the organizational chart facilitate many hours of strategic conversations to get it just right. Organizations that do not regularly evaluate their organizational chart can find their organizational health begin to decline.

One aspect these org charts do not address is the distance between each level vertically. It would be recommended that top executives also spend time determining the length of the vertical lines representing the distance in the boss–subordinate relationship. Although difficult to accurately determine, the exercise would be very fruitful toward improving these relationships.

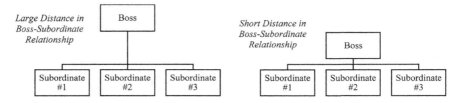

Figure 5.8 Boss-Subordinate Relationship Distance

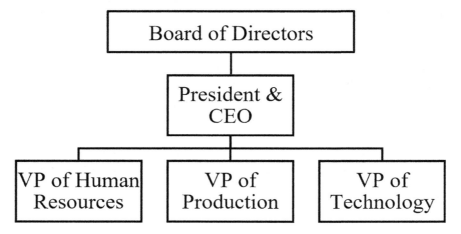

Figure 5.9 Functional Org Chart

Functional Org Charts

The most common type of organizational chart divides up the labor into functional categories. For example, the top line could be the Board of Directors, followed on the second line with the President and CEO. On the third line, the vice presidents would be listed with their titles of the department or function they oversee, such as VP of Human Resources, VP of Production, and VP of Technology. Then, the fourth line would be the directors of each department, followed by other middle management positions.

Divisional Org Charts

In a division organizational chart, the labor may be divided by the product, the geographical area it serves, or the customer type it targets. The vice presidents and their titles denoting that division are on the third line (reporting directly to the

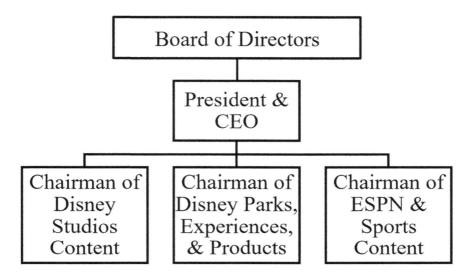

Figure 5.10 Divisional Org Chart

President and CEO). For example, in an entertainment company like the Walt Disney Company, the company offers several different products, and thus the divisions denote that product. In Disney's case, they have a Chairman of Disney Studios Content; a Chairman of Disney Parks, Experiences, and Products; and a Chairman of ESPN and Sports Content. In an insurance company, the division may be by customer types such as VP of Personal Auto, VP of Homeowners, and VP of Recreational Vehicles. Lastly, the division may be geographical, such as VP of Southwest Sales, Northeast Sales, and Pacific Islands.

Matrix Systems

Some workplaces have seen that those traditional structures don't clearly define how work is supervised. For example, in the movie *Office Space*, Peter Gibbons makes a mistake and is subsequently given coaching by eight different bosses since their office's structure includes several different people who oversee his work. As companies realize the need for more formal lines of authority to be drawn, they may turn to a Matrix System in which each employee may have both a function supervisor and a product supervisor. For example, a book publishing company may have functional departments such as Production, Design, and Editing while also having someone assigned to oversee one book. This Book Manager would be responsible for ensuring that the production, design, and editing of that book was done well and on time. Still, they'd also understand that the editor of their book may be working on two other books simultaneously. With a Matrix System, the editor may report directly to the Editorial Manager and indirectly report to the Book Manager. In the Matrix Organizational Chart, the direct supervisor may have a solid line connecting them, while the indirect supervisor would have a dotted line. When laid out, the organizational chart no longer looks like a pyramid or family tree illustration but instead like an interwoven quilt or matrix.

Matrix Systems work well when new products are being developed. It encourages employees from different functional departments to work under a project manager and draw from different perspectives and skill sets. And, since a team working on a new product would be disbanded once the product was created, it is much easier and cheaper to draw upon other departments for a short time and then dissolve that team once the project is completed. However, if the company regularly develops new products, creating a designated product development team would make more sense. Another drawback of using the Matrix System is that sometimes an employee is crucial to their department because they possess a unique skill (Reh, 2019). In these cases, sharing this employee may dilute their ability to focus on the company's function.

Some modifications of the Matrix System could be valuable by designating the system's strength. Reh describes these as Weak Matrix, Balanced Matrix, and Strong Matrix Teams (Reh, 2019):

- **Strong Matrix** – team members directly report to the project manager until the end of the project.
- **Balanced Matrix** – team members work for both their direct manager and their project manager. It is up to the worker to keep both managers up to date on the progress of the project.
- **Weak Matrix** – team members don't report to the project manager. It is up to the project manager to borrow workers from their functional manager (Reh, 2019).

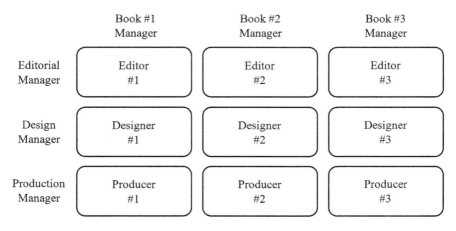

Figure 5.11 Matrix System

One of the challenges of using a Matrix Management system is that employees can become confused about their performance evaluation and which manager is responsible for coaching. There also is potential for conflicts between managers as the employee becomes too stretched across several projects and the functional team starts to slip in productivity.

A lot of this can be alleviated if there is clarity in the project charter and lots of communication between managers from the start. In addition, managers need to discuss each employee's capabilities as they are assigned to other managers. Employees should also be encouraged to discuss all their work with their direct supervisor to keep them appraised (Reh, 2019).

Project Management and Special Assignments

Another form of improving the boss–subordinate relationship is to assign the employee to a project team or other special assignment as mentioned in the Matrix System. This gives the employee the chance to do something a little different to break the monotony of their regular role for a short time without losing them to that function forever. This also allows the employee to demonstrate additional skills and talents that may not be drawn upon in their regular role. In addition, the more inexperienced team members may benefit from working closely with more experienced employees they usually wouldn't come into contact with.

This also allows the employer to see what internal talent there may be for upcoming promotions or new roles being developed. And, of course, this will also increase the likely success of the project itself (Duggan, 2017).

Flattening the Org Chart

As more companies employ organizational design strategies and find ways to improve productivity and employee relations, there is a strong motivation to "Flatten the Org Chart". Flattening the Org Chart is meant to reduce the number of tier levels between the top management and the frontline worker. The owners work alongside the dishwashers in a small business, such as a local mom-and-pop café. This move reduces labor costs and empowers decision-making to the lower tier levels in larger organizations. Another benefit of Flattening the Org Chart is that employees have much better access to top-level management and can better influence changes in the organization.

Current Working Conditions

Of course, back during the Industrial Revolution, factory owners found ways to distance themselves from their subordinates. Many viewed workers as assets or machines within the factory system and employed humans simply because there wasn't a way to design machines to make those motions.

This made the boss–subordinate relationship a point of contention to the extreme of abusive labor practices. As factory owners began to see the benefits of increased productivity, they realized that they could make more money if they pushed harder. And, as there seemed to be a long flow of workers wanting to work for them, they began to view their workers in this negative light. Hours got longer, physical demands got tougher, and injuries resulted. In addition, a father would see the benefit of having his children work at the factory to increase the family pay. Owners welcomed this since there were tasks that were better suited for shorter and thinner workers, but very few adults fit that profile. This era led to many injuries, illnesses, and deaths as there were little to no regulations that owners had to adhere to.

Role of Unions

During the twentieth century, the role of unions became a powerful driver to improve the boss–subordinate relationship. As workers were encouraged to collectively bargain and find strength in numbers to address workplace concerns, business owners were forced to become more sensitive to these concerns. As victories were tough but increasing, professional labor unions began growing in size and power. As employers became more overbearing, it only took a few employees to contact a professional labor union and gain support to address these overreaches.

Throughout the twentieth century, labor unions won several significant victories in the fight to level out the power structure in the boss–subordinate relationship. For example, one of the significant roles of a local labor union is to go through the collective bargaining process. When the current collective bargaining agreement expires, some employees are voted to participate on the negotiation team, meeting with management to set pay scales, benefits packages, vacation and sick days, working hours and days, and other working conditions.

As many of the terms of collective bargaining agreements have made it into state and national labor laws, most professional labor unions see their memberships decline. Although the role of labor unions will always exist, it is to their credit that the perceived need for them is a victory in itself (Cornell Law School, n.d.). In today's digitized workplace, there are new challenges that pose a threat to workers that could use union support to continue these workplace improvements. As we will discuss later in the book, employers are beginning to violate worker privacy in online environments, and many of the current labor laws are becoming obsolete or at best ineffective in these realms.

Role of Occupational Safety and Health Administration

In addition to the role of labor unions, the Occupational Safety and Health Administration (or OSHA) has improved working conditions for employees, especially in health and safety. According to the U.S. Department of Labor (n.d.), over the twentieth century, unhealthy and dangerous working conditions caused the injuries and deaths of employees across all industries. As many business owners did not feel their employees' health and safety were their responsibility, local, state, and federal law-makers began to address these businesses with increased regulations. These efforts culminated in the formation of OSHA with the Occupational Safety & Health Act of 1970. Since then, workplace injuries and deaths have dramatically reduced. In addition, the boss-subordinate relationship has improved since many perceive their boss as concerned about the employee's health and safety as their priority.

Role of Technology and Artificial Intelligence Systems

As managers work to meet the federal, state, and local regulations, they begin to see their labor force as their most expensive asset and their highest main-tenance component. So, the logical conclusion they come to is offshore that labor, outsource that labor, or replace it using automation.

During the Industrial Revolution, owners had found numerous ways to bring in technology to replace that labor. Inventors came up with amazing machines such as the steam engine, cotton harvesters, grain elevators, and esca-lators. As factory owners began to purchase these items in large quantities, inventors had even more motivation to solve other factory challenges with new inventions (History.com, 2009).

As workers began to notice these machines replacing them, some of them even conspired together to destroy those machines in the middle of the night to help save those jobs. These conspirators were led by Ned Ludd and are com-monly known as "Luddites".

In the British factories, the first "Luddites" were weavers and textile work-ers. These workers saw that the time they had invested in becoming skilled was going to be easily replaced by unskilled workers operating these new machines. Their reaction was to break into the factories after hours and destroy the machines (Andrews, 2015).

The "Luddites" are still represented today in all industries but still do not pose such a threat to overshadow the financial benefits of today's and tomorrow's tech-nological advancements. As mentioned earlier, there is a big motivation to "Flat-ten the Org Chart" and push decision-making closer to the frontline worker. The first place organizations look to flatten the org chart is in middle management. And, since the rise of computers, top managers have found that many of the functions of middle managers can be replaced by software while simultaneously requiring potential middle managers to be proficient in using these software pro-grams. Ironically, middle managers load the bullet that will later kill them.

Administrative Functions of Management Now Performed by Software

Computers were designed to process large amounts of information in very little time. The human capacity to do so is very limited. Still, with the use of com-puters, managers can feed data into the system, convert that data into informa-tion, and then view the outputs as useful insights.

Over the past 70 years, many software companies have created computer programs to replace some or most of the administrative functions of management, as they were rudimentary tasks that could be automated in some fashion.

- In the 1950s, IBM began using the punch card system to quickly receive and analyze large sets of data. These punch card systems were used to store data, process information, and validate the information.
- Microsoft unveiled the MS-DOS command-line interface in 1980. MS-DOS allowed users to enter, store, and retrieve data from floppy disks using the single command line.
- In 1983, Lotus 1–2–3 was introduced as the first digital spreadsheet. Lotus 1–2–3 allowed users to store data in columns and rows and print out results.
- Microsoft introduced Windows in 1985 as a graphical representation of the MS-DOS systems. Windows made using computers much easier as the user no longer had to understand the DOS coding. As Windows grew in use, many popular management programs have been created to work on the platform, including the Microsoft Suite of products such as Microsoft Word, Microsoft PowerPoint, and Microsoft Excel.
- One prevalent customer relationship management (CRM) system is Salesforce, formed in 1999. Salesforce is a database that collects, stores, and queries customer or client information. It allows both employee and manager to have varying access to input data and create reports.
- A growing management software from Microsoft is Power BI. The Power BI program is much like Salesforce in that it is a database that can collect and analyze data quickly. In addition, it allows the user to use filters much like a simple Excel spreadsheet.

Management Dashboards

As top executives began to see the numerous applications these software programs could provide, they used them to replace the middle manager. As executives analyze the desired outcomes of production, they begin to discover the tasks that lead to higher production. They find that these "Key Performance Indicators", or KPIs, are the workers' tasks to concentrate on. These KPIs are laid out in job descriptions, one-on-ones, and annual reviews in most companies. When employees know their goals and what tasks lead to those goals, productivity increases. The middle manager's role, then, is to monitor these KPIs, and often their own KPIs are the roll-up of their subordinate's KPIs. However, the most difficult aspect is knowing what data to collect and feed into that system.

In the past, middle managers would monitor these KPIs by walking around with a clipboard and checking off items. This allowed them to "walk the floor" and be around the workers they monitored. In recent decades, computer programmers have created digital "Dashboards" that display all of the KPIs and many other metrics on one screen of a computer, laptop, or tablet. This has decreased the need for the middle manager to "walk the floor" and has created distance in the boss–subordinate relationship.

As these management dashboards have become more commonplace, the next frontier of computer programmers is to create artificial intelligence (AI) machines that can analyze the KPIs and the dashboards to make decisions. These AI machines will be programmed to make adjustments to increase productivity. Of course, these machines will only be as good as their creators program them. It is hoped that AI can incorporate the human element better than their human counterparts.

Tyranny of the Metrics

From the management perspective, these dashboards and the prospect of AI managers feel like a massive leap toward increased productivity. Many of the issues discussed thus far are due to human beings' complex nature, leading to many improvements in the boss–subordinate relationship. Managers have become better at using intuition and experience to drive increased results and retention. Simultaneously, business owners have seen the overwhelmingly positive results of automation in robotic assembly lines, inventory control systems, and even self-checkout registers. The allure to replace humans with machines has paid off both emotionally and financially. However, even though it may be faint at times, there is a sense that disconnecting the human element from these movements and transactions leads us closer and closer to a return to Taylorism and the removal of emotion and connection from the passions that began in the heart of the business owner.

The result of ignoring this faint signal leads to what Jerry Muller describes in the title of his book from 2018, the *Tyranny of the Metrics*. Muller expresses that collecting and displaying as much data as possible is a very good thing but needs to be balanced by the human element of intuition and experience. Managers can easily be hypnotized by the readily available data points to drive decisions when their "guts" may be leading them elsewhere. As many motivation theories demonstrate, an organization's most powerful asset is its people. The best way to leverage that asset is by implementing boss–subordinate relationships that come as close to an equal partnership as possible while still focusing on meeting and exceeding the organizational goals. This begins with the design of the dashboards and the constant need to choose which data to collect and analyze that will lead to the desired results (Muller, 2018).

International Business – Reducing Travel

As our capitalistic economy has grown from the local marketplace to becoming a global marketplace, the need for international business travel has grown. As most business deals and contracts require extensive face-to-face negotiations, relationship-building, and ongoing touchpoints, the international business travel industry has also grown to accommodate this and make it easier than ever before. Flying business class has become quite an enjoyable experience with extended legroom, champagne cocktails, heated towels, and a cocoon for a seat.

Of course, these types of working conditions are not without their challenges. For example, employees may need to be away from their families for extended periods, they may need to live in societies or conditions they are not comfortable with, or they may find that their extensive travel prevents them from having a personal life at all.

With increasing costs, many businesses have been looking to reduce international business travel in many ways. With the internet and other communication technological advancements, companies have scaled back. And with the Covid-19 Pandemic and the subsequent travel bans, it became impossible virtually overnight.

In the early months of 2020, it became clear that a flu-like virus originating in Wuhan, China, was spreading rapidly with no way of containing or treating it. As the number of cases increased, many governments began to restrict air travel from China and subsequently from all international destinations. But international travel could not be restricted forever, so governmental agencies began working on recommendations on international travel with the help of the World Health Organization (WHO).

In the United States, the Centers for Disease Control and Prevention (CDC) issued international travel recommendations for those countries where travel was not banned. As of early 2021, the CDC was still recommending not to travel internationally unless necessary, but if travel was required, these were some of the recommendations:

- Follow entry requirements at your destination, including testing, quarantine, and providing contact information.
- Understand that you may be restricted to return to the United States.
- Avoid all cruise ships worldwide.
- Get tested one to three days before your flight.
- Get tested three to five days after travel and stay at home for seven days after travel.
- Keep a distance of at least 6 feet apart from anyone who did not accompany you on your trip. If there are people in your household who did not travel with you, wear a mask in your home for 14 days (CDC, n.d.).

As these destination countries continue to struggle to stop the spread of Covid-19, they see international travelers as both carriers of the disease and the solution to their struggling economies. And, the airlines are experiencing a similar struggle as they attempt to increase the number of passengers on a flight to make these profitable flights while also helping reduce transmission (Nunes, 2020).

Air Travel Has Changed

After the September 11, 2001, attacks in New York, the airline industry made many changes to the comfort of air travel. This included only guests with boarding passes allowed past the initial front door security, increased baggage screenings, reduced items allowed in carry-ons, and increased body pat-downs. Unfortunately, with the hyper-infectious spread of Covid-19, air travel has already been massively impacted and will continue so in the future.

Like many of the changes that September 11 prompted, passengers and policymakers will likely see these temporary restrictions as general good ideas and keep them around. As mentioned earlier, prior to Covid-19, first-class passengers enjoyed many amazing amenities that made international business travel much more palatable. In addition, even though reduced, airlines treated coach passengers with some comfort amenities as well. However, with the infectious nature of Covid-19, and other transmissible diseases, restrictions have been implemented to reduce the number of touchpoints that increase the likelihood of transmission. This means that no in-flight magazines, no pillows, and no meals.

Airlines have had to take a layered approach to create a safe travel environment, including security, passenger medical screenings, reduction of touchpoints, personal protective equipment (PPE) for flight attendants, and passenger mask mandates while balancing out their economic concerns. And now, with the vaccine becoming more widely available, they may even begin collecting and verifying vaccine status. As each one of these in isolation is not 100 percent effective, while this layered approach may seem redundant, it will likely continue to be necessary for some time in the future (Nunes, 2020).

Technology for Flying After Corona

As seen in much of the twentieth and early twenty-first centuries, advances in technology can be a great solution to help reduce some of these restrictions. For example, technologies like touchless passports, robotic cleaners, streamlined and fashionable PPE suits for flight attendants, and nanotechnology passenger sterilization could be implemented soon.

For years, passengers have used their smartphones to do all sorts of tasks they previously did on paper. More technologically savvy passengers have been using apps to check in and store their boarding passes to scan when prompted. Airlines can also require passengers to use these apps like many restaurants requiring patrons to scan a QR code to view the menu. In addition, face recognition technology could be utilized to serve as a boarding pass. And, although many people are nervous about contact tracing apps, airlines and airports could use the location services data from passengers to help guide future crowd control movements within the airport to avoid gatherings in close proximity, much like the amusement parks use a fast pass system to reduce the number of visitors in lines.

Scientists have found that using UV lights can more effectively sanitize surfaces than chemical products with odors that can linger and be dangerous to people. UV light rays send a wavelength that damages a virus's DNA and RNA, causing it to stop replicating and die. This light ray can be harmful to the humans who administer it, so some companies have tested using robots to roll down the plane's aisles and shine the light on all the surfaces. This helps to quickly sanitize the airplane while allowing the cleaning staff to focus on other areas. In addition, installing high-efficiency particulate air (HEPA) filters in the air system can help reduce passengers' germs after the cleaning.

In 2020 and 2021, mask mandates on flights were commonplace, and many passengers and flight attendants were concerned about the comfort of wearing a mask and other PPE for the entire flight and felt it diminished from the fashion sense that had been prevalent pre-Covid. As these restrictions will foreseeably be around for some time, some airlines are looking to create a more attractive flight attendant outfit that blends the PPE into the uniform. These could be sleek jumpsuits with matching face coverings and germ-resistant materials. Face coverings for passengers have become much of a fashion statement with various colors, logos, and sayings.

With the heightened state of health and safety brought on by the pandemic, many passengers are now used to technologies being used as quick health screenings. Still, with innovations, this could become even more effective. For example, some airports have cameras that can scan a body temperature, but these can miss asymptomatic passengers. The Symptom Sense is a system that appears to be a metal detector, but it can gather biometrics quickly like temperature, oxygen levels, and heart rate. Another system called Cleantech uses "nano needles" and a sanitizing spray to protect them from viruses (Snow, 2021).

As vaccines get better and herd immunity is reached, these restrictions will likely remain in place to help mitigate the spread of other infectious diseases and any future pandemics as well. As a result, international business travel may become much more strategic, and perhaps businesses should leverage remote technologies as much as possible instead.

Telecommuting

In the late twentieth century, businesses began to experiment with the idea of "Telecommuting". Instead of coming into the office, workers would work remotely using their telephones to stay connected. Telecommuting was a highly desired perk in larger cities as it meant avoiding traffic jams and long drives. In addition, as companies began to expand nationally and internationally, telecommuting became necessary to reduce travel costs (Shrivastava, 2012).

Virtual Teams

As the internet became more and more robust, companies began seeing the possibility of converting telecommuters into virtual workers. Not only could the worker use their phone to work remotely, but they could now use email and videoconferencing software to hold meetings. The demand for these technologies spurred companies like Skype and CISCO to develop additional virtual tools to mimic the in-person experience, including screen sharing and chat. Google was one of the first companies to introduce file sharing through their Google Drive software. In contrast, other companies such as OWL Labs developed 360-degree cameras with embedded microphones and speakers to further eliminate the perceived distance barriers. Recently, Microsoft has developed Microsoft Teams to encompass all these technologies into one software. Microsoft Teams features the ability to instantly chat, videoconference, file share, and screen share. As virtual workers use these technologies regularly, the team begins to form closer bonds. Some virtual teams are high-performing teams that have never actually met each other!

Remote Work Before Corona

Before the Covid-19 Pandemic in early 2020, many companies felt the remote work experiment was dead. Chiefly among them was Yahoo! CEO Marissa Mayer, who, as the new CEO in 2012, announced that all remote workers were expected to come back to the office. In the now-famous leaked internal memo, Yahoo! felt their outcomes had suffered under remote work. The memo explained that in order for Yahoo! to be the best, communication and collaboration were essential, and that required employees working next to each other physically. It further tried to persuade workers by reminding them how some of their best ideas happen when employees bump into each other in the hallways or at lunch (Goudreau, 2013).

The initial reactions were mixed as the opponents of remote work cited lower productivity, difficulty in supervision, challenges in collaboration, and more. Meanwhile, remote work proponent Jennifer Owens, former Editorial Director of Working Mother Media, believed Yahoo! was coming from a place of fear. "Fear that I can't see you, I don't know what you're working on. It's a distrust of your workforce" (Goudreau, 2013).

Other factors found by Dana Wilkie writing for Society for HR Management were that:

- Workers weren't trained to work remotely
- Managers were not trained in remote supervision
- Supervisors felt like they lost control or couldn't trust their workers
- Employers found that remote workers aren't as productive as on-site employees (Wilkie, 2019)

Supervision of work was the biggest hurdle to overcome. It made sense back before the pandemic because high-speed internet and conferencing software were high-priced connection tools managed by a staff of IT workers at the office. In contrast, many workers did not have the hardware capabilities, network speeds, or IT knowledge to keep these connections working from home. As a result, when something happened either technologically or work-related, and the remote worker "got stuck", there were major delays in productivity to resolve these issues (Ingram, 2013).

Remote Work After Corona

As companies faced the shutdowns in response to the Covid-19 Pandemic in early 2020, they stitched together ways to manage remote workers quickly. Although they felt these were temporary fixes, many significant innovations in remote work emerged, and companies began to see the value in remote work once again.

One of the primary reasons was that the connection technology and the software innovations matured. Companies like Zoom, Cisco, and Microsoft improved their videoconferencing platforms and expanded quickly. Most neighborhoods and city apartment high-rises had high-speed internet infrastructure installed and was widely accessible. Companies had already shifted from tower computers to laptops and other mobile devices at the workplace and easily shifted those resources to their employees' homes. Remote third-party IT solutions had also emerged as a viable option at the campus but easily converted to service existing remote workers. And, dashboard software, already being used by management on location, could supervise workers whether they were two offices away or two zip codes away.

Remote workers of today have even found flexibility in working locations. Some workers took road trips in Recreational Vehicles and used their personal cell phone hotspot and unlimited data to work along the way. Employees could visit family members in other states and work from their homes. As companies found their on-site costs dramatically increasing, they began offering stipends for the remote workers to help cover these costs.

As companies have now started to desire some of their workforces to return to the office, there is a heightened understanding that it doesn't make sense to cram a lot of employees into cubicles anymore (Kelly, 2021).

In his article in Forbes titled "The Future Will Entail Working Anywhere You'd Like and the Hours You Want, While Receiving the Same Pay", Jack Kelly says that after the Covid-19 Pandemic is over, many workers will still be fearful of using mass transit and some will refuse to go back to the office. This has been a topic of businesses and their lawyers as they try to navigate the health and safety requirements while balancing the needs of the organization. Most companies have determined that it is best to stagger their employees return to the New Normal (Kelly, 2021).

As workers have embraced the benefits of remote work and employers have seen increased productivity and the decrease of costs, remote work will continue to grow.

References

Andrews, E. (2015, August 7). Who were the Luddites? Retrieved December 29, 2021 from www.history.com/news/who-were-the-luddites

Bartolome, F., & Laurent, A. (1986). The manager: Master and servant of power. Retrieved December 29, 2021 from https://hbr.org/1986/11/the-manager-master-and-servant-of-power

CDC. (n.d.). CDC's interim guidance for general population disaster shelters during the Covid-19 Pandemic. Retrieved December 29, 2021 from www.cdc.gov/coronavirus/2019-ncov/php/eh-practitioners/general-population-disaster-shelters.html

Cornell Law School. (n.d.). Collective bargaining. Retrieved December 29, 2021 from www.law.cornell.edu/wex/collective_bargaining

Duggan, T. (2017, November 21). The advantages of project teams. Retrieved December 29, 2021 from https://smallbusiness.chron.com/advantages-project-teams-56232.html

Goudreau, J. (2013, February 25). Back to the stone age? New Yahoo! CEO Marissa Mayer bans working from home. Retrieved December 29, 2021 from www.forbes.com/sites/jennagoudreau/2013/02/25/back-to-the-stone-age-new-yahoo-ceo-marissa-mayer-bans-working-from-home/?sh=10eb514c1667

History.com. (2009, October 29). Industrial revolution. Retrieved December 29, 2021 from www.history.com/topics/industrial-revolution/industrial-revolution

Ingram, D. (2015, August 7). Yahoo's Mayer is right: Work-from-home employees are less efficient. Retrieved December 29, 2021 from www.wired.com/insights/2013/05/yahoos-mayer-is-right-work-from-home-employees-are-less-efficient/

Kelly, J. (2021, February 1). The future will entail working anywhere you'd like and the hours you want, while receiving the same pay. Retrieved December 29, 2021 from www.forbes.com/sites/jackkelly/2021/02/01/the-future-will-entail-working-anywhere-youd-like-and-the-hours-you-want-while-receiving-the-same-pay/

Kinicki, A., & Williams, B. K. (2020). *Management: A practical introduction*. New York, NY: McGraw-Hill Education.

Maxwell, J. C. (2013). *The 5 levels of leadership*. Center Street.

Muller, J. Z. (2018). *The tyranny of metrics*.

Nunes, A. (2020, July 9). How Covid-19 will change air travel as we know it. Retrieved December 29, 2021 from www.bbc.com/future/article/20200709-how-covid-19-will-change-air-travel-as-we-know-it

Pink, D. H. (2011). *Drive*. Edinburgh: Canongate Books.

Reh, F. (2019, August 30). Understanding the challenges and benefits of matrix management. Retrieved December 29, 2021 from www.thebalancecareers.com/matrix-management-2276122

Ryan, R. M., & Deci, E. L. (2017). *Self-determination theory: Basic psychological needs in motivation, development, and Wellness*, p. 457

Shrivastava, M. (2012). Reducing the need of travel through ICT. *IRACST – International Journal of Computer Science and Information Technology & Security (IJCSITS)* 2: 1262–1265.

Snow, J. (2021, May 3). The future of air travel is going high tech due to coronavirus. Retrieved December 29, 2021 from www.nationalgeographic.com/travel/2020/08/the-future-of-flying-is-going-high-tech-due-to-coronavirus-cvd/

United States Department of Labor. (n.d.). Retrieved December 29, 2021 from www.osha.gov/laws-regs/oshact/completeoshact

University of Rochester Medical Center. Our approach. (n.d.). Retrieved December 29, 2021 from www.urmc.rochester.edu/community-health/patient-care/self-determination-theory.aspx

Wilkie, D. (2019, August 16). Why are companies ending remote work? Retrieved December 29, 2021 from www.shrm.org/ResourcesAndTools/hr-topics/employee-relations/Pages/drawbacks-to-working-at-home-.aspx

Chapter 6

Managing Human Resources in the "Gig Economy"

William Garrison and Bashker Biswas

Thomas Jefferson wrote that all men and women were created equal in the Declaration of Independence. Their Creator had endowed them with inalienable rights, such as life, liberty, and the pursuit of happiness. One of the concepts that arose out of that spirit is the idea that an individual should be their own boss, and thus, the American Dream of having your own business was born.

As the factory owners began hiring people to leave their farms, that Dream was still pursued by many. Of course, owning your own business comes with many risks in today's world, but those who figure it out are highly rewarded in our Capitalist Economy.

Many people still hold this Dream but don't want to take the associated risk. This is because they don't know how to form a Business Plan, don't have the credit history to take out a small business loan, and have the luxury of having a steady paycheck to pay the bills. However, some of these people have found a similar Dream in what is known as the "Gig Economy".

As mentioned in previous chapters, workers have many subsets and distinctions. In the traditional definition, an employee works for an organization in a part-time or a full-time role. They are paid per hour or on a salary basis with some obtaining additional perks such as health insurance and stock options. The company hires these workers to perform a job laid out by a job description and placed within the organizational chart. They are subject to the policies and procedures laid out in the employee handbook and the code of conduct. They are evaluated regularly using the company's performance review system, and, if necessary, they are terminated following a document-rich series of events. In most states, employees can quit their job anytime but typically stay employed as long as they satisfy the requirements set out before them by their supervising managers and top executives.

The "Gig Economy" is the world in which unemployed workers and the companies that hire them interact. In the past, these independent contractors were temporary or freelance workers who had very short-term ties to organizations and enjoyed more freedom in the Employment Contract. The "Gig Economy" encompasses all those traditional independent contractors but adds in technological advances that help remove much of the friction points

DOI: 10.4324/9781003122272-6

previously encountered by these workers. So, in a way, there isn't much new about "Gig Workers", but that technology has helped connect organizations and workers better.

Who Are "Gig Workers"?

In 2021, the Academy Award for Best Picture went to the film *Nomadland* that portrayed an American Baby Boomer female who quit her job and lived around the country in her van, taking on "Gig" work along the way. The film mentioned that a growing segment of Americans is not homeless, just houseless. These nomads can find work to pay for their free lifestyle due to the "Gig Economy" (Zhao, 2020).

One man who has been able to lift himself out of poverty through "Gig" work is Eric Jacobs, aka the Nomadic Fanatic.

> Eric and his furry cat sidekicks Tara & Opie, travel around the country while chasing 70 degrees and sharing life's adventures while living in an RV. Adventures range from national parks, theme parks, museums, LARGER THAN LIFE, to Americana and historic drives as they're always looking for adventure and excitement on the road.
>
> (Jacobs, n.d.)

He goes on these adventures and then uploads these videos to YouTube and is compensated based on his number of subscribers and views through YouTube's advertising revenue. Before YouTube, Jacobs attended Evergreen State College and studied film production, and it shows. As a result, his vlogs on YouTube have a superior quality to most recreational vehicle (RV) dwellers. Still, he is a legend and a mentor to many other YouTubers, including Campervan Kevin, RV Prepper Wayne, and others. He supports them in running their own YouTube channels to cover the expenses of living in an RV full-time. Currently, Nomadic Fanatic has over 228 thousand YouTube subscribers, and typically, he uploads a video every three days, with each of them viewed over 50,000 times (Jacobs, n.d.).

YouTube is a great place to find "Gig Workers". There are all sorts of industries they work in, and many have found that YouTube is an excellent way to create yet another "Gig", or as many of them refer to it, as another "side hustle".

"Gig Workers" are Uber drivers, code writers, journalists, YouTubers, adjunct professors, nurses, editors, accountants, babysitters, truck drivers, political campaign workers, authors, IT Workers, event coordinators, business consultants, airplane pilots, sound and light technicians, graphic designers, web developers, and even Macy's Thanksgiving Day Parade Santas. Also, they come in all shapes and sizes, including singles, college-aged students, mothers, foreigners, and moonlighters.

"Gig Worker" Mindset

Although the term "Gig Worker" is relatively new, the personality has been around for some time. This form of labor is described as "moonlighting" or, more popularly in today's jargon, a "side hustle". These terms infer that the work is being done on the side or after hours from their regular full-time employment, but many today can stitch together several "Gigs" to earn enough money without being an employee. "Gig Workers" are free spirits who mostly seek flexibility in choosing when to work. They enjoy working in intense spurts but equally enjoy their time off. They are looking to do something with purpose, and many establish themselves as a personal brand through social media. They enjoy the hustle and are eager to overcome obstacles because, in the end, they are the ones making the decisions. They can choose to repeatedly work for a company, but they can also quit and find something else much more easily than most full-time employees. Yes, there are downsides and pitfalls, but they know that being a full-time or part-time employee has its own sets of downsides and pitfalls as well. Most have tried living that lifestyle and found that the "Gig Lifestyle" fits their personality best.

The Strategic Importance of "Gig Workers"

So, how can established organizations with a well-established part-time and full-time workforce of employees leverage these workers to meet their organizational goals? They fit in well to solve some of the biggest challenges that HR departments have recently faced.

Many companies have been struggling with high employee turnover as replacing these workers is costly both in dollars and time. Employee retention programs have helped reduce some of these costs, but Employee Engagement Surveys demonstrate that some workers are not interested in the long-term plans of their companies.

Meanwhile, "Gig Workers" don't intend to stay in the first place. Companies could mix "Gig Workers" into their strategic plan to increase productivity while keeping costs lower and reducing the turnover of those employees who want to stay. The key to this recipe is to ensure that traditional employees fill key roles and have the "Gig Workers" fill the gaps.

Human Resources Processes Need to Be Different

HR departments need to modify their process to seize these opportunities, especially in the hiring process. The biggest hurdle to most organizations bringing "Gig Workers" into the mix is the high cost and the time spent hiring. Many HR managers cite these costs as significant enough to avoid the conversation altogether. However, if HR departments could find efficiencies and automation in the hiring process, they could fold "Gig Workers" into their workforce.

This would include carving out roles and tasks that are short-term in nature and need very little supervision. By doing so, companies would find their retention of employees increase, and their regular workforce will benefit from career-growth opportunities within the company. To truly become proficient at hiring and supervising "Gig Workers", most HR departments will need to hire a Gig Specialist with the right managerial mindset to embrace these workers.

"Gig Worker" Employment Contracts and Legal Status

One of the advantages of hiring "Gig Workers" is that they are considered contract employees. They are paid to take on tasks and not retained on the payroll for an indefinite period. They are hired for a contract that can include a defined period. This gives both the "Gig Worker" and the company a mutually agreed upon release date.

As contract workers, "Gig Workers" are paid using a 1099 tax form that places any tax liability on the "Gig Worker". This means the company does not need to withhold or spend time delineating additional benefits to the worker.

This also means that there is a limited liability on behalf of the company as the "Gig Worker" is doing their tasks independently. The worker's responsibility is to ensure they are covered for any damages they inflict. Many new cooperative insurance companies are beginning to offer great packages for "Gig Workers" to provide that security. "Gig Workers" are also responsible for adhering to its policies and procedures, as the company can be held responsible for some of its actions (HG.org., n.d.).

Many opponents of the "Gig Economy" cite these mutual advantages as a way to skirt labor laws. This has been seen most recently in California with Assembly Bill 5, also known as AB5. Many workers in the "Gig Economy" and labor groups felt that companies were taking advantage of this arrangement by misclassifying them. The result of AB5 in California is that a worker can only be classified as an independent contractor if their tasks are not part of the company's core business. Also, their supervisors do not direct the way they complete the tasks, and they have established themselves as a business or belong to an independent trade group. This has become quite a challenge for both companies and "Gig Workers" and will continue to be addressed. However, companies should not be discouraged by these efforts but instead concentrate on ensuring the "Gig Workers" are treated well from the beginning of the hiring process to being folded into the overall employee relations strategy (Myers & Roosevelt, 2019).

"Gig Workers" and Human Capital Acquisition (Staffing) Processes

When an organization hires "Gig Workers", it usually fosters Employee Engagement. In addition, it opens up new organizational outcomes, for example, discovering innovation through crowdsourcing, encouraging creative thinking through special project teams, and managing labor expenses by hiring flexible employment categories.

The most common avenue companies use to secure the services of "Gig Workers" is through "Gig" employment platforms. These are digital marketplaces called platforms that allow employers to hire and manage "Gig Workers".

As evidenced by the plethora of these platforms, it can be said that the category of "Gig Workers" is going to be a growing part of the worker acquisition in many companies and in all types of industries for a while.

But as has been discussed earlier, employing "Gig Workers" as an important element of the workforce requires a different mindset. Organizations must realize that today, top talent often comes in the form of flexible contractual employment of various kinds, understanding that going forward, organizations must accept that using this huge flexible talent pool is an important strategic way of utilizing and managing the human element of the digital workplace. With this realization, corporate leaders will be removing the first barrier to harnessing the power of this significant talent pool. The conventional wisdom was that online "Gigs" worked best for one-off or exploratory work with low impact. Changing this closed paradigm requires a fundamental shift in the mindset at the top leadership level. With the hiring of "Gig Workers", they must follow a strategically conceptualized attract-engage-retain talent model. The first step is to ensure that the organization is ready.

The Employer Value Proposition for hiring "Gig Workers" should be based on a specific value proposition that ties into the real motivations of "Gig Workers". The HR professionals responsible for hiring a "Gig Worker" must probe into the real motivations of the "Gig" talent by asking, "Why do you do 'Gig' work?". Then, further probing needs to be done, asking the candidate why they want to take on the genuine challenges of this type of work. Some of these challenges are losing stability and professional credibility while only gaining limited company benefits. In this manner, organizations must, therefore, tap into the real "motivators" for doing "Gig" work, which quite often include flexibility, work-life balance, independence, and the need to do varied work. A digitally enabled organization will naturally attract savvy, "Gig" talent if the hiring organization understands these real motivations.

Many digital start-ups have built digital platforms to connect "Gig Workers" and employers as the demand for "Gig Workers" develops in the digital workplace. Some of these platforms are:

1   AppJobs GAP
2   Catalant
3   Contently
4   crowdSPRING
5   FreelanceDiary
6   GIG
7   Guru
8   PeoplePerHour

And there are many more.

Successful "Gig" models are Freelancer, Upwork, Task Rabbit, and even Uber. Talent acquisition specialists must explore, evaluate, and experiment with these platforms. In addition, they need to find the right platform depending on the nature of the work offered.

Several organizations have started their own in-house platforms and networking possibilities using databases, such as alumni networks, to develop a community of contractors.

Another intriguing concept is the "flash organization", which assembles teams on demand and then disbands once the project is completed. Much of this "Gig"-hiring is done using artificial intelligence (AI)-based platforms that intelligently match talent needs with available "Gig" talent, so talent acquisition teams must invest time and money in understanding and using these emerging technologies.

Integrating "Gig Workers" into the work teams professionally, culturally, and socially requires new initiatives. The first step needs to be implementing a digital onboarding process, including online background verification, digital documentation, team and leadership connection sessions, and cultural orientations.

"Gig Work" flexible policies and processes must be designed and communicated keeping in mind that most "Gig" employees would be working on irregular schedules, from remote locations, and in varying time zones. In addition, "Gig Workers" should be given an orientation on required legal, compliance, and intellectual property rules, thus ensuring a safe and sound working relationship between "Gig" employees and their employers.

Finally, the success of the "Gig Economy" is driven by a healthy partnership between the hiring organizations and the "Gig Workforce". Employers should first resolve the ambiguous areas related to hiring "Gig Workers" and create the necessary, appropriate policies. The "Gig Economy" is sure to grow in the future, but whether it truly creates value for both the "Gig Employee" and the employer depends on developing the correct strategies and then using the right "Gig" digital work platforms.

"Gig Worker" Compensation and Benefits

"Gig" platforms are everywhere, from Amazon's Mechanical Turk to Fiverr, TaskRabbit, Upwork, and Behance. So whatever an employer's needs, whether they need a simple microtask or a complete redo of the overall business strategy, chances are there's a "Gig Worker" on a platform somewhere that can do it for the employer.

"Gig Workers" are no longer exclusively for tiny businesses. In a recent report from the Oxford University, many Fortune 500 companies and multinational enterprises are using platform-based sourcing of "Gig Workers" into their business models. Platform sourcing is growing in popularity due to simple access to scalable sources of labor, skills, and experience at cheaper start-up and transaction costs.

But for many, the "Gig Economy" is still novel and difficult to understand. There isn't a lot of trustworthy data on how this workforce is becoming more popular. But all the evidence is not very clear at this time. The U.S. Bureau of Labor Statistics (BLS) has been slow to collect data and conduct surveys on this workforce category. That is also changing with BLS announcing that a survey is in progress.

If an employer is thinking of hiring from the pool of "Gig Workers", employers need to think about how these "Gig Workers" will be paid. Most microtasks on Mechanical Turk are paid at a set rate; a "Gig Worker" can earn a few cents if they perform the task correctly. Over the course of a full day, you can earn an average of $6.00 to $12.00 per hour. Other platforms pay workers hundreds or even thousands of dollars per month for more complicated jobs.

Compensation is typically output-based regardless of the type of task or platform used. The compensation the "Gig Workers" receive is based on the "Gig" outcomes. So, if the outcome can be measured in a "yes/no" binary manner, then the payment amount can be easily ascertained. However, when the "quality" of the job is in question, determining the appropriate payment amount becomes more complex.

By the very nature of "Gig" work, the worker has a lot of latitude over how much and when they will work. "Gig Workers" also have discretion over how much effort they put into that work. As "Gig Workers" perform tasks more complex and mission-critical, employers need to consider how to bake discretionary effort into the "Gig Worker" compensation structures.

Performance-Based Pay for "Gig Workers"

While there is some interesting new research in progress examining performance pay for "Gig Workers", we want to present some easy and practical suggestions for paying them now based on performance.

Early Delivery Bonus

The first idea is based on the timing of deliverables and hard deadlines critical to a project. So, consideration should be given to paying an early delivery bonus if quality standards are met. A little early delivery bonus can be the extra motivation a "Gig Worker" needs to ensure assignments are performed on time for time-sensitive activities.

Cost Savings Bonus

When it comes to allocated jobs, cost containment is always a priority. But if cost savings are critical to the project, then offering the "Gig Worker" a percentage of the cost savings generated will also be a good incentive. This commission or incentive may encourage the "Gig Worker" to seek out other resource and Supplier sources that offer the same high-quality inputs at a reduced cost. This can become a winning proposition, the structure of which will be similar to a Gain-Sharing Plan.

Quality Bonus

Quality bonuses can be challenging to design. First, it's hard to know the right standards for quality measures. The degree of quality work is hard to establish. The use of a quality matrix can be useful here. A quality matrix is nothing more than a document that states the expectations for an assignment by listing the criteria and then describing levels of quality from poor to excellent. If there is agreement on the continuum of the range of quality, good to bad, then a simple bonus payment matrix can be integrated into the quality matrix.

Retention Bonus

A performance/merit/retention payment scheme can also be developed to pay the better "Gig Workers" an annual one-time lump-sum payment. This will lead to retaining the better-performing "Gig Workers" in the company. This might also reduce the constant churn in the company. According to a JP Morgan survey, one out of every six online platform "Gig Workers" is new to the platform every month, and more than half of platform users leave after a year. Therefore, if the company finds a "Gig Worker" who does a great job and is a great fit for the organization, then an incentive payment might just be the glue to retain that "Gig Worker" and can motivate them to sign up for more future "Gigs" in your organization.

Consultation Stipend

Performance pay cannot necessarily become a regular component of the "Gig Worker" pay strategy for all "Gig" work types. On the other hand, a pay-for-performance system could be a realistic choice for more difficult time-sensitive activities or need a little more effort than a "normal" effort. Another creative option can involve a team of "Gig Workers" to advise the employer to develop an optimum "Gig Worker" compensation system. This has many benefits, among them "Gig Worker" commitment, motivation, and worker engagement.

"Gig Worker" Training and Development

One of the challenges for the "Gig Worker" is the ability and facility to continuously update and improve their skills and thus their ability to find more and more "Gigs".

"Gig Workers" usually ask themselves the following questions:

• What skills do I need?
• Where can I learn online?
• How much does it cost?

"Gig Workers" often face a lack of funds and time, and thus, they face a level of inadequacy as to what training they should do and how to acquire the required training.

There is a huge number of opportunities for inexpensive skill training opportunities online. The issue is figuring out where to find them and which ones are valuable in the marketplace.

There is a host of inexpensive and convenient courses and training resources available both for entry-level "Gig Workers" and experienced workers.

A range of courses and programs are available from the world's largest digital corporations to teach freelancers how to utilize their technologies efficiently. As a result, all categories of "Gig Workers" can find suitable and valuable training opportunities on these platforms. In addition, "Gig Workers" who are beginning their "Gig" work journey and who have limited resources can find many pieces of training and no-cost opportunities on various platforms. Here are some examples:

1 **Facebook Blueprint** offers a wealth of free, self-guided courses and programs to help build marketing and business skills using social media platforms such as Instagram, Messenger, WhatsApp, and Facebook.

   A "Gig Worker" can choose from seven portals instead of a basic program: people looking for work, students, and those already employed are all included in this group.

   These "Gig Workers" can promote their credentials by showing prospective "Gig" employers an official certification. For example, Facebook Blueprint offers nine Certified Professional examination options at increasingly advanced levels of competence. The training materials are free, but the "Gig Worker" has to pay around $100–150 to take the certification exams.

2 It's beneficial to know about Adobe's capabilities if the "Gig Worker" works in the graphic arts field. They're the industry standard for freelance photographers, videographers, graphic designers, and even writers who are frequently required to provide relevant photos to clients.

   Adobe's free online classes cover all their programs, including Photoshop and Illustrator.

3 Apple offers a variety of training courses and certifications that cover topics such as writing software for Macs and iOS devices and providing support for Apple technology in business settings. It's worth checking out **macOS**

Support Essentials 11 because it provides a relatively simple path to becoming an Apple Certified Support Professional. A "Gig Worker" can study the course materials by studying the textbook and then pay to take an exam if they so desire. Apple's **Deployment and Management** course consists of papers and guided exercises that teach "Gig Workers" how to handle Apple devices in the workplace. **App Development with Swift** is a 12-hour course that explains the tools, language, and design ideas that enable apps to function flawlessly with Apple platforms. It is absolutely free.

4   Google offers **Google Digital Garage**. Google has partnered with training providers worldwide to deliver free courses to assist people in improving their business or job abilities. One can select from individual modules or entire courses in three categories: Digital Marketing, Career Development, and Data and Tech. In addition, if the "Gig Worker" wants to acquire and use a Google certificate for promotion, they can explore the process of earning Google's Professional Certificates.

5   If the "Gig Worker" is looking for work around video content, as a potential option, the **YouTube Creator Academy** provides a wealth of resources and learning tools to help new YouTubers learn how to produce and advertise their own channels and videos. But, again, this is a high-demand skill.

Other training opportunities are also available via software companies' great free training resources. However, it is not just the online giants offering free training for "Gig Workers". There are hundreds of organizational, financial, and marketing tools available online, with more coming into the market all the time. Clients often look for "Gig Workers" with detailed knowledge of these apps and tools.

Fortunately, many of the tool vendors offer free or low-cost videos, tutorials, and even whole courses to assist users in navigating the complexities. A "Gig Worker" can often become an expert in a specific tool simply by working through all the materials provided for free. Here are some software platforms that fit this category.

- **Ahrefs** prides itself on being an "all-in-one SEO toolbox". Many bloggers and website owners use it as their go-to tool, but it's also quite strong and complex. So knowing how to utilize it effectively can provide a "Gig Worker" with an employable skill. In addition, the Ahrefs Academy, which includes the company's comprehensive Blogging for Business course, offers hundreds of hours of free SEO and marketing courses. On the company's YouTube channel, there are also more video tutorials.
- **ConvertKit Email Marketing** is quite popular for many businesses, and many of them frequently search for "Gig Workers" to help. Some of the most well-known email service companies provide excellent training materials.

- With **Trello**, learning to manage projects can help the "Gig Worker" with their work juggling many clients. As a result, learning to use a modern project management system is a good use of time. Trello uses online boards, lists, and cards to help individuals and teams manage their projects. Thanks to comprehensive instruction on getting started with Trello, it's easy to get up and running with the system.

- **FreshBooks** and **Xero** – no guide to the training of "Gig Workers" would be complete without mentioning accounting software. Among the most popular solutions for freelancers are FreshBooks and Xero. These are paid tools, but both offer free tutorials, webinars, case studies, and blog articles on getting the most out of systems.

- **Free Training Resources** from Upwork is a great place to find new freelance work. Aside from finding "Gig" work, Upwork also provides some great training resources for "Gig Workers". As a freelancer or a client, you'll find a wealth of information in the Upwork resource section.

Online e-Learning Portals

There is now a slew of online e-learning portals that offer thousands of courses, as well as full degrees, instead of requiring you to attend a physical campus. In many cases, there are plenty of studies that can be done for free on these sites; one has only to pay if you wish to receive a formal certificate at the end of a course.

Almost any skill or discipline can now be learned online, thanks to the efforts of universities around the world, individual course developers, and well-known corporations.

- There are over 5,000 courses available on **Coursera**, which provides a wide range of educational options. Short courses and accredited online degrees are just a few alternatives available. While you won't get any feedback (or an official certificate) by "auditing a course", many of them do allow you to study for free.

  In addition, Coursera offers Google Professional Certificates. Google's new Professional Certificates for UX designers, IT developers, and support specialists are being offered via Coursera to meet the growing demand in the tech industry. Technical support, project management, data analytics, automation, and design are topics covered in these self-paced programs, all of which prepare students for careers in these rapidly expanding technological fields. Google has said that these online credentials will be deemed comparable to a complete degree.

- **edX** has formed partnerships with universities such as Harvard and Cambridge, corporations such as Amazon and IBM, and international organizations such as the World Bank and Amnesty International to train in various fields. Many courses provide a free audit track or a charge for graded assignments and a course certificate upon completion. Financial aid is also available through edX for students who demonstrate financial need. In addition, the program allows these students to earn verified certificates at a reduced cost.

Learning about Python programming or project management, for example, can be found by exploring the edX subject options further. In addition, some of the more expensive, instructor-led writing classes, like How to Write a Novel Structure and Outline, are included in their tuition as well as many other self-paced writing courses.

- As a for-profit company, **Alison** is committed to making it possible for anyone to learn at any time, from any location, and at any level of education. They want to be a catalyst for positive social change, creating opportunities, prosperity, and equality for all people. Certificates and diplomas (3–5 hours of learning) are free, but you must pay for the longer courses (8–15 learning hours).
- And then there is **Open Culture**. An important part of its mission is to compile and make easily accessible a wide range of free, high-quality cultural and educational resources available online. Free university courses, movies, documentaries, audiobooks, and tens of thousands of massive open online courses (MOOCs), as well as language learning and other resources, are all available. As this description shows, the "Gig Worker" need not worry about continuing education to stay ahead of the needed learning to ensure for themselves a continual flow of profitable "Gigs".

Modified Employee Relations for "Gig Workers"

Employers undoubtedly need to adapt as all workgroups – including "Gig Workers" – demand interesting work. The good news is that a lot of what worked in the past can be applied today. What remains a guiding principle is treating new employees with respect and help making them feel integral to the organization regardless of work category. In addition, most "Gig Workers" desire recognition and commitment from their employers and support throughout their tenure. This includes providing feedback regularly as managers would do with their traditional teams. By constantly evaluating procedures and "Gig" talent, organizations will create a "Gig" talent management process that will provide strategic value to the evolving digital workplace.

So, there needs to be a clear understanding that managing a "Gig Workforce" takes planning due to the complexity and diversity of this type of work. This includes maintaining a system that keeps the "Gig Workforce" included in the process. The "Gig Workforce" is all about customization. A productive, "Gig Worker" relationship model will fill the company's skills gap. Continually acknowledging the strengths that "Gig Workers" bring to the company will build a flourishing relationship.

In today's digitized workplace, flexibility is critical to attracting talented employees. Employers willing to give up traditional job requirements can attract and retain highly qualified and flexible "Gig Worker" talent. All types and categories of employees need to be resilient to transitions quickly and, therefore, become productive members of the workforce. With "Gig Workers", companies get a flexible, agile individual who acts with conviction instead of reacting to change.

Helping an employee grow is powerful in any setting, but it is especially powerful in the "Gig Economy". Proper onboarding and training should be clear about the organization's growth and development criteria, both intrinsically and extrinsically. Data analytics and evaluations enable leaders to identify opportunities for improvement and growth. To meet expectations and work objectives, employees need to understand them and be given a clear line of sight. Any expectations or requirements that employees do not meet should be seen as opportunities for improvement. To this end, managers should help coach, guide, and lead "Gig Workers" with performance improvement strategies as well as their traditional workers as the productivity dividends are massive.

Integrating "Gig Workers" Into the Company Culture

Since "Gig Workers" are not real employees, some may assume they are not a part of the organization. This is the wrong way to view the opportunity. Instead, organizations should integrate "Gig Workers" into the organization's overall culture.

Since many "Gig Workers" will not be working the traditional 40-hour workweek, they may feel isolated from the company. However, it should be impressed that its policies still apply to them. This includes safety procedures, communication protocols, and codes of ethics.

HR departments should make every effort to fold these workers into both the spoken and the unspoken culture of the organization because the work done will still impact both the internal and the external stakeholders. "Gig Workers" should be invited to staff meetings, participate in employee training, and even participate in other rites and rituals such as off-site activities and employee birthday parties. A lot of a company's culture is caught, not taught, and having the "Gig Workers" be indiscernible from regular employees from Outsiders is highly beneficial. A key starting point is to orient "Gig Workers" to the mission and vision of the organization.

How HR Can Benefit From "Gig Workers"

As previously stated, the high cost of staff turnover is one of the most critical difficulties in today's businesses. By carving out the tasks that most regular employees find tedious or consuming, HR departments will find these employees staying around longer and finding opportunities for growth within the company. HR departments can then position transitory workers into a different turnover equation. The Gig Specialist within the HR department could then manage a roster of "Gig Workers" who may complete their tasks and leave or complete their tasks and return for another without impacting the full-time workforce.

Companies could also hire half-workers for shorter tasks, including projects, developments, and the on-demand workforce. Then, companies can quickly downsize these "Gig Workers" when economic challenges arise without impacting the employee workforce by simply not offering new contracts. And the beauty of it is that the "Gig Worker" will find a new opportunity quickly.

References

Beck, D. (1992). Implementing a gainsharing plan: What companies need to know. *Compensation & Benefits Review* 24.

HG.org. (n.d.). Legal issues involved in the gig economy. Retrieved December 29, 2021 from www.hg.org/legal-articles/legal-issues-involved-in-the-gig-economy-51956

Jacobs, E. [Nomadic Fanatic] (n.d.). Home [YouTube Channel]. Retrieved from www.youtube.com/user/nomadicfanatic/about

Myers, B., & Roosevelt, M. (2019, September 18). Newsom signs Bill rewriting California employment law, limiting use of independent contractors. Retrieved December 29, 2021 from www.latimes.com/california/story/2019-09-18/gavin-newsom-signs-ab5-employees0independent-contractors-california

Zhao, C. (Director). (2020). *Nomadland. [Film].* Century City, CA: Searchlight Pictures

Chapter 7

Managing the Remote Employee

Robert L. Ramirez

Threats like the coronavirus will continue to disrupt the workforce as we know it. As a result, the need for managing remote employees is critical. This chapter deals with the most up-to-date strategies that managers and leaders can use to ensure their staff and teams collaborate effectively and maintain momentum in productivity. For many professionals, the promise of working from home is now a reality, and it is gradually becoming the standard. As this has occurred over the last two-year normal work patterns, modes of communication and team dynamics have been disrupted while new strategies are being implemented to manage the remote employee. The task of adjusting to these work adjustments will become even more difficult as the coronavirus variants continue to spread over the world heightening uncertainty and worry about personal hazards from the pandemic and its economic consequences. First, we'll go over some of the day-to-day issues of working remotely and then present recommended management tactics to maximize remote worker productivity.

Benefits of a Remote Workforce

According to globalization partners, a remote global team gives you two specific advantages: proven efficiency and increased success (Krasno, 2021). The remote aspect leads to efficiency, and the international perspective improves company productivity. Companies that have a remote workforce can benefit by having a more significant potential labor pool. If the employee workforce pool is not geographically bound, the chances of finding the right employee increases. Out-of-area employees can also be more cost-effective, saving employers money.

Recent evidence shows that remote workers are more productive, including during the Covid-19 Pandemic. In mid-2020, over 3,000 employees responded to the Global Work-from-Home Experience Survey, making it one of the most extensive global Covid-19 Pandemic employee surveys (Global Workplace Analytics, 2021). According to this survey, a full 53 percent of remote workers reported they were likely to work overtime to meet productivity goals. That's compared to just 28 percent of in-office workers. According to a recent Prodoscore Research Council (PRC) survey, remote workers put in longer hours

DOI: 10.4324/9781003122272-7

than when working on-site. However, 86 percent of respondents felt fully productive at home (77 percent globally). They also stated that they gained back 35 minutes a day due to fewer unwanted interruptions (43 minutes/day at home vs. 78 minutes/day in the office). It's also important to note that 76 percent of worldwide employees desire to work from home in the future. On average, their preference is for 2.5 days a week in the office.

For the work from home employees, here are some of the benefits:

- Saving time from the commute to work and back
- Setting your working schedule
- The comfort of being at home
- Chance to travel more
- Less stress and more satisfying
- Dressing in more of a relaxed way
- Better time management for personal life
- Closer to your loved ones

Challenges of Remote Working

First, managers need to understand the job aspects that can make remote work challenging for many employees. Good performing employees may experience job performance and engagement declines when they begin working remotely. The environment and home distraction could lead to productivity issues. They also may experience a lack of communication, motivation, preparation, and training. Challenges inherent in remote work include the following issues.

Remote Issue #1 – Lack of Face-to-Face Supervision

Both supervisors, managers, and staff members have new concerns about the lack of face-to-face interaction. Management's fear is that their staff will not be as productive and may not work as hard from home. Many employees are concerned about the reduced access to managerial support, training, and company communication. Since information won't be gathered at the water cooler anymore, employees will begin to feel isolated. Some employees believe that remote bosses are unresponsive to their demands and are neither supportive nor helpful in completing their tasks. Traditionally, face-to-face meetings have been key to building solid relationships. The employee may feel better connected with you when you meet them in person than via email or phone. Face-to-face communication also allows you to interpret body language and facial expressions better.

Remote Issue #2 – Lack of Access to Information

Remote employees can get frustrated by the additional time and effort required to access other coworkers or management information. While in the office, the employee can easily ask other staff members how to locate the required information without delay. Now, gathering information to what could be simple questions can become an obstacle to remote employees. Due to the lack of necessary information, business opportunities could be lost if not provided in a timely fashion. The information must be available to employees in a timely manner.

Remote Issue #3 – Social Isolation

Social isolation is an absence of social connections. Social isolation may lead to loneliness for some employees, while others can feel lonely without being socially isolated. One of the most typical complaints from remote employees is loneliness; the staff member misses the informal social interaction of the office setting. Extroverts may suffer from isolation even more in the short term if their remote work environment does not provide them with the opportunity to engage with others. Furthermore, loneliness and isolation can cause many employees to feel a lack of belonging and community with their employer over a longer period. This can also result in less loyalty to remain at the job and increased motivation to look for new opportunities.

Remote Issue #4 – Work From Home Distractions

Working from home can present itself with many interruptions not found in the office such as interruptions from children, expectations from a significant other, the temptation of television and other entertainment options, the perceived opportunity of running errands, and the attraction of other hobbies. In addition, due to a lack of space, the employee may not have the proper home office space or desk. We've all seen the photos of the mother trying to work on her laptop while holding her toddler. Companies encourage employers to provide specialized workspace and suitable childcare for their remote employees before allowing them to work remotely, but this is not always the case. However, in the event of a quick change to virtual work, such as the Covid-19 Pandemic, many employees did not have suitable workspaces. In some situations, employees had new, unanticipated parental responsibilities like monitoring their students attending school remotely. Even in normal circumstances, family and home obligations can interfere with remote employment.

Strategies for Managing the Remote Employee

The recommendations in this chapter can bring positive change to managing remote employees. Managers and leaders must realize that their staff is stressed out due to uncertainty and anxiety. While remote work has its drawbacks, there are several things that managers may do to ease the transition more smoothly. The strategies are not listed in any order of importance as they are all equally important.

Strategy #1 – Clarify Goals

The first recommendation addresses the issue of clarifying departments' goals and roles. Leaders and managers need to review and determine how the goals and objectives for the department are set. The move to remote work is an excellent opportunity for managers to revisit the basics to ensure everyone understands the team's goals and objectives. Each staff member has individual roles to play and contributions to make toward those outcomes. Clarifying roles allows employees to identify when they can turn to peers rather than the leader, minimizing the need to wait on the leader. This improved communication within the organization also aids peripheral members to remain involved. Business department goals need to be written clearly and be specific. The goals are best written when they include the five "W's" as listed next:

- What is the goal to be accomplished?
- Why is the goal important?
- Who will be involved in completing this objective?
- Where will the goal be implemented?
- Which barriers are you likely to face?

Once you have the five "W"'s, make sure the goals are specific, measurable, achievable, relevant, and time-bound, or SMART Goals. This will provide the team with an anchor on which to base all the department's focus and decision-making.

Like the Covid-19 Pandemic, future disruptive events will generate new and competing tasks across the business. Thus, the leaders will need to continually address and clarify goals to the team to keep them focused on productivity.

Strategy #2 – Schedule Regular Virtual Meetings

It is the responsibility of the manager to set expectations for the frequency, means, and ideal timing of communication for their teams. For example, teams can use videoconferencing software for the essential daily or weekly check-in meetings. Teams can use instant messaging (IM) or texting when communication is more urgent or quick and use the telephone when a discussion or dialog is needed. The employer should communicate the best way and time to reach them during the workday. Finally, managers should monitor team member communication (to the extent possible) to ensure that they exchange information as needed. Employee "rules of engagement" should be established as soon as feasible, preferably during the initial online check-in meeting.

By creating consistent weekly or biweekly meetings, you can communicate to the team what to expect. Sending an agenda in advance with the meeting notice helps remind employees of the meeting and keep the meeting running on schedule. Scheduling these meetings in advance will help the team come together virtually. During the Covid-19 Pandemic, virtual meetings became the New Normal for employees and companies worldwide. Zoom reported that over 200 million people were using the app daily in 2020 compared to 10 million in December 2019 and then shortly after, over 300 million people (Iqbal, 2021). A regularly scheduled virtual meeting is much better than having a meeting on an ad hoc basis. If you meet only ad hoc, the staff will not be prepared or may not attend the meeting. Try to stick to your agenda and time allocated for the meeting. These regular meetings will serve to bring the group together. This will be your opportunity to help the staff rethink how to accomplish their tasks and ensure that everyone understands their role. These meetings will be accessible for all employees to engage with clients and colleagues in other locations. The meeting should also be recorded for those who could not attend or wanted to relisten to the meeting.

Virtual WebEx or Zoom meetings can provide the staff with that crucial "in-person" feel. Requesting that everyone turn on their camera provides for a more personal connection and the capacity to pick up on facial emotions, exactly like in a face-to-face meeting. Being able to schedule regular shorter virtual meetings increases the productivity of time used. Pre-Covid, meetings held at the central office conference room could run longer as the staff had to gather in a central location. Having your meetings virtual removes the commute time allowing for shorter, more concise, and efficient meetings. Decision-making is sped up, and time is used better. The meeting will usually start on time because they are recorded for anyone who arrives late. In addition, removing all that travel, paperwork handouts, and possible food expense creates an advantage.

Another benefit of the virtual meeting is that you can add attendees allowing for a diverse range of opinions and sharing of information across the organizations. Being able to invite individuals from across your company to the meeting simply will bring different perspectives and knowledge that you might not have had access to in a typical location-specific meeting. Finally, individuals can join from any part of the world and in any time zone because distance is no longer an issue.

Strategy #3 – Humanize Good Communication, Not Products

Personalize and humanize your virtual meeting by showcasing the staff and real people in the meeting. You may want to start your discussion by featuring their interests, hobbies, and other information that make them seem relatable. Structuring ways for employees to interact socially by having informal chats about nonwork issues is one of the most significant actions a manager can take. This holds true for all remote workers, but it holds true even more so for those who have been forced to leave the office unexpectedly. Another suggestion is to hold a virtual party where each employee brings their favorite alcoholic or nonalcoholic beverage to the videoconference or have each member share a favorite recipe. While these events may sound artificial, they may reduce the feelings of isolation and promote a sense of company comradery.

Emails and spreadsheets are good informational tools and present lots of data. When discussing data using videoconferencing software, encourage all team members to have their cameras on so they may be able to see nonverbal movements to help with interpreting emotions.

Strategy #4 – Help the New Work Environment to Become the Norm

Leaders and supervisors must recognize stress, listen to employees' anxieties and concerns, and empathize with their problems, especially in the context of a rapid move to remote work. Ask newer remote workers how they're doing, especially if they're struggling but not communicating their stress or concern. You can simply begin by asking a general question, such as How is working remotely going for you right now? This will open the door to conversations with important information that you might not otherwise hear. Make sure you pay attention to the response and briefly restate it back to the employee to ensure you got it right. Next, allow the employees to talk about their stress or concerns. According to research on emotional intelligence and emotional contagion, employees look to their bosses for indications on how to react to rapid changes or crises. If a manager expresses tension and hopelessness, the employee will pick up on it.

Working remotely creates new distractions and potential misunderstandings with other team members. Working from home means working from the bedroom, dining room, or office. It could also mean that you could be distracted by the kids, gardeners, or others in the household. So, the more the team members understand each other's environment, the better they will make sense of their behavior. For example, if the team members understand that you have kids in the background, they will know why you are frequently on mute or have to leave for short periods of time.

You could encourage each participant to take a few minutes at the outset of the new group meeting to show the team their home workstation and give some personal context. That would then explain the possible distractions like barking dogs, noisy passing trucks, or kids coming home from school.

Strategy #5 – Track Your Employee's Progress

Have your employees provide a work from home schedule, but be flexible. For example, some employees like to work early in the morning, while others want to work late into the night. Request that the staff supplies you with regular tasks and deadlines for which they are responsible. These self-reporting items will provide management with information to oversee the work from home.

The second alternative is to track how your employees use their weekday time using an employee productivity tracking tool. When your employees start a new task, these tools normally urge them to start and stop a built-in timer as needed. Depending on how you manage this implementation, you may require employees to log all their work throughout the day or only utilize it for special projects.

Strategy #6 – Increase Employee Recognition

Vice president of Gartner©, Brian Kropp, points out that "during periods of disruption, employees' desire for being recognized for their contribution increases by about 30%" (Baker, 2021). It is even more important to motivate the remote staff member. Effective recognition not only motivates the employee but also serves as a leading signal to other staff members with behaviors they should emulate. Recognition doesn't need to be a bonus or a pay raise. Simple public acknowledgment, tokens of appreciation, development opportunities, and low-cost perks are enough to motivate most employees. Employees want and require recognition for their efforts. Managers in firms experiencing a slowdown might use this time to provide development opportunities to staff who usually do not have capacity. Earlier managers identified employees' work and contributions within the traditional office space; however, they must recognize more with less visibility. Remote workers and managers have limited unintentional interactions and fewer group interactions where colleagues can meet and share stories.

With a lack of visibility in a remote environment, try to improve your monitoring techniques and relationships with direct reports. Use simple pulse surveys to ask specific questions or track output to collect data and find recognition areas. By meeting with employees virtually and asking what obstacles they have overcome or ways colleagues have helped them, you can identify elements to recognize, celebrate, and share their accomplishments to the employee and teams.

Work From Home Software for the Remote Employee

Work from home software can provide the employer with software tools that can assist in managing employees working remotely. Remote working software includes communication and networking technologies such as video chat applications or messaging tools, cloud storage, task and project management systems, and remote team management programs. To support remote collaboration, it is critical that the remote working software integrates with various other applications and is simple to use for other team members. With effective remote working software, onboarding new staff should be a breeze.

The work from home software is generally broken down into six types of software tools needed to have productive employees:

- **Project Management Tools** – track project road maps in real time through online dashboards.
- **Real-Time** – communication tools allow entire teams to post messages within appropriate groups; it's simple for a remote worker to join in on a conversation or catch up on communications they missed earlier if they were busy.
- **Collaboration** – lets remote workers contribute to shared files to work with a team in real time.
- **Team Monitoring and Management** – let you survey your team on their engagement and how they feel about their work.
- **Remote Access** – makes your work computers accessible to you at any time. You can use your work computer at home as if you were sitting in front of it. While remoting in from another device, open any file and utilize any application on your work computer.
- **Videoconferencing Software** – enables online communication for audio meetings, video meetings, and seminars, with built-in features such as chat, screen sharing, and recording. Video meeting apps are trusted teleconferencing platforms ideal for organizations of any size.

While being able to work from home is a nice perk, you and your team must have the necessary software solutions to ensure that you can meet your objectives even with remote workers. Here are 25 of some of the more popular work from home software programs:

1. **Hubstaff** – to help teams make the most of their time, develop trust, and generate accountability through time tracking, timesheets, and team management.
2. **Todoist** – for tracking to-dos and creating subtasks; shows you your productivity trends for the day or week.
3. **Asana** – a ticketing system that helps teams stay focused on projects and daily tasks for collective team knowledge.
4. **10to8** – meeting scheduling software that enables distant teams to organize and sync meetings like daily stand-ups, cross-departmental meetings, virtual coffees, and more.
5. **TalentLMS** – an award-winning Learning Management System (LMS) ideal for training remote employees and delivering engaging online training.
6. **Userlane** – a flexible digital adoption solution for employee onboarding and training.
7. **Culture Amp** – a people and culture platform that raises the bar for Employee Engagement. It gives managers vital information about employee satisfaction, performance, feedback, and planning tools.

8   **F4S (Fingerprint for Success)** – an online people analytics tool that helps identify your strengths and your blind spots, which, when optimized, will help unlock greater productivity in the workplace.

9   **HiveDesk** – time and project tracking, activity management, timesheets, and screenshots are all part of this all-in-one remote team management software. It's a one-stop shop for managing distributed teams.

10 **Sold0** – software to manage work from home employee purchases on company expenses.

11 **Connecteam** – an all-in-one employee management app that allows you to manage your remote teams quickly and effectively, keeping everyone on the same page, creating schedules, and celebrating success.

12 **Kissflow** – a digital workplace and project management platform that enables distant team leaders to optimize, monitor, and track all of their work.

13 **HelloSign** – an eSignature solution that allows you to design flexible signing workflows.

14 **PukkaTeam** – a tool for bringing distant teams closer together. It takes photos of your coworkers' faces throughout the day, allowing you to see their faces throughout the day.

15 **Slack** – a solution to some of the communication issues that occur with remote working. It lets you have real-time chats with anybody in your team, create channels for various reasons, and organize your conversations with threads within messages.

16 **Zoom** – feature-rich videoconferencing with various plans based on business size and needs. The enterprise-level subscription includes up to 200 meeting participants, personalized emails, unlimited cloud storage, and a vanity meeting URL.

17 **Cisco WebEx** – industry-standard videoconferencing service, especially for companies with many team members or a huge enterprise.

18 **Microsoft Teams** – chat-based workspace in Office 365. It brings people, conversations, and content together and tools that teams need to collaborate to achieve more easily.

19 **Skype** – make free internet calls for business, family, and friends with your Go and Pay Monthly subscriptions.

20 **GoToMeeting** – online videoconferencing for companies worldwide or real-time virtual communication and collaboration.

21 **1Password** – all your passwords may be stored in a safe, online password vault with this password management program. You won't have to remember dozens of different passwords, and you won't have to worry about someone finding out your passwords if you write them down.

22 **Email Analytics** – displays information about employees' email activity, such as how many emails they send and receive, typical email response times, and even their busiest hours and days of the week.

23 **ActivTrak** – employee monitoring software to track activities like website visits and app usage and apply content filters and other controls.

24   **Teramind** – software solution for staff monitoring that includes time and activity tracking. It also allows administrators to define and enforce certain regulations, such as blocking traffic to select websites and notifying you of any problematic user activity.

25   **iDoneThis** – a unique entry on this list, giving your team the ability to self-report on their daily progress. With this employee monitoring tool, everyone on your team will participate in a daily check-in, where they'll explain the tasks they've completed, their current projects, and any challenges standing in the way of their productivity.

Managers need to understand these factors that make remote work incredibly demanding. If not, even high-performing employees may experience job performance and engagement declines when they begin working remotely, especially in the absence of preparation and training.

References

Baker, M. (2021, January 04). 9 tips for managing remote employees. Retrieved December 30, 2021 from www.gartner.com/smarterwithgartner/9-tips-for-managing-remote-employees

Global Workplace Analytics. (2021). The work-from-home survey results are in! Retrieved December 30, 2021 from https://globalworkplaceanalytics.com/global-work-from-home-experience-survey

Iqbal, M. (2021, November 11). Zoom revenue and usage statistics (2021). Retrieved December 30, 2021 from www.businessofapps.com/data/zoom-statistics/

Krasno, A. (2021, August 21). New study by globalization partners underlines the critical role employee experience plays in remote team working environments. Retrieved from www.globalization-partners.com/about-us/company-news/new-study-by-globalization-partners-underlines-the-critical-role-employee-experience-plays-in-remote-team-working-environments/#gref/

Chapter 8

Corporate Cultures in The Digital Age

Robert L. Ramirez

What does the culture in the new digital office look like today? Take a look at the office, and you will see a plethora of diverse individuals working together while also working with others from diverse locations including homes and from different countries, all striving toward a common mission. The most important asset of all companies is arguably its people. Without the employees, there will be no new generation of ideas nor the creation of intellectual properties such as patents, trademarks, and brands. No new products would be designed, and no orders would be fulfilled.

In today's Digital Age, our customers, employees, and investors are global. This is both a great challenge and a great opportunity for Human Resource professionals attempting to build high-performing, collaborative work teams.

In his book *The Culture Code: The Secrets of Highly Successful Groups*, Daniel Coyle shared that strong cultures improved revenue by 765 percent over 11 years for more than 200 companies (Coyle, 2018). So, the challenge for Human Resources lies in building a culture of social cohesion in a diverse workplace.

Corporate Cultures and Cultural Intelligence in The Digital Age

Culture is the intensely rooted patterns of values, customs, attitudes, and beliefs that distinguish one group of people from another, and at the foundation of every organization is the company culture (Schmit, 2015). A strong culture acknowledges that the most critical asset for a company is its people. Protecting its people is one of the surest ways to continued success.

National Cultural Differences

National cultural differences influence the conduct of business internationally (Hill, 2017). As business becomes progressively global, managers require a skill set that combines technical leadership, strategic management, and cultural competence. Even managers working in their native cultures often work with

DOI: 10.4324/9781003122272-8

employees from various cultural and religious backgrounds in today's environment. A great company culture has many positive values that not only help employees feel supported but also lead to higher productivity.

Workplace Involvement

Great company cultures support workplace involvement. They offer positive and fun ways for their employees to get along by hosting personal and professional development activities, both within and outside regular company hours, thus enhancing their performance.

Global Collaboration and Cultural Intelligence

Global leaders and skilled managers are critical to the interconnected economy, implementing complex business processes with teams of workers from across the world. Seventy percent of international ventures fail because of cultural differences (Economist Intelligence Unit, 2012). Success in today's globalized economy requires a learned talent to adapt to various cultural situations. For example, managers may be implementing a project using programmers located in India, product developers in China, research development in Poland, customer service in the Philippines, assembly in Mexico, and management from various other countries. As governance and globalization have become more complex and competitive, the ability of managers to function effectively in diverse cultural contexts, called Cultural Intelligence (C.Q.), has never been more critical for organizations (Lee & Liao, 2015).

Even though technology is one of the forces of global convergence, deep-rooted cultural differences and cultural diversity present critical challenges to leaders worldwide. Ang et al. (2012) observed in their study that with an increase in globalization, there is also an increase in intercultural interactions that can exacerbate cultural misunderstandings, tensions, and conflicts. Erin Mayer, international business professor and author of the book *The Culture Map*, states that organizational leaders who are not aware of cultural differences and do not know the strategies for managing cultural differences can upset team meetings, demotivate employees, aggravate Suppliers, and end up making it very difficult for the businesses to achieve their goals (Meyer, 2016).

Multigenerational Workforce

As discussed in Chapter 3, the multigenerational makeup of the workforce is also a challenge for companies; the next generation of managers is beginning to take on new management roles as the Baby Boomers retire at a pace of 10,000 per day (America Counts Staff, 2019). The majority of the corporate workforce comprises three generational cohorts: Baby Boomers, born from 1946 to 1964; Gen Xers, born from 1965 to 1980; and Millennials, born from 1981 to 2000 (Fry, 2020). In the United States, Millennials have surpassed Baby Boomers as the largest living generation (Fry, 2020). This generation shift, reflected in the workforce, necessitates Gen Xers and Millennials to take on more management roles in organizations. Each generation making up the workforce communicates and sees the world differently. Therefore, leaders must be skilled in managing the variances between generations and understanding the differences of their generational characteristics (Rivers, 2012).

This mix of generational and cultural workforce diversity challenges organizations to ensure that all the positive attributes of the various generations are fully utilized in order to maintain a competitive advantage. Employees and leaders need to learn how to create a teamwork environment so that all the generations can share knowledge (Rivers, 2012). Business today is global, and success requires a new set of skills. Managers must lead these workforce teams to work collaboratively toward achieving organizational goals. Using C.Q. to optimize the performance of these diverse teams is critical.

Corporate Culture and Religion

The relationship between culture and religion is subtle and sophisticated. Religion can be defined as a system of shared beliefs and rituals concerned with the realm of the sacred (Hill, 2017). Due to an increasingly global society, people are much more likely to deal with international business relationships, trade agreements, commodity exchanges, and overlapping cultures; therefore, it is important to understand religions, customs, and beliefs worldwide. Religion plays an important role in shaping attitudes toward work, culture, and entrepreneurship in some places. According to Hill (2017), religious ethics affect the cost of doing business in a country. Among the 12 classical world religions, the four largest are Christianity, with around 2.1 billion followers; Islam, with approximately 1.3 billion; Hinduism, with about 900 million; and Buddhism, with around 376 million (Hill, 2017). Christianity is the most prominent religion in the United States (Hill, 2017), but worldwide, the differences in religion can inhibit any organization if not managed well.

Avoiding Ethnocentrism and Prejudice

The core of C.Q. involves recognizing one's tendencies toward ethnocentrism and prejudice. Learning and having a meaningful dialogue about other religions can demonstrate significant respect when interacting with leaders from different parts of the world. Many cultural problems begin when people from different cultures misunderstand the culturally based actions of others. It also includes examining one's own core beliefs and integrating them into one's daily life.

Corporate Culture Evolution From the Industrial Revolution

Fueled by considerable advances in technology and scientific understanding over the past several centuries, modern business and corporate cultures have evolved.

The First Industrial Revolution – The Manufacturing Age

The Industrial Revolution's first wave began around the late 1700s to the mid-1800s. It initiated the transition of textile production from homes to factories by industrializing textile manufacturing. During this time, steam power and the cotton gin were highly significant.

For many entrepreneurs, these machines allowed for an explosion of productivity turned out by the factories. The corporate culture began to emerge as owners needed increased man power to run the machines. This began the concept of the boss-subordinate relationship marked by a large separation between the two. Men who were used to working on their own farms and working alongside their family to sustain themselves now were placed into a subordinate role. This also began to erode some of the communities these men lived in as they were often absent.

The Second Industrial Revolution – The Technological Revolution

The Second Industrial Revolution followed this from around the mid-1800s to the early 1900s. In this phase, large factories and companies started using more technologies and railroads to produce and transport goods in mass. The introduction of division of labor and mass manufacturing powered by electrical energy ushered in the Second Industrial Revolution in 1870 with the first assembly line. Key innovations during this period include the use of electricity, the telephone, the production line, the Bessemer steel process, electric light, and the typewriter.

Many cultural changes occurred as a result of the Industrial Revolution. Before the Revolution, most people lived in rural areas and worked on farms, while some lived on farms and traveled to the factory each day. In most cases, workers moved to the cities to work in factories. As a result, cities expanded in population and became overcrowded, filthy, and polluted. Poor laborers in many cities lived in crowded and dangerous buildings. For the typical person, this was a significant change in their way of life.

Transportation changed dramatically throughout the Industrial Revolution. Before people traveled by horse, by foot, or by boat. New ways of travel were introduced, including railroads, steamboats, and cars. This altered the way people and goods traveled across the country and world. Poor factory working conditions were one of the Industrial Revolution's drawbacks. At the time, there were few rules protecting workers, and working conditions were frequently hazardous. People had to work long hours regularly, and child labor was prevalent. However, by the end of the 1900s, labor unions and new legislation made the workplace safer.

The Third Industrial Revolution – The Information Age

Around 1969, we witnessed the Third Industrial Revolution, as electronics and programmable IT systems began to automate tasks and production further. The Information Age's democratization of energy, information, manufacturing, marketing, and logistics made productivity much easier and accessible to many more aspiring entrepreneurs. Along with that, the dawning of a new era of distributed capitalism resulted in a rapid reduction in transaction costs bringing in a new generation of distributed capitalism that has reduced the traditional barriers of entry enjoyed by larger businesses.

Since workers could possibly start their own companies using these systems, the power of the employer over the employee weakened. Workers had more leverage now in their desires to improve working conditions, and employers had to address these concerns reactively or proactively.

Today's Fourth Industrial Revolution – The Digital Age

The Digital Age we live in now is the Fourth Industrial Revolution. The Digital Age is marked by large amounts of information that is widely available, primarily through computer technology. There has been an explosion of disruptive technologies by digitizing corporate processes like free access to enormous amounts of data, hyper-connectivity, artificial intelligence, and the Internet of Things. As a result, business evolution has resulted in massive increases in productivity and speed adding more and more value to the global gross domestic product (GDP) and many individuals' well-being. Similarly, our understanding, application, and approach to corporate culture have had to evolve to keep up with these changes.

Corporate Culture Disruptors of The Digital Age

The Digital Age offers so much opportunity to utilize the power of computing data and providing collaboration tools. As these new emerging technologies have entered the World of Work, many companies struggle to blend them in and, as a result, disrupt the corporate culture. And, although the term "disruptors" sounds destructive, they should be viewed as great opportunities to enhance the corporate culture.

Digital Communities

Business tools and technology are quickly changing and making the old ways of brand management obsolete while providing new and exciting ways of engaging with our customers. A thriving digital community increases customer engagement. Digital communities use technologies such as cloud computing, the internet, cell phones, social media, and email to effectively communicate at all levels with customers. Companies can now connect 24/7 and on demand to engage with followers and customers in this digital community.

In 2012, the University of Michigan study found that customers spend 19 percent more after joining a company's online community (University of Michigan, 2012). In addition, the study shared that companies profit more from personally created social communities than third-party social networks like Facebook. Engaged people in a digital community provide the kind of transparent, real-time feedback that helps a company stay ahead of the competition. This input enables businesses to enhance their products and consumer experiences continuously. It also aids in maintaining your brand's reputation.

Digital Collaboration With "Gig Workers" and Contractors

Companies find it more cost-efficient to hire a remote social media team and work with them online using digital collaboration tools. This includes hiring "Gig Workers" domestically and internationally. With online collaboration tools, small businesses can employ workers or outsource a team of experts from different parts of the world and bring them together on one online platform. Companies use collaborative platforms as a virtual workspace where centralized resources and tools facilitate communication and personal interaction. As seen in Chapter 7, there is a collaboration tool for any business project need. Most online collaboration tools support multiple communication such as videoconferencing, chat, instant messaging, and file sharing.

Globalization and a Diverse Workforce

Another disruptor is that today, generationally and culturally mixed workforce environments cause conflict in the workplace (Brett, 2018). Ang et al. (2012) found that globalization intensifies intercultural interactions and increases the probability of cultural misunderstanding, tension, and conflict. As organizations and globalization have become more complex and competitive, the ability of managers to function effectively in various cultural contexts, called C.Q., has never been more critical for organizations (Lee & Liao, 2015). In the growing global world, the development of cross-cultural competencies is vital as employees and organizations become increasingly culturally diverse (Eisenberg et al., 2013). In addition, there are four generational cohorts of workers as well that have different aptitudes concerning their C.Q. capabilities.

C.Q. – The Key to Thriving in The Digital Age

Functioning effectively in intercultural contexts has never been more critical than today (Rockstuhl & Van Dyne, 2018). Little research has been performed to help leaders manage multicultural work environments to facilitate creative and practical solutions to cultural conflict. Previous C.Q. work has had some limitations but has laid the foundation for future research (Alexandra, 2018).

So far, the research has provided some valuable concepts to help explain the relationship between C.Q. and the working generational cohorts of the leaders in today's organizations. Janssens and Cappellen (2008) have stated that global leaders require an increased set of C.Q. capabilities to work effectively with multiple cultures simultaneously. C.Q. levels in the workforce need to be better understood so that business leaders, scholars, and Human Resources professionals can facilitate conflict resolution and train and educate their global workforce and multicultural teams. This current research could help improve individual and organizational performance.

Early Culture and Intelligence Theory

Measuring intelligence is a core element in understanding individual differences in the field of psychology (Gottfredson & Saklofake, 2009). Research began to explain psychological differences scientifically in the nineteenth century, focusing on measuring intelligence factors (Gardner, 1983). Charles Spearmen was widely recognized as the formative author for general intelligence testing (Gottfredson & Saklofake, 2009; Sternberg & Detterman, 1986). Spearman led influential research in the field of psychology using factor analysis as the statistical method to explain intelligence factors. His study concluded that intelligence testing of individuals across unrelated subjects led to similar outcomes. This relationship suggested general intelligence related to cognitive performance (Spearman, 1927).

Overall, intelligence research has provided insight into psychology and into social theories and constructs (Gottfredson & Saklofake, 2009). C.Q. builds on these past theories of intelligence and culture. Geert Hofstede's Cultural Dimensions Theory, published in 1980, established a framework that aided in cross-cultural communication. Between 1967 and 1973, Hofstede developed this structure using the results of a worldwide survey of IBM employee values. It was one of the most comprehensive theoretical framework studies of how culture influences values in the workplace. In the study, Hofstede described the effects of culture on society, how it influences values in the workplace, and how it relates to behavior by using a structure derived from this factor analysis. Hofstede and Hofstede (2005) defined four dimensions of national culture, each having its own mental or behavioral characteristics (Hofstede & Hofstede, 2005).

1   Power Distance

People in cultures with a higher power distance place some people as superior to others because of their social status, sex, ethnicity, age, level of education, birth, or personal achievements. Conversely, people in cultures with lower power distance tend to assume equality among people, emphasizing earned status rather than a recognized state. Usually, the more unevenly wealth is distributed, the higher the power distance.

2   Individualism versus Collectivism

Individualism is defined as a desire for a loosely knit social framework in which people wish to care for their family or only themselves. Its opposite, collectivism, represents a desire for a tightly knit community in which people can expect their kin or members of a particular in-group to look after them in exchange for unquestioning loyalty.

3   Masculinity versus Femininity

Hofstede used the language of masculinity and femininity to denote how a culture values decisiveness or nurturing and social support. This distinction was also used to refer to the degree to which acceptable social roles operate for men and women.

4   Uncertainty Avoidance

This is the extent to which culture programs its people to feel either uncomfortable or comfortable in unstructured situations. Trust is bestowed only on close family and friends in high uncertainty avoidance cultures. As a result, it is hard for outside negotiators to establish relationships of confidence and trust with members of these cultures.

These dimensions provide the basis for understanding behavioral patterns in different cultures.

Multidimensional Construct Theory

Earley and Ang (2003) developed C.Q. further based on the theory of multiple intelligences by Sternberg and Detterman (1986). The theory of multiple intelligences includes:

- Interpersonal and Intrapersonal Intelligence (Gardner, 1983)
- Cognitive Intelligence (I.Q.)
- Social Intelligence (S.I.) (Cantor & Kihlstrom, 1987; Goleman, 1997)
- Emotional intelligence (E.Q.) (Boyatzis & McKee, 2005; Goleman, 1995)

C.Q. is proposed to be one component of intelligence and complementary to I.Q. and E.Q. (Livermore, 2018). Neither I.Q. nor E.Q. includes understanding cross-cultural settings (Rockstuhl et al., 2011). Ang et al. (2012) argued that C.Q. has four distinct intelligence loci:

1   **Metacognitive C.Q.** – the capability of processing information during and after a culturally diverse experience
2   **Cognitive C.Q.** – the available knowledge of norms, practices, and customs in different cultures

3   **Motivational C.Q.** – the willingness and drive to seek out and partici-
    pate in intercultural experiences and the motivation to learn about cultural
    differences
4   **Behavioral C.Q.** – appropriate verbal and nonverbal actions in intercul-
    tural environments

It was also found that C.Q. is not culture-bound. However, it constitutes a
culture-free ability that transfers across cultures and various cultural environments (Ang et al., 2012; Ng & Earley, 2006).

Current Cultural Intelligence Theory

Kim and Van Dyne (2012) developed and tested a moderated mediation model
of international leadership potential to close two significant gaps in the previous literature on Global Leadership Potential. First, they found that critical gaps
existed in understanding the C.Q. dynamic. The first gap reviewed was about
predictors of Global Leadership Potential. Global Leadership Potential is the
judgments observers make about future global leadership performance. The
second gap was from previous international leading research and its inconsist-
ency regarding intercultural contact and global leadership.

Kim and Van Dyne (2012) went beyond previous research by indicating
support for a new set of predictors of Global Leadership Potential. The moderated mediation model can lead to better leadership potential in international
contexts. Their research results add support to contact theory and provide clarity on the long-standing issue about the value of prior intercultural contact by
showing that cross-cultural communication is positively related to C.Q. and
Global Leadership Potential (Kim & Van Dyne, 2012).

Generations in the Workforce Theory

The workforce includes a diverse age range of employees. The more conventional
hierarchy of the organizational workforce, in which older workers, such as the
Baby Boomers, hold senior-level positions, middle-aged employees have middle
management positions, and younger employees hold more entry-level positions,
is no longer the trend (Howe & Strauss, 2007). In today's workplace, there are
three to four generations working together. Seniority is no longer due to age,
and sometimes the least tenured workers are often asked to participate in the
daily decision-making processes and are consulted to improve policies (Weston,
2001). As the workforce becomes older, an increasing number of generational
cohorts will work side by side, as four generational cohorts (Baby Boomers, Gen
Xers, Millennials, and Gen Z) take on essential roles within organizations. The
Boomers remaining in the workforce will have to accept sharing positions once
reserved for those who had seniority grown from a long tenure at a company.

Eisner (2005) cautioned that managers should not oversimplify workplace
differences between generations. Instead, they should consider the differences

and adopt them as a form of diversity. Managers can use this diversity to move an organization forward using the various generational cohorts' experiences, C.Q.s, opinions, and skill sets. However, if managers fail to embrace this adequately, such diversity can turn into conflict within the organization.

New Opportunities for HR Professionals

The Covid-19 Pandemic forced companies to speed up the concept of remote work drastically. As a result, up to half of American workers worked from home in 2020 and 2021, more than double from 2017 to 2018. In the past, the biggest holdbacks of work from home was the boss-subordinate trust factor; management did not trust their employees to work untethered. However, employees, wanting to prove that they could work remotely, jumped at the opportunity and have proven to be very productive (Kamouri, 2021). Now, according to Iometrics and other global associations, working remotely on multiple days per week will be the norm for 25–30 percent of the workforce.

The remote work trend has created a challenge for Human Resources to build better, high-performance virtual teams. Remote employment is made possible by digital communication, but it also introduces a slew of new issues.

Building High-Performance Teams (Virtual Teams)

To build a high-performance team, one of the first things that must be done is to ensure that the corporate leaders are on board and properly aligned with the vision of managing and hiring virtual talent. Company leaders have to make it clear to employees that they are responsible for their actions and their impact on the rest of the team (Hirsch, 2021). DeRosa, a managing partner at OnPoint Consulting, suggests that managers of remote employees observe the following guidelines with those workers:

- Communicate clearly about who will be held accountable for what to all team members
- Jointly agree upon a timetable for every project and assignment
- Monitor progress by scheduling regular check-ins
- Avoid blame if a deadline is missed or another issue arises
- Use regular check-ins to help keep track of progress

Managing the Digital Environment

Many organizations may change their technologies, infrastructure, and processes; however, if they do not address the human elements of change, successful transformation is unlikely to happen. When people grow overly reliant on technology to mediate their connections, a phenomenon known as "Virtual

Distance" develops. "Virtual Distance" is the sense of emotional and psychological separation that develops over time. According to Virtual Distance International (VDI) and Karen Sobel Lojeski, co-author of *The Power of Virtual Distance* (Sobel Lojeski, 2020), the greater the "Virtual Distance", the larger the negative impact is on the team in terms of innovation effectiveness, trust, work happiness, role and objective clarity, and project success.

Solutions and Problem-Solving

Culture encompasses the whole way of life for people, including material and symbolic elements. It is the operating system or the lens through which one views the world. Culture is passed on from one generation to the next. As a result, cultural issues have existed throughout history, and people often judge other people's cultures according to their own cultural values. This can cause misunderstandings when people from different cultures interact.

In a world where business is global, organizational leaders are experiencing considerable challenges managing cultural differences. They also have difficulties finding exemplary leadership to handle complex cultural differences (Law et al., 2004). New research on leadership competencies provides us with growing awareness and understanding of cultural differences in business.

- **Biases** – affect us and our decision-making
- **Attitude** – how we react to particular people
- **Perception** – how we perceive people and reality
- **How We Act** – how receptive/friendly we are to specific individuals
- **Our Listening Skills** – how attentive we are to what others have to say
- **Our Attention** – which qualities of a person we pay the most attention to
- **Our Micro-Affirmations** – how much we console individual people in particular situations

How to Recognize, Avoid, and Stop Stereotype Biases and Threats

Many times, our natural ethnocentrism leaves us exposed to potential blind spots on how we perceive, judge, and treat others. For a great corporate culture to exist, it is important to help leaders, managers, and team members to be able to know these blind spots exist so they may be able to adjust their behavior. Today, this is called Unconscious Bias. Here are five reasons to help your workforce identify their Unconscious Bias and modify their actions in your organization:

1 **Business and People Management** – since managers are leading a diverse set of workers, they need to be aware of their own biases and how they can be sure to supervise their teams fairly

2   **Team Efficiency** – since teams must collaborate often, understanding their own biases will help prevent unintentional acts that could slow down the team process

3   **Making Decisions** – as teams are working on making decisions, they need to be able to bring up different points of view and engage in conflict while understanding different cultures view conflict in different ways

4   **Communications** – as teams communicate with each other, they need to be able to voice their opinions and ensure connection without fear of using offensive terms

5   **To Be a Good Manager and Human** – as leaders, it is important to be empathetic to their team in a way that is meaningful based on their cultural beliefs

Recommendations for Practice

Leaders can bring positive change to their organizations by developing C.Q. in the workforce. The primary reasons leaders need to develop C.Q. is (1) the growth of diverse markets and (2) an increasingly diverse workforce (Schmit, 2015). If the following recommendations are applied, it will lead to a workforce with a higher C.Q. that would be better able to adjust and adapt to the complex situations of today's globalized world.

Recommendation #1 – Help Your Workforce Explore Their Own Cultural Beliefs

Taking a personal inventory of why a person believes, why they believe, and where those beliefs come from will help them understand others. Studies have shown that the Baby Boomers scored below the Gen Xers and Millennials on the four dimensions and would benefit most from C.Q. training from learning strategies for improving their cross-cultural interactions, emphasizing problem-solving, and adapting their own behaviors. Before people can begin to understand other people's cultures, they need to understand their own culture. C.Q. training can help ensure that all employees understand what the organization and the law consider appropriate and inappropriate behavior toward people based on their race, ethnicity, age, gender, religion, or sexual orientation.

Recommendation #2 – Help Your Workforce Understand Other Cultures

The second recommendation address the issues around the cultural understanding. It includes the ways communication styles, religious beliefs, and role expectations differ across cultures. It takes time to learn about a different culture; aspects of a culture, such as dress, mannerisms, behaviors, customs, and symbols, are visually apparent. However, several pieces are unseen and take some time to know and understand. These include assumptions, beliefs, world-views, attitudes, and more. Each generation can learn to be more mindful of other visible and invisible cultures. Professor of Psychology Harry Triandis (1994) believes in learning C.Q. through learning the local language, embedding oneself in a cross-cultural work experience, and spending time in diverse cultural settings. Working and traveling abroad and taking even short trips to other cultures can increase C.Q.

The SHRM Foundation (2015) recommends strategizing before, during, and after crossing cultures to develop C.Q. First, plan to prepare for an intercultural encounter and foresee how to approach the people, how to discuss the topics that may come up in conversation, and how to handle various situations in light of cultural differences. Second, a person must be in tune with their mind and the minds of others during these intercultural encounters. Finally, after the meeting, the person should compare the experience with prior expectations and make mental adjustments as needed (Schmit, 2015). C.Q. strategy highlights the importance of thinking consciously and is the key to understanding and knowing how to be more effective in the workplace.

Recommendation #3 – Help Your Workforce by Using Reverse Mentoring

The unique characteristics of the younger generation of Millennials allow reverse mentoring to help the older generations of the Baby Boomers and Gen Xers so they may become more culturally sensitive. Reverse mentoring involves a more youthful, junior employee engaging a more senior employee to encourage cross-generational learning (Murphy, 2012). Reverse mentoring can provide an essential role in bridging the gap between the generations currently in the workforce. The generational cohort has experienced vastly different social and cultural situations, which have resulted in varied work ethics, mindsets, and attitudes (Myers & Sadaghiani, 2010). Reverse mentoring can help challenge C.Q. issues and benefit team members and organizations as a whole.

Recommendation #4 – Help Your Workforce by Using C.Q. Assessment Tools

The C.Q. assessment can be a Human Resources and Management tool to improve and predict various effectiveness outcomes in culturally diverse situations. Intercultural competency inventories have been one of the most significant breakthroughs in intercultural competence (Schmit, 2015). The assessment data can reduce the sense that intercultural skills are vague and elusive and provide Management and Human Resources professionals a way to benchmark C.Q. performance against norms and standards. This can also become part of the onboarding process to help new employees succeed in culturally diverse environments. C.Q. assessments can also help companies assess their

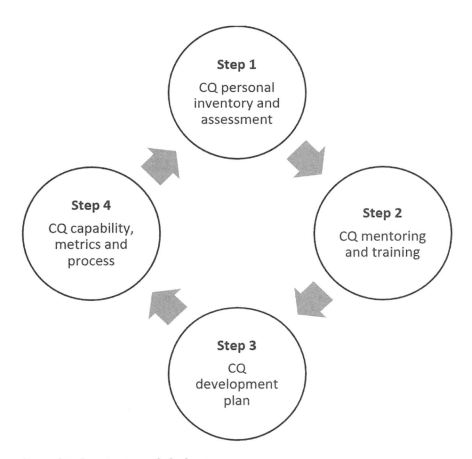

Figure 8.1 Developing a C.Q. Strategy

staff members worldwide to see how their company compares against other organizations. This can also offer workers individual insights into where they can most profitably focus their energies, use their strengths, and improve their skills for working across cultures (Schmit, 2015).

In order for companies to fully experience the benefits C.Q. training can provide, they must implement this four-part cycle that will also perpetuate their learning.

In the first step, the employee would take the C.Q. assessment to identify their strengths and development opportunities for functioning effectively in multicultural settings. The employee would also take a personal inventory of their own beliefs and why they believe a certain way. The assessment would provide the employee with a C.Q. profile summary breaking their scores into the four dimensions of drive, knowledge, strategy, and action.

In Step 2, the employee would be enrolled in a training course to learn about specific cultures and worldwide norms. They would learn about individual cultural values by countries or clusters. This training would provide an opportunity to learn and develop new skills in low-risk, diverse simulated environments in the safety of a classroom setting. A coach or mentor would help the employee review their C.Q. scores and create a training path to build their C.Q. skill set.

In Step 3, the employee and their mentor or trainer would create a C.Q. development plan.

In Step 4, the company would develop a plan for accountability and metrics. Employees would share their plans with their supervisors and peers. After a specific time, the employee would retake the assessment to ensure C.Q. development. The results will enhance the employee and benefit the individual and company with experience, reflection, time, coaching, and personal growth.

By going through this cycle repeatedly, workers learn to slow down their thinking to allow the brain to recognize where their Unconscious Biases originate. Then they begin to allow their conscious rational thought occur. Managing bias requires slowing down the system 1 part of your brain so that system 2 has a chance to make conscious choices (Kahneman, 2011).

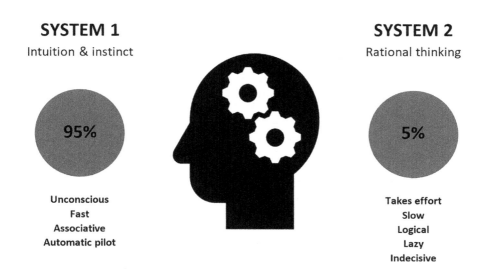

SYSTEM 1
Intuition & instinct

95%

Unconscious
Fast
Associative
Automatic pilot

SYSTEM 2
Rational thinking

5%

Takes effort
Slow
Logical
Lazy
Indecisive

Figure 8.2 Thinking Fast and Slow

Succeeding in Today's Global Marketplace

Companies now can use this research and recommendations to provide targeted training to the generations in their workforce. Targeted C.Q. training can give companies tremendous success in culturally diverse markets. It can also speed up efficiency when working across borders and increase multicultural and global team effectiveness. Companies should combine C.Q. assessments, training, and coaching as part of their management development. This training will help multicultural teams work together more effectively in both virtual and in-person teams. Companies that invest in C.Q. training can improve the work performance of culturally diverse employees (Azevedo, 2018).

References

Alexandra, V. (2018). Predicting C.Q. development in the context of experiential cross-cultural training: The role of social dominance orientation and the propensity to change stereotypes. *Academy of Management Learning & Education* 17(1): 62–78. https://doi-org.proxy1.ncu.edu/10.5465/amle.2015.0096

America Counts Staff. (2019, December 10). 2020 census will help policymakers prepare for the incoming wave of aging boomers. U.S. Census Bureau. Retrieved July 15, 2022 from https://www.census.gov/library/stories/2019/12/by-2030-all-baby-boomers-will-be-age-65-or-older.html

Ang, S., Van Dyne, L., & Tan, M. (2012). Cultural intelligence. In R. Sternberg & S. Kaufman (Eds.), *The Cambridge handbook of intelligence* (Cambridge handbooks in psychology, pp. 582–602). Cambridge: Cambridge University Press.

Azevedo, A. (2018). Cultural intelligence: Key benefits to individuals, teams and organizations. *American Journal of Economics and Business Administration* 10: 52–56. doi:10.3844/ajebasp.2018.52.56

Boyatzis, R., & McKee, A. (2005). *Resonant leadership*. New York: Harvard Business Press.

Brett, J. (2018). Intercultural challenges in managing workplace conflict – A call for research. *Cross Cultural and Strategic Management* 25(1): 32–52. https://doi.org/10.1108/CCSM-11-2016-0190

Cantor, N., & Kihlstrom, J. F. (1987). *Personality and social intelligence*. Englewood Cliffs, NJ: Prentice-Hall.

Coyle, D. (2018). *The culture code: The secrets of highly successful groups*. New York: Bantam.

Earley, P. C., & Ang, S. (2003). *Cultural intelligence: Individual interactions across cultures*. Stanford, CA: Stanford Business Books.

Economist Intelligence Unit. (2012). Competing across borders: How cultural and communication barriers affect business. Retrieved April 14, 2022 from www.cfoinnovation.com/competing-across-borders-how-cultural-and-communication-barriers-affect-business

Eisenberg, J., Lee, H., Brück, F., Brenner, B., Claes, M., Mironski, J., & Bell, R. (2013). Can business schools make students culturally competent? effects of cross-cultural management courses on cultural intelligence. *Academy of Management Learning & Education* 12(4): 603–621. https://doi.org/10.5465/amle.2012.0022

Eisner, S. P. (2005). Managing generation Y. *SAM Advanced Management Journal* 70: 4–15. doi:10.1109/emr.2011.5876168.

Fry, R. (2020, April 28). Millennials overtake baby boomers as America's largest generation. Retrieved December 30, 2021 from www.pewresearch.org/fact-tank/2020/04/28/
millennials-overtake-baby-boomers-as-americas-largest-generation/

Gardner, H. (1983). *Frames of mind: The theory of multiple intelligence.* New York: Basic Books.

Goleman, D. (1995). *Emotional intelligence: Why it can matter more than IQ.* New York: Bantam Books.

Goleman, D. (1997). *Emotional intelligence.* New York: Bantam Books.

Gottfredson, L., & Saklofake, D. H. (2009). Intelligence: Foundations and issues in assessment. *Canadian Psychology* 50(3): 183–196. Retrieved from http://proquest.umi.com.
proxy1.ncu.edu/

Hill, W. L. (2017). *International business: Competing in the global marketplace* (10th ed.). New
York: McGraw-Hill Higher Education.

Hirsch, A. (2021, July 6). Building and leading high-performing remote teams. Retrieved
December 29, 2021 from www.shrm.org/resourcesandtools/hr-topics/technology/
pages/building-leading-high-performing-remote-teams.aspx

Hofstede, G., Hofstede, G. J., & Minkov, M. (2005). *Cultures and organizations: Software of the
mind* (Vol. 2). New York: McGraw-Hill.

Howe, N., & Strauss, W. (2007). The next 20 years: How customer and workforce attitudes
will evolve. *Harvard Business Review* 85(7/8): 41–52

Janssens, M., & Cappellen, T. (2008). Contextualizing cultural intelligence: The case of
global managers. In M S. Ang & L. Van Dyne (Eds.), *Handbook on cultural intelligence:
Theory, measurement and applications* (pp. 356–371). New York: M.E. Sharpe.

Kahneman. (2011). *Thinking fast and slow* (1st ed.). New York: Farrar, Straus and Giroux.

Kamouri, A. (2021, November 20). Work-at-home after Covid-19 – Our forecast. Retrieved
from https://globalworkplaceanalytics.com/work-at-home-after-covid-19-our-forecast/

Kim, Y. J., & Van Dyne, L. (2012). Cultural intelligence and international leadership potential: The importance of contact for members of the majority. *Applied Psychology: An
International Review* 61: 272–294

Law, K. S., Wong, C. S., & Song, L. J. (2004). The construct and criterion validity of
emotional intelligence and its potential utility for management studies. *Journal of Applied
Psychology* 89: 483–496.

Lee, Y.-T., & Liao, Y. (2015). Cultural competence: Why it matters and how you can acquire
it. *IESE Insight* 26: 23–30. https://doi-org.proxy1.ncu.edu/10.15581/002.ART-2746

Livermore, D. (2018, September 13). E.Q. does not equal C.Q. Retrieved from https://
culturalq.com/blog/eq-does-not-equal-cq/

Meyer, E. (2016). *The culture map.* New York: PublicAffairs.

Murphy, W. M. (2012). Reverse mentoring at work: Fostering cross-generational learning and developing Millennial leaders. *Human Resource Management* 51(4): 549–574.
doi:10.1002/hrm.21489

Myers, K. K. and Sadaghiani, K. (2010). Millennials in the workplace: A communication
perspective on Millennials' organizational relationships and performance. *Journal of Business and Psychology* 25(2).

Ng, K.-Y., and Earley, P. C. (2006). Culture + intelligence: Old constructs, new frontiers.
Group & Organization Management 31(1): 4–19.

Rivers, M. (2012). Bridging the knowledge gap between the Baby Boomers and the multi-
generations. Retrieved from http://search.proquest.com.proxy1.ncu.edu/docview/1271
758049?accountid=28180

Rockstuhl, T., Seiler, S., Ang, S., Van Dyne, L., & Annen, H. (2011). Beyond general intelligence (I.Q.) and emotional intelligence (E.Q.): The role of cultural intelligence (C.Q.) on cross-border leadership effectiveness in a globalized world. *Journal of Social Issues* 67: 825–840.

Rockstuhl, T., & Van Dyne, L. (2018). A bi-factor theory of the four-factor model of cultural intelligence: Meta-analysis and theoretical extensions. *Organizational Behavior & Human Decision Processes* 148: 124–144. https://doi-org.proxy1.ncu.edu/10.1016/j.obhdp.2018.07.005

Schmit, M. (2015). Cultural intelligences: The essential intelligence for the 21st century. Retrieved from www.shrm.org/hr-today/trends-and-forecasting/special-reports-and-expert-views/Documents/Cultural-Intelligence.pdf

SHRM Foundation. (2015). Cultural intelligence: The essential intelligence for the 21st century. Retrieved from https://www.shrm.org/hr-today/trends-and-forecasting/special-reports-and-expert-views/Documents/Cultural-Intelligence.pdf

Sobel Lojeski, K., & Reilly, R. R. (2020). *The power of virtual distance: A guide to productivity and happiness in the age of remote work*. Hoboken, NJ: John Wiley & Sons.

Spearman, C. (1927). *The abilities of man: Their nature and measurement*. Oxford: Macmillan

Sternberg, R.J., & Detterman, D. K. (1986). *What is intelligence? Contemporary viewpoints on its nature and definition*. Norwood, NJ: Ablex.

Triandis, H.C. (1994). Cross-cultural industrial and organizational psychology. In H.C. Triandis, M.D. Dunnette, & L.M. Hough (Eds.), *Handbook of industrial and organizational psychology* (pp. 103–172). Palo Alto, CA: Consulting Psychologists Press.

University of Michigan. (2012). Firms' own social networks better for business than Facebook. Retrieved December 30, 2021 from https://news.umich.edu/firms-own-social-networks-better-for-business-than-facebook/

Weston, M. (2001). Coaching generations in the workplace. *Nursing Administration Quarterly* 25(2): 11–21.

Chapter 9

Organizational Behavior in The Digital Age

Robert L. Ramirez

We are now living in The Digital Age, the period in human history shaped by the explosion and widespread availability of digital information and communication technologies (Lengsfeld, 2019). In his book, *Digital Era Framework*, Dr. Lengsfeld discusses that quick knowledge transfer is vitally essential in periods of disruptive change. For knowledge to be practical, new ideas and concepts must be able to spread rapidly. Today, in our modern digital era, companies are being forced to change at a breakneck pace by their customers and competitors alike. Digital leadership innovation is not motionless but changes through time. In a time when social media encourages consumers to share and rate their experiences with companies, products, and services within social media communities of potential consumers, companies need to ensure that those experiences are positive. Consumers have learned to expect products and services that were previously unavailable, and firms competing for their business must now provide them. For example, consumers now expect that their smartphones will have the ability to "learn" about their owner's preferences, so it is important that businesses ensure their products can be found by algorithms and other artificial intelligence systems accessed by these smartphones.

When businesses are faced with the need to transform, leaders usually think about the required core components. Then, they leverage deep data analytics, real-time customer insights, digitized solutions, process reengineering, and the latest transformation tactics (Moore, 2019). To understand customer requirements and facilitate change, a group of talented leaders, business analysts, and data scientists come together.

Work from home and the use of applications on the internet are changing modern workplaces and have introduced new options for employee behavior, including organizational citizenship behavior (OCB). This chapter introduces the OCB in The Digital Age.

DOI: 10.4324/9781003122272-9

Organizational Behavior

Organizational behavior examines individual and team behavior in the workplace of an organization. This leads to an analysis of human behavior and its impact on work performance. In addition, organizational behavior examines challenge areas, including motivation, leadership, conversation, and teamwork. This chapter will study how these concepts have been impacted by the digitization of work and recommends the required changes in organizational behavior needed to ensure ongoing increases in productivity in The Digital Age.

Organizational Citizenship Behavior

OCB has become a key concept in the industrial-organizational psychology literature because of its relationships with performance and other desirable outcomes (Organ & Ryan, 1995; Podsakoff et al., 2009). OCB describes all the positive and constructive employee actions and behaviors that aren't part of their formal job description. It's anything that employees do, out of their own free will, that supports their colleagues and benefits the organization as a whole. While OCB interest has endured, the nature of the workplace has changed due to significant technological advances. Employees have integrated internet-enabled social media resources into their work routines leading to work-related social behavior changes (Pillemer & Rothbard, 2018). These changes call for examining how two researchers understand OCB in the internet age. First, social media platforms and digital environments allow employees to engage in behaviors that impact their professional relationships and the companies for which they work. Workplace by Facebook is an example where colleagues can post pictures, stories, and other items that other colleagues can interact with. In addition, the convenience and ubiquity of these technology-enabled spaces may allow for desirable prosocial behaviors, such as OCB, to be completed with increased ease and frequency compared to traditional in-person settings.

Pre-Digital Era Theories Leading to the Current Motivational Theories

Motivating the best employees to join the organization and stay with it is crucial for managers. Top-performing employees usually surround top-performing leaders. Employees are encouraged by various things, such as appreciation of their work efforts, ideas, contribution to the organization, achievement, and status. An intrinsic reward is a personal satisfaction you feel when you perform well and complete goals. Intrinsic reward is the belief that your effort substantially contributes to the business or society. Someone else bestows an extrinsic reward on you as a token of appreciation for your actions. This reward can come in the way of pay raises. In the pre-digital era of motivation, some traditional theories of motivation evolved from the studies of Taylor, Mayo, Maslow, Herzberg, and McGregor. We will review these theories next.

Taylor Scientific Management Theory

In 1911, Frederick Taylor was known as the "Father" of Scientific Management. Taylor's goal was to boost worker productivity, which would benefit both the company and the employee. His Scientific Management approach included a three elements approach: time, methods, and work rules. Taylor's thinking has helped streamline current operations such as FedEx and McDonalds.

Elton Mayo and the Hawthorne Studies

Following Taylor, Elton Mayo and his colleagues from Harvard University went to the Hawthorne plant to test how much light would be best for optimum productivity. They kept detailed records of the worker's productivity under different lighting levels. The researchers were expecting productivity to lower if the factory was lightly dimmed. However, the experimental group's productivity went up regardless of whether the lighting was bright or dim, even when it was reduced to set to moonlight. Later in a series of 13 more experiments, another test room was set up where researchers could operate the temperature, humidity, and other environmental factors. They learned that productivity increased each time; the study showed that productivity grew by 50 percent. When the study was repeated under the original conditions (expecting productivity to fall to actual levels), productivity increased again. As a result, Mayo guessed that some human or psychological factor was at play.

The study at the Hawthorne plant of Western Electric gave birth to the concept of human-based motivation by detailing that employees behaved differently simply because they were involved in planning and executing the experiments. Mayo's findings led to new assumptions about employees: pay is not the only motivator. Mayo found that money was a relatively ineffective motivator. New beliefs then led to many new theories about the human side of motivation (Hill, 2018).

Maslow's Hierarchy of Needs Theory

One of the most well-known motivation theorists at the time was Abraham Maslow. Human needs, from basic physiological requirements to safety, social, and esteem needs to self-actualization wants, are all unsatisfied in this theory of motivation (Nickels et al., 2015). Maslow's hierarchy of needs is founded on the premise that necessities drive motivation. When a condition is met, it ceases to be a motivation, and a higher-level need takes its place. Higher-level

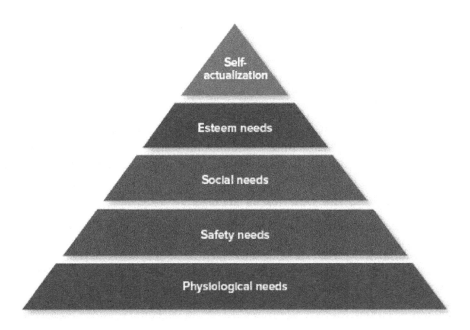

Figure 9.1 Maslow's Hierarchy of Needs

requirements necessitate lower-level needs' assistance. The various levels of deprivation are depicted in Figure 9.1 (Nickels et al., 2015).

- **Physiological Needs**: Food, water, and shelter are essential survival requirements
- **Safety Needs**: They want to feel secure at work and home
- **Social Needs**: The desire to be loved, welcomed, and included in a group
- Self-esteem, self-respect, and a sense of status or importance are required for self-esteem
- Self-actualization needs the desire to reach one's full potential (Nickels et al., 2015)

When one need is satisfied, another higher-level need emerges and motivates us to fulfill it. The satisfied condition is no longer a motivator. Hunger, for example, would not be a motivator (at least for several hours) if you had just eaten a four-course dinner, and your focus would shift to your surroundings (safety needs) or family (social needs). Lower-level needs (such as thirst) may resurface if they are not fulfilled, diverting your focus away from higher-level needs (Nickels et al., 2015).

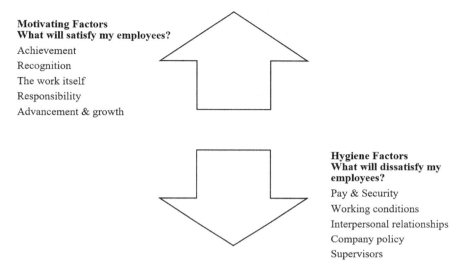

Figure 9.2 Herzberg's Motivating Factors Theory

Herzberg's Motivating Factors Theory

Frederick Herzberg, a psychologist, completed the most widely publicized study in this area in the mid-1960s. Workers were asked to rate several job-related criteria in order of significance in terms of motivation by Herzberg. The topic was: What inspires employees to work hard and to their full potential? The most important factors are shown in Figure 9.2.

Herzberg found that certain factors, which he called Motivators, made employees productive and satisfied. For example, workers wanted to know that they contribute to the company (feeling of achievement was number one). As you can see, these factors are mostly related to Job Factors. Herzberg called the other elements of the job as Hygiene Factors or Maintenance Factors. Those related to the job environment could cause dissatisfaction if missing but would not necessarily motivate employees if increased (Nickels et al., 2015).

Motivation in The Digital Age

Motivation is both an emotion and a process that originates, guides, and maintains goal-oriented behaviors. It operates in the nonverbal area of our brain; therefore, by asking a direct question like this, we are more likely to engage our rational and logical brain. We need questions that go to the heart of what drives us. Questions elicit feelings. Similarly, managers should not assume that they know what motivates someone merely because of their age or stage of life. When a manager has actual conversations with a team member about their motivations, they send an unmistakable message that they care (Turner, 2019). In today's workplace of automation, globalization, and virtualization, recognizing the human element is crucial to engendering the loyalty and engagement of your teams. Here are some tips to motivate employees in The Digital Age:

1   **Set Clear Target Objectives** – Setting targets is a much more meaningful technique of pushing people to accomplish than assigning jobs.
2   **Use Effective Communication** – Be explicit about how you expect people to interact with clients and anybody relevant to the task. For example, they understand when the right time is to email, call, text, or take time out from a meeting to stop any misunderstanding in its tracks.
3   **Be Clear about Praise** – Let colleagues know why it has made a difference and, if appropriate, reward them. It will have the most significant impact if you do it personally and on the spot. Using social recognition tools, you can distribute kudos between teams and throughout the firm (Philpott, 2021).

Leadership Theories Before The Digital Age

Managers and leaders usually do not fit neatly into a box containing any category. Instead, leadership is more fluid when it's a continuum along which employee participation varies, from purely boss-centered leadership to subordinate-centered leadership.

Autocratic Leadership

Autocratic Leadership is defined as making managerial decisions without consulting others. However, Autocratic Leadership can be effective when young, somewhat unskilled personnel require clear direction and guidance (Nickels et al., 2018).

Participative (Democratic) Leadership

Participative (Democratic) Leadership involves leaders, managers, and staff working together to make decisions. Employee participation in decisions does not always increase effectiveness; however, it usually does increase job satisfaction. Many mega organizations like Google, Apple, IBM, Cisco, AT&T, and most smaller companies have used a democratic leadership style. One values traits such as flexibility, good listening skills, and empathy. Employees will meet to discuss and resolve management issues by giving everyone some opportunity to contribute to decisions.

Free-Rein Leadership

Managers set objectives, and employees can do whatever they need to meet those goals. Free-Rein Leadership is often the most successful leadership style in many specific companies, such as managers supervising doctors, professors, engineers, or other experts. Warmth, kindness, and understanding are qualities that managers in such organizations require. As a result, more and more firms adopt this leadership style with at least some employees.

There is no one best leadership style or "best practice". Research tells us that it depends mainly on its goals, values, leaders, and situations. This would mean using a "best fit" approach instead. For example, with a fresh trainee, a manager might be authoritarian but personable and democratic with an experienced employee while using a free-rein approach with a long-term supervisor. There is no such thing as a universally effective leadership quality or leadership style. In some cases, a successful leader in one organization may not be successful in another. However, a very successful leader can adopt the leadership style most appropriate to the situation and the employees (Nickels et al., 2018).

Leadership in The Digital Age

Nicholas Negroponte's 1996 book, *Being Digital*, foreshadowed The Digital Age, which came to fruition around two decades after Nicholas wrote his book. The advent of The Digital Age only happened recently, mainly because of massive improvements in technology. Computing power grew exponentially with Moore's law. Moore's law states that every two years, chip densities double, and the cost of computers is cut in half. He was also emerging as quantum computing and artificial intelligence expert. We now have almost infinite amounts of storage space becoming available in the cloud. As the internet became more widely used, it became feasible for anyone or anything to instantly connect with anyone or anything else or for near-zero cost (Dubey, 2019).

These developments ensured that practically everything humans had done would be reinvented at some point in the future. To achieve them, however, we needed to abandon industrial-era management and employ a new type of leadership. Success in The Digital Age will be dependent on how quickly teams can execute and deliver in a rapidly changing market. The faster digital teams can innovate with new ideas in the market, the better their chance to win. Digital teams need leaders who both trust and empower them to act quickly. Leaders who are product-focused relentlessly deliver business value.

Digital leadership empowers employees to lead and create self-organized teams that optimize their day-to-day operations (Dubey, 2019). Leadership is no longer hierarchical; it needs everyone's participation, involvement, and contribution. Rapid ongoing developments drive the digital economy. Leaders can no longer take ownership and control of everything. A leader can't know

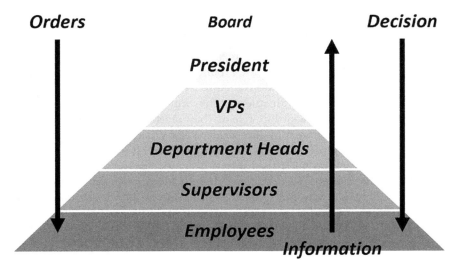

Figure 9.3 Digital Age Leadership (Grimsley & Scalia, 2021)

it all, and the top-down approach is no longer sustainable. The need for rapid response to frequent changes in The Digital Age changes old, slow hierarchical models into flat organizations where employees are more empowered to make decisions (Mihai & Crețu, 2019).

Digital Age Leadership is almost the opposite of Industrial Age Management (Denning, 2021). The steep vertical hierarchy of authority where orders and decisions move from the President to the employees, pictured in Figure 9.3, needs to be replaced with a horizontal network of competent workers who are self-organizing teams, driven by common goals, that can quickly change strategy and direction. A new mindset is required to transition from an internal focus on outputs and efficiency to an external focus on value for services, goods, and consumers in this new period. In addition, leadership must pull from the talents of those doing the work. Leaders need to engage the brain and the heart through inspiration and collaboration in Digital leadership.

The new leaders will have to empower their teams to work with autonomy and freedom to make decisions. Organizations will need to build leaders at all levels by ensuring participation and accountability. They need to learn from the employees working on the ground who are customer-facing and take inputs and trust them. To achieve common goals, every team member must be encouraged to contribute ideas, insights, and information. Leaders must create an environment where individuals take responsibility for their actions and are held accountable. Great things are possible when staff members care about their tasks and work with their hearts, soul, and mind.

FLAT ORGANIZATIONS

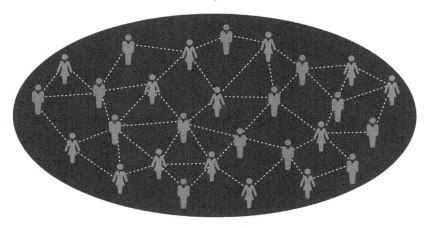

© Jacob Morgan *(thefutureorganization.com)*

Figure 9.4 Flat Structure (Morgan, 2015)

Advantages of a Flat Organizational Structure

The new flat structure elevates the employees' level of responsibility. It removes excess layers of management and improves the coordination and speed of communication between employees. Fewer levels of management encourage a more straightforward decision-making process among employees and speed up communications and the sharing of ideas.

Currently, most organizations still follow a hierarchical structure of authority. Ideas or decisions came from the top (from the President), the VP was in charge of implementing them, and then power trickled down through the many layers of management. This work structure is bureaucratic, where the staff filled roles and followed the job description guidelines and rules. The mindset is internal, focused on results and efficiency. Attention was achieved with carrots and sticks. And the management tactics usually involved telling people what to do, and if necessary, coercing them (Denning, 2021).

To be successful and drive up productivity in The Digital Age, we need to turn the Industrial Age upside down. Companies now need to maximize creativity, freedom, and flexibility while inspiring collaboration instead of maximizing control. Only those leaders who understand how to optimize productivity while maximizing liberty simultaneously will thrive in the new, fast-paced digital error. This involves creating a work culture based on values rather than rules (Peshawaria, 2021).

Industrial Age Management			
Organization	*Mindset*	*Attention*	*Tactics*
Hierarchy Top-Down Siloed	Internal	Carrots and Sticks	Telling and Coercing

Digital Age Leadership			
Organization	*Mindset*	*Attention*	*Tactics*
Flat Interconnected Remote	External	Feeling and Creativity	Inspiring and Collaborating

Source: Denning (2021)

Because motivation is a sensation that acts in the part of our brain that doesn't have words, we're more likely to engage our rational and logical brain by asking a direct question. We require questions that probe to the core of our motivations, such as feelings–inducing questions. Similarly, managers should not presume that they understand what motivates someone merely because of their age. When a manager has actual conversations with a team member about their motivations, they send an unmistakable message that they care (Turner, 2019). It's easy to set work tasks, but setting targets is a much more meaningful way of motivating people to perform and places importance on the human element of work.

References

Denning, S. (2021, March 14). How new leadership succeeds in The Digital Age. Retrieved December 29, 2021 from www.forbes.com/sites/stevedenning/2021/03/14/how-new-leadership-succeeds-in-the-digital-age/

Dubey, A. (2019, April 24) This is what great leadership looks like in The Digital Age. Retrieved December 29, 2021 from www.weforum.org/agenda/2019/04/leadership-digital-age-leader/

Grimsley, S. & Scalia, S. (2021, September 28). Organizational chart and hierarchy: Definition & examples. Retrieved February 7, 2022 from https://study.com/academy/lesson/organizational-chart-and-hierarchy-definition-examples.html

Hill, C. (2018). *Reformation to industrial revolution: 1530–1780*. London: Verso Books.

Lengsfeld, J. (2019). Digital era framework. Retrieved December 29, 2021 from https://joernlengsfeld.com/en/?publication=digital-era-framework

Mihai, R. L., & Crețu, A. (2019). Leadership in the digital era. *Valahian Journal of Economic Studies* 10(1): 65–72.

Moore, D. (2019, November 11). Corporate culture in The Digital Age. Retrieved December 29, 2021 from www.northridgegroup.com/blog/corporate-culture-is-more-critical-than-ever-in-the-digital-age/

Morgan, J. (2015, July 13) The 5 types of organizational structures: Part 3, flat organizations. Retrieved from www.forbes.com/sites/jacobmorgan/2015/07/13/the-5-types-of-organizational-structures-part-3-flat-organizations/?sh=42355cd16caa/

Nickels, W. G., McHugh, J. M., & McHugh, S. M. (2015). *Understanding business.* Boston, MA: McGraw-Hill/Irwin.

Nickels, W. G., McHugh, J. M., & McHugh, S. M. (2018). *Understanding business.* Boston, MA: McGraw-Hill/Irwin.

Organ, D. W., & Ryan, K. (1995). A meta-analytic review of attitudinal and dispositional predictors of organizational citizenship behavior. *Personnel Psychology* 48(4): 775–802.

Peshawaria, R. (2020, February 28). Leading in the digital era – Two most needed changes. Retrieved December 29, 2021 from www.forbes.com/sites/rajeevpeshawaria/2020/02/27/leading-in-the-digital-era-two-most-needed-changes/?sh=1b9007b6247f

Philpott, A. (n.d.). How to motivate employees in The Digital Age. (n.d.). Retrieved December 29, 2021 from www.professionalacademy.com/blogs/how-to-motivate-employees-in-the-digital-age/

Pillemer, J., & Rothbard, N. P. (2018). Friends without benefits: Understanding the dark sides of workplace friendship. *Academy of Management Review* 43(4): 635–660.

Podsakoff, N. P., Whiting, S. W., Podsakoff, P. M., & Blume, B. D. (2009). Individual- and organizational-level consequences of organizational citizenship behaviors: A meta-analysis. *Journal of Applied Psychology* 94(1): 122.

Turner, K. (2019, November 08). Leadership and development in a digital era – Why conversation is still key. Retrieved December 29, 2021 from www.hrdconnect.com/2019/09/03/leadership-and-development-in-a-digital-era-why-conversation-is-still-key/

Chapter 10

Green Human Resource Management

William Garrison

In 1987, in the hit movie *Wall Street*, starring Michael Douglas and Charlie Sheen, Douglas's character, Gordon Gekko, gave an impassioned speech as the main shareholder of Teldar Paper to the other shareholders. In that speech, Gekko extolls the virtues of greed with the phrase, "Greed, for lack of a better word, is good". In taking liberties with that speech,

> The point is, ladies and gentleman, that "GREEN" – for lack of a better word – is good.
> "GREEN" is right.
> "GREEN" works.
> "GREEN" clarifies, cuts through, and captures the essence of the evolutionary spirit.
> "GREEN", in all its forms – "GREEN" for life, for money, for love, knowledge – has marked the upward surge of mankind.

The Green Movement is a worldwide phenomenon that appeals to our best natures and is a noble aspiration.

However, even those who believe in The Green Movement haven't placed their money where their mouth is, although the movement has been met with hostility. Green has become a political football carried by environmental groups and is often times associated with the Hippies of the 70s. The Green Movement has seen a lot of progress, but there is still a lot of disagreement over how to proceed.

There are two methods to bring The Green Movement closer to consensus: first, come up with fresh phrases that appeal to a wider audience, and second, have HR departments take the lead in their enterprises.

A Rose by Any Other Name

According to PBS, The Green Movement began in the post–World War II era in 1948 when the first federal water pollution regulation passed, called the Federal Water Pollution Control Act. This was the first of many regulations

DOI: 10.4324/9781003122272-10

targeted at protecting the environment from businesses and others that were irresponsibly disposing of waste and other materials. When the Sierra Club challenged the construction of the Echo Park Dam on the Colorado River in 1956, it attracted national attention. In 1970, the first Earth Day saw nearly 20 million people protest against environmental ignorance and was the largest demonstration in American history (PBS, n.d.).

As The Green Movement began to gain supporters, it became associated primarily with environmentalists and the Democratic Party. And, with the split in ideologies between Liberals and Conservatives over the past 30 years, The Green Movement seems to be owned by half the country. The other half of the countries are perceived to be the Resistance Movement. This verbiage and the tactics by which The Green Movement has achieved victories further sew this division. Meanwhile, Republicans, Conservatives, and Moderates all essentially believe in protecting the environment, cleaning the water and air, and finding new sustainable production methods. Perhaps the marketing approaches of The Green Movement should follow the old adage, "Honey is more effective at catching flies than vinegar".

"Earth Day and the Polling of America"

Joel Makower, chairman, and co-founder of the GreenBiz Group, has been conducting surveys on The Green Movement since 2007. Each year, Makower would conduct a survey and deliver his results in what he named "Earth Day and the Polling of America". The series of questions were meant to ascertain both the beliefs and the actions on The Green Movement of those he polled. What he found in 2007 was that overwhelmingly, "Americans want clean, affordable, and care-free solutions to climate change and every other environmental challenge" (Makower, 2007). As most would agree, it's comforting to know that there is a high level of support for such efforts. However, in the same poll, he also discovered that most respondents were either unwilling or hadn't yet changed their spending habits to support their beliefs (Makower, 2007).

By 2021, Makower had become more cynical in The Green Movement since his poll results have changed very little since 2007. "In general, a large swath of consumers – typically, two-thirds to three-fourths – claim they are ready, willing, and able to make green choices at home and when they shop. The reality, of course, suggests otherwise" (Makower, 2021).

In the 2021 poll, however, there was some good news. Makower claims that over two-thirds of economists believe that "reaching net-zero emissions by 2050 would likely outweigh the costs" (Makower, 2021).

Most adherents to The Green Movement look to Washington to write laws governing our society and add regulations to businesses. However, politicians are only as strong as the public that votes for them.

In 2019, New York Congresswoman Alexandria Ocasio-Cortez and Massachusetts Senator Ed Markey presented the framework for a series of environmental solutions named the Green New Deal. Ocasio-Cortez touted that the problems of Climate Change demanded that we implement aggressive solutions. However, even though Ocasio-Cortez and Markey could get the Green New Deal passed through a Democratic Congress, they weren't able to get it through a Republican Senate (Kurtzleben, 2019).

So the first solution to solving the issues of Climate Change could be rebranding The Green Movement into a more inclusive and moderate approach that would gain traction over time. This would mean uniting Americans from differing political spectrum points under one banner – quite a difficult undertaking.

Could Business Leaders Be the Solution?

Or, perhaps, The Green Movement just makes common sense, and business leaders could be the answer!

If economists are right that reaching the benefits of The Green Movement would outweigh the costs, CFOs and small business owners alike would be foolish not to adopt the Green HR Management Model.

Many companies currently have environmental, social, and governance (ESG) initiatives to address the concerns of both their employees and stakeholders. Some companies list their ESG score on a prospectus to help attract socially conscious investors in the finance world. However, as Joel Makower noted in his 2021 Earth Day article, most top managers reported not achieving their ESG goals. And their employees agree.

> Although an overwhelming majority of respondents (81 percent) said their company has a formal ESG program in place, they did not express a high level of confidence their organization was following through as measured against its standards. Only 50 percent said their company performs very effectively in meeting its environmental goals; only 37 percent rated its performance as "very effective" on social issues.
>
> (Makower, 2021)

Corporate Social Responsibility and The Green Movement

Organizations have already experienced similar success in other social initiatives within the business world. For example, Corporate Social Responsibility (CSR) efforts within an organization focus on giving back to its community. In the initial stages, these activities are more philanthropic; the company's ownership donates a lot of money toward social programs they believe in and support. However, from society's perspective, the response is not appropriate for the company's impact on that society. For example, a logging operation that donates toward homeless shelters looks more like a personal choice. Instead, as logging operations do impact the cleanliness of the rivers and lakes in the area, emit lots of exhaust from their heavy equipment, and remove trees from the forest, their CSR efforts should center on cleaning up the waterways, contributing toward research for clean-burning tractors and electric chainsaw technology, and replanting trees in the forest. These conservation and replenishment efforts are seen as the company putting back what they took away. The companies that do CSR well have it as a critical component in their strategic plan, and the HR department is the key owner of these efforts.

The Green Movement comprises many different areas of environmental protection. Overall, The Green Movement views the natural environment as a gift to humanity rich with resources to sustain life. However, mainly since the Industrial Revolution, the desire by business owners and managers to increase productivity and sales has led to the decline of the environment, and the fear is that if nothing is done to protect and sustain these natural resources, they will become scarce. Therefore, although The Green Movement began as a social campaign outside of organizations, there is now a much bigger push from within those organizations from their employees.

Earth-Friendly Practices

At the heart of The Green Movement is encouraging earth-friendly practices within organizations. These include reducing pollution, reducing waste, recycling, and other energy-saving efforts spurned on by employees passionate about protecting the environment. In some cases, these individuals organize volunteer groups to clean up parts of the community or go door-to-door, informing citizens about community efforts. In these instances, the volunteers unite under a purpose, receive a T-shirt and a lunch, and possibly get a photo-op for the bulletin board in the company break room. Nearly always, there is little to no executive support, but the employee may receive encouragement from their manager and/or fellow colleagues. Although these opportunities provide the employees an outlet, they do very little to address the company's impact on the local environment.

Environmental Management Systems (EMS)

Companies began to adopt official environmental measures that promoted The Green Movement during the end of the twentieth century and the beginning of the twenty-first century. Besides just focusing on the company's productivity today, they are looking for ways to create sustainable processes to build upon those accomplishments. In that equation is the ability to procure and convert local resources while reducing the emissions and other impacts on local society.

Many efforts have grown to become part of the workplace culture and even strategic choices in capital projects within the organization's walls. These include:

- **Recycling and Waste Management** – The entry-level to Green Practices are to provide bins where the company can include recycling in their waste management processes. These include different bins for aluminum, glass, compost, paper, and other materials.
- **Paperless Office** – Another common practice is to reduce the need for paper. As more and more business happens online, these reduction efforts have been very effective.
- **Energy Reduction** – The pollution caused by fossil-fuel energy production can be reduced when implementing energy reduction programs. Installing motion-detective lights with auto-shutoff timers, purchasing energy-efficient laptops, and installing smart thermostats to save on heating and cooling bills are all examples of this.
- **Green Building** – In the construction process, companies can install recycled and energy-efficient insulation in the walls and ceilings, install solar panels and battery walls to capture green energy, use water preservation systems, and build near public transportation. Many of these same conversions can be made in existing buildings as well.

Why EMS Is Not Enough and What Needs to Change

As these initiatives and projects go a long way in helping employees feel that the company supports their personal beliefs, they don't become part of the organization's DNA. Instead, these smaller communities within the larger organization go only as far as somebody takes the reigns and sustains the efforts. Although these programs help attract and retain high-performing Millennial workers, the company will only achieve long-term sustainability if executive support exists.

According to Patrick Lencioni's book, *The Advantage*, the leadership of an organization needs to be on the same page to increase their overall organizational health. He recommends that the executives of the company take the time and answer these six critical questions:

1   Why do we exist?
2   How do we behave?
3   What do we do?
4   How will we succeed?
5   What is most important right now?
6   Who must do what? (Lencioni, 2012)

These questions must result in a consensus answer from each team member. This goes far beyond the EMS, but it encapsulates the organization's soul. For a company to overachieve at its sustainability goals, the tenants of The Green Movement must be part of these answers. Executive leadership and ownership are everything.

ESG Rating

In the past ten years, the official measurement of how an organization is doing toward being a sustainable, Green organization is the ESG rating. According to the financial advisor website, Motley Fool, "An ESG rating measures a company's exposure to long-term environmental, social, and governance risks. These risks – involving issues such as energy efficiency, worker safety, and board independence – have financial implications" (Brock, 2021).

*   Under the **Environmental** component, the company is scored on how well they address Climate Change, water usage, and pollution.
*   For the **Social** score, they are rated on how they manage issues such as labor practices, training, safety protocols, product safety, and access to healthcare.
*   The **Governance** score includes accounting practices, approaches to diversity and inclusion, and business ethics.

These scores are reported publicly to help investors decide which companies to place their dollars with but can also be used by potential employees to get an inside look into the company's Green Practices. Finally, for top management, the ESG rating can be an excellent metric to include in the company's overall performance since it has been established that Green, for lack of a better term, is good for the environment, the community, and the bottom line (Brock, 2021).

Why HR Is the Home of Green

After this executive ownership is attained and the ESG rating is a core metric, a department must drive these results. In many cases, the Operations department has led these efforts. This is a strange choice as The Green Movement is not a productivity concept. Since Human Resources is the department that focuses on the human element, and the elements of ESG (the Environment, the Society, and how we Govern ourselves) impact the humans in the organization and the society it operates within, HR should be the Home of Green.

Operations Managers have been highly successful in implementing Waste Reduction Programs that impact productivity. These have been primarily focused on reducing costs to impact the productivity equation.

*   **Waste Reduction Programs** – organization-wide programs that train employees to reduce waste in the production process. These could include negotiating with Suppliers, changing Suppliers, improving methodologies, and even automating.

- **Lean Methodologies** – a popular, formal efficiency practice in which inventory space is reduced and waste of raw materials is minimized. These include Just-In-Time inventory where Suppliers deliver the raw products just before they are needed, thus reducing the need for a large warehouse carbon footprint. These also include finding ways to eliminate steps in inefficient processes.
- **Lean Six Sigma** – combining the principles of Six Sigma (reducing flaws in production that lead to fewer returns or product failures) with Lean Principles, these combination practices implement a culture of waste reduction, efficiency, and excellence that, in effect, is a Green Practice.

Although these practices have been implemented to increase productivity, the motivation for these improvements was not from The Green Movement perspective. In addition, the reason these practices became so effective was partially due to the supervisors in Operations monitoring these methods but primarily due to the impactful training and mindset shift led by the Human Resources department.

Green Human Resource Management Framework

The Human Resources department is the ideal home for Green. HR leaders constantly think about increasing efficiency while also organizing a sustainable workforce. Green HR Management is much more than reducing waste; it is also a great source to foster a purpose-driven culture among the workforce that sees their company's mission is to fulfill the needs of their customers and their community truly. As mentioned before, the Millennial Mindset is to work passionately for others in an organization that genuinely cares. Solidifying a Green HRM Framework throughout the organization will increase the retention of valuable Millennial workers.

With just a few adjustments to the existing HR approach, a Green HRM Framework will convert the organization into an expressed, purpose-driven, and sustainable force for all stakeholders involved. In addition, these practices send a clear message to potential employees and the current workforce that Green Practices are a way of life.

- **Recruitment and Selection** – all recruitment can be paperless, and the selection process can be completely digitized. Since potential employees create, edit, and revise their resumes on a device, the company should have a way to collect them digitally. Having the candidate's application and resume as a soft copy can be duplicated and shared electronically. Interviews could be done remotely using virtual software or even conference call systems. Many companies also employ assessment software that can ascertain the personality and skills of recruits. The software must be compatible with mobile devices in today's world since many younger candidates do not operate on desktop or laptop computers but instead use their smartphones, tablets, or Chromebooks.

- **Orientation** – as workers enter the organization, there is never a better time to lay out the organization's purpose, code of conduct, and beliefs. When hiring managers and those involved with the onboarding process are bought into Green Practices, that culture is caught. During the set of orientation tasks, employees will catch more of "what is not said" than "what is said". They are assessing to see if the organization truly means what it says. The leaders involved here must be the best representatives of the company's Green Practices.

- **Training** – as opportunities arise to implement new systems and processes, it is important that Green concepts are embedded within the training processes. These include new hire training, management training, and new systems training. Trainers should reduce waste where possible and state the priority of Green Practices throughout all training activities. These training activities could include communicating scientific and research-based findings in the area of the environment, including debunking myths in the areas of Climate Change. Since employees spend a lot of time at work, there is an opportunity to impact social change. Green Practices also include many elements of Diversity, Equity, and Inclusion and can be paired together easily. As stated at the outset of this chapter, it is critical to develop strategies to persuade all coworkers, regardless of political affiliation. It is best to find training programs and trainers that can appeal to all sides of the topic to find common ground for how the organization wants to behave in these areas. Many prior attempts have been one-sided and led to more conflict than intended.

- **Supervision** – it is the role of supervisors to ensure that the methods employees are using are getting the results the company wants. When a safety culture is implemented, the supervisor's role is to ensure the employees are operating safely using the processes and policies laid out by management. For Green Practices, this also needs to be true. Employees should be provided clear directions on operating, and supervisors should be trained to reinforce these methods.

- **Performance Review** – during performance reviews, the employee and their manager are heightened to the job description and job expectations. By embedding a Green component into the performance review system, Green Practices can be reinforced. If they are not reviewed, it is easy for the employee to deem them not as important as the aspects that are being reviewed. Green Practices should also be used to monitor and deliver the performance review that includes paperless communication, remote conversations, and other waste reduction practices.

- **Reward Management (Bonuses and performance-related pay [PRP])** – bonuses and other PRP could be used to reinforce the Green Practices as well. When considering compensation packages, HR managers typically think of what behaviors they want to see repeated. While performance outcomes are paramount, the values and practices demonstrated by the employee can impact the organization's culture as well.

- **Termination** – when HR managers need to sever working relationships, it can be done with Green Practices in mind. For example, while remote off-boarding should be avoided as much as possible, off-boarding materials can be emailed to the former employees' personal email address.

How Green HRM Improves Employee Engagement and Retention

As employees begin to see the Green HR Management Framework become part of the organization's culture, they see their workplace as nearly a human entity. The pride of working for an organization that genuinely cares about its customers and its community is rewarding itself. Employees can walk around the community with pride, knowing that their employer is esteemed as a responsible contributor to society. This is especially true for the Millennial workforce who considers the purpose of the organization a motivating factor in choosing a job. Employee Engagement measures the emotional tie that an employee has in the company's productivity. When more workers are engaged, they come to work with a sense of meaning, knowing that they are adding to their community in meaningful ways. Employees who wake up on Monday morning excited to move that purpose forward surely stay longer and increase employee retention numbers.

Support of Senior Management

As HR is the true Home of Green, it must be said that the culture and reputation of any organization are solidified in how the Senior Management leads. If the CEO and other C-Suite Leaders only give lip service to Green Practices and leave it to the HR department to monitor, the company will be exposed. Being close to Green is viewed as worse than not Green at all. When companies fake their Green approach, and it is revealed, the backlash can be brutal. Therefore, all Senior Management must be the first to be united in their Green Framework. Working through the six critical questions from the aforementioned book *The Advantage* by Patrick Lencioni can be a very valuable experience (Lencioni, 2012).

References

Brock, C. (2021, October 13). What is an ESG rating? Retrieved December 29, 2021 from www.fool.com/investing/stock-market/types-of-stocks/esg-investing/esg-rating/

Kurtzleben, D. (2019, February 07). Rep. Alexandria Ocasio-Cortez releases Green New Deal outline. Retrieved December 29, 2021 from www.npr.org/2019/02/07/691997301/rep-alexandria-ocasio-cortez-releases-green-new-deal-outline

Lencioni, P. (2012). *The advantage: Why organizational health trumps everything else in business.* New York: Jossey-Bass.

Makower, J. (2007, April 22). Earth Day and the polling of America, 2007. Retrieved December 30, 2021 from www.greenbiz.com/article/earth-day-and-polling-america-2007

Makower, J. (2021, April 6). Matter of opinion: What the 2021 Earth Day polls reveal. Retrieved December 29, 2021 from www.greenbiz.com/article/matter-opinion-what-2021-earth-day-polls-reveal

PBS. (n.d.). The modern environmental movement. Retrieved December 29, 2021 from www.pbs.org/wgbh/americanexperience/features/earth-days-modern-environmental-movement/

Chapter 11

Employees as Owners

Bashker Biswas

The primary goal of this book is to highlight and discuss the changing paradigms that are creating a need to rethink the traditional concepts and structures of Human Resource Management. New forces are at play in the organizational and business environments and their associated context requiring a pivot or a change of direction. The majority of the chapters in this book lay out the changing landscape and then propose structural pivots or even wholesale organizational restructuring.

The concept of having employees as owners, however, is not a new concept but an old one that is already in the Human Resource playbook but has not been widely known, widely practiced, and, in some cases, widely condemned. So, in some cases, for organizations to move forward, they must look backward. In a sense, the concept of Industrial Democracy (2021) is a natural endpoint as companies look for ways to increase Employee Engagement and employee empowerment that lead to increased productivity.

Reviving Industrial Democracy

Industrial Democracy is an arrangement that involves workers making decisions, sharing responsibility and authority in the workplace. Industrial Democracy is a concept where worker rights in the employment arrangement include participation by the workforce in the organization's running. The term is often based on an ideological thought process. At one extreme, Industrial Democracy implies worker control over industry, possibly through worker ownership of the factors of production as demonstrated by the operation of worker cooperatives. Another strategy is to appoint worker or union representatives to corporate boards or governing bodies. Others define Industrial Democracy as "worker participation", such as collective bargaining, in which trade unions act as a countervailing force to management's decision-making authority. Here managements propose strategies, plans, programs, and actions, and employees (or their Unions) offer reactions. If necessary, opposition and negotiation subsequently lead to collective agreements, which are more or less satisfactory to both sides. Another approach emphasizes consultation and communication

DOI: 10.4324/9781003122272-11

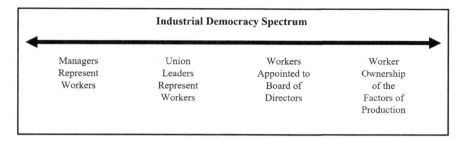

Figure 11.1 Industrial Democracy Spectrum

over power-sharing. Managers are seen as bearing sole responsibility for decisions, but management consults with worker representatives before implementing changes.

Industrial Democracy challenges the characteristically authoritarian and bureaucratic structures of the capitalist enterprise and centralized decision-making in the planned economies of socialist societies. Without worker participation, many argue that it will be difficult for management to maintain workforce stability, engagement, and job satisfaction. Actual examples show that the degree of power achieved by or delegated to the workforce is crucial. Skeptics argue that, even in the extensive worker self-management of the decentralized state socialism, underlining control is maintained by management types.

In Germany, a system of codetermination has been in practice because of labor-movement pressure to find a middle ground between capitalism and socialism. The German model has influenced the labor policies of most countries in the European Community. Profit-sharing, gainsharing, and Employee Stock Ownership programs may be regarded as examples of management-initiated participation systems, including self-managed workgroups and teams. Participatory leadership styles reflect the building blocks of an Industrial Democracy philosophical mindset.

A Historical Perspective

Allowing employees to earn and own stock in the company where they work is a fundamental component of the American economy that dates back to its founding.

Benjamin Franklin pursued Employee Ownership as early as 1733 when he dispatched the first of many journeyman employees to various cities to establish new print shops. Franklin covered one-third of the expenses and paid for the shop's initial capital costs, which were substantial because most of the equipment had to be shipped from England. He took one-third of the profits for the next six years; after that, the journeymen could buy the equipment with the profits they earned and own the business (Patrick Williams, 2021).

Employees earned their shares in the company through sweat equity, which was more readily available than cash, as with some modern Employee Ownership options.

According to Benjamin Franklin's memoirs, "most of them fared well", and many of them were able to "carry on working for themselves" when their six-year terms were up.

It was a belief shared by George Washington, Thomas Jefferson, and Alexander Hamilton that employees should be permitted to own shares in the companies they worked for. New England cod fishery was severely depleted following the Revolutionary War, so the three founding fathers agreed to cut taxes on the fishing industry to help it recover.

However, the three Founding Fathers agreed that there had to be a catch: federal assistance would be available only if employees shared in profits.

Jefferson and Hamilton were bitter political rivals who rarely agreed on anything. Nonetheless, the concept of economic fairness – which was central to the Revolution itself – was powerful enough to persuade them to support a plan that gave employees a stake in the company.

By the mid-nineteenth century, the United States was transitioning to an industrial economy, and leaders of national corporations (including Procter & Gamble, Railway Express, and Sears & Roebuck) recognized that long-term employees might end their working careers and find themselves without a source of income. As a result, those leaders set aside company stock to be given to employees upon retirement, giving them a stake in the company based on their efforts.

Employee stock was one of the most contentious problems when the United States imposed a federal income tax on everyone in the early twentieth century. The formalization of employee stock ownership schemes directly affected the treatment Congress chose more than 50 years later.

Louis Kelso, an economist and attorney, shared his ideas for equal distribution of wealth in the 1940s. According to Kelso, widespread lack of capital was a fundamental factor in the Great Depression and other periods of economic inequality. Too few people had the start-up capital needed to start their own business. Kelso told Bill Moyers a year before his death in 1990 that "capital is too magnificent, too important, too critical" to be possessed by the few.

Kelso discovered innovative techniques to divide wealth evenly among more employees and began leaders others to do so. He founded Kelso & Co., which assisted businesses in establishing a type of Employee Ownership known as an Employee Stock Ownership Plan (ESOP) while also practicing that same plan within the company.

In 1974, the U.S. Congress passed legislation to respond to the increasing uncertainty associated with employee pension plans. As a result, there is legal protection for employees who participate in ESOPs. Today, the most common and effective form of Employee Ownership in the United States is an ESOP.

In the United States, ESOP and Employee Stock Purchase Plan (ESPP) employees can acquire a share in their employer in the following ways:

- Buying the stock directly
- Participating in an employee-owned cooperative
- Converting their stock options into a stock purchase in the future
- Making an employee stock purchase plan contribution
- Contributing to a 401(k) plan that includes company stock as an asset

Many different forms of Employee Ownership exist in North America, and they have played an important role in the country's economy since the United States was founded. As more companies understand the increased productivity when employees as invested in the companies they work for, more Employee Ownership setups will occur and labor-management collaboration will increase.

Labor-Management Collaboration

Labor-management collaboration to improve product quality, employee work-life balance, and company productivity can be traced back to the early nineteenth century. However, the true forerunners of our modern labor relations system emerged in the nineteenth century, coinciding with rapid industrialization. Class distinctions between employers and employees were once hazy and ill-defined. Most masters graduated from working ranks until rapidly expanding economies of scale soon drew definable, if not bold, lines. During this period, developing political institutions tried to gain working-class support by emphasizing that workers and employers had a mutual dependency. This was aided by the declining economic conditions of the time. Cheaper, inferior goods imported from Europe captured portions of the American market, adversely affecting both workers and domestic manufacturers. This, at times, created a common bond between highly skilled workers and their employers.

The "Ascendancy of the Common Man"

In the words of Alexis de Tocqueville, the "ascendancy of the common man" occurred between 1820 and 1840. Developing political institutions tried to gain working-class support by emphasizing that workers and employers had a mutual dependency.

The Cooperative Movement

The cooperative movement developed on a broader scale in England. One of the most celebrated and most frequently cited by historians was in the town of Rochdale. Working-class shareholders in jointly owned enterprises received fixed dividends on invested capital in the so-called Rochdale Experiment. In addition, excess profits were reinvested in new ventures such as insurance companies, foundries, and factories. This experiment aimed to (1) manufacture articles deemed necessary by society to employ members, (2) provide high-quality products for distribution in expanding markets, and (3) foster the belief that working people are not inferior.

The cooperative experiments in factory ownership were almost entirely the result of organized labor input. There developed a model for electing shop workers' representatives to industry- or plant-wide problem-solving body of managers and employees. Each body debated issues related to product quality and working conditions separately before presenting them in joint sessions, with all results being forwarded to the plant superintendent.

Industrial Democracy in America

As John D. Rockefeller launched one of the most controversial Industrial Democracy programs in American history, he declared that capital cannot move a wheel without labor, nor can labor evolve beyond a more primitive existence without capital. Rockefeller is referred to as a "Welfare Capitalist" by historians. The Industrial Democracy movement was one that he supported (Guzda, n.d.).

President Woodrow Wilson's administration attempted to avoid work stoppages in critical war production and related industries following the United States' entry into World War I. Among the many suggestions made was forming plant-level advisory committees of employees and managers to study and suggest ways to improve production expenditures while maintaining industrial peace. Secretary of Labor William B. Wilson enthusiastically supported the plan, believing that the spirit of cooperation between labor and management would endure beyond the war and into peacetime. In most cases, organized labor took full advantage of the employee representation plans established by government orders. Although these plans were officially operating under the "open shop" principle, they quickly became avenues for organized labor to meet with employers on an equitable level. Other labor programs were impacted by the war's end. Employers, for the most part, desired a return to prewar normalcy. As a result, employers unilaterally disbanded cooperative plans in many industries, particularly those where government boards ordered worker-manager councils. During the 1920s and 1930s, there were just a few Industrial Democracy projects in the United States, mainly in the textile, railroad, and garment industries.

The Great Depression of the 1930s necessitated that both workers and companies increase their output.

Labor and management were forced to experiment with new ideas due to the poor economic conditions. Employers, for example, began to collaborate with the Steel Workers' Organizing Committee of the new Congress of Industrial Organizations (CIO) to solve problems by the late 1930s, when many small steel mills were on the verge of bankruptcy. Two pioneers in this drive were Clinton Golden, Pittsburgh area director of the committee, and Joseph Scanlon, open-hearth furnace operator, local union president, and father of the Scanlon joint-stock ownership plan.

These men approached several steel plant superintendents in the area and proposed that union participation in the managerial process would improve production, stabilize employment fluctuations, and participate in productivity research. As a result of following the recommendations of labor-management committees, several plants in the upper Ohio Valley improved efficiency and achieved solvency.

CIO President Philip Murray enthusiastically supported the concept. He co-wrote a book on the Golden-Scanlon model with Morris Cooke (Frederick Taylor's prize student), establishing standards for the codetermination of production procedures and administrative policies to increase the distribution and output of goods and services. Their concept, known as the Murray plan, called for cooperation at the shop and factory levels, and eventually at the "intra and inter-industry levels". Murray and Cooke referred to their representative bodies as "Industry Councils", which sparked considerable debate during World War II.

As with the previous conflict, the United States' entry into the war required cooperation from both management and labor. As a result, Franklin D. Roosevelt founded the War Production Board just a few weeks after the attack on Pearl Harbor. Intending to boost productivity, board director Donald Nelson tinkered with Murray's ideas.

The Death of Industrial Democracy

On the other hand, Donald Nelson knew that employers would not accept such a proposal and instead advocated for forming voluntary labor-management committees at the plant level as a compromise. For the sake of the War Production Board's cooperative production program, Murray and Clinton Golden agreed to this. As a result, labor-management committees were established, but employees were not involved in decision-making to a substantial degree, and Murray's suggested industrywide councils were not implemented. However, employers refused to "give" when it came to labor encroachment on managerial prerogatives, as shown in internal War Production Board memos when they stated that the entire push would wither succeed or fail depending on their ability to create a give-and-take spirit between labor and management. As a result of this confusion, Murray backed the committees and said that they were directly in line with their industry council's ideas. Donald Nelson was accused of "sabotaging" and "Sovietizing" industry by overly cautious employers. General Motors (GM) President Charles Wilson also emphatically declared that there would be no equal voice at GM. Even though the Industrial Democracy movement was born in the United States, it lost its momentum during these Industrial Relations battles.

A Second Look

The past deserves a second look now as U.S. companies experiment with Industrial Democracy in the shape of quality of work-life balance, Employee Engagement initiatives, and other comparable endeavors. The majority of the previous initiatives at labor-management cooperation failed, but this does not mean that they were all for naught. The term "productive failures" was coined by a historian to describe presidential labor-management committees, and it may apply to the vast majority of historical participatory management committees. When the going got tough, they delivered, and they only fell short when the going got better. In the American labor relations system, Industrial Democracy has a position because it was first developed in the United States.

Under the Industrial Democracy philosophical framework discussed earlier, two specific employee programs have had operational traction over the years in various organizations. These programs were mentioned in previous paragraphs. These two programs are ESOPs and Gain-Sharing Plans.

As part of the current trends in the changing Nature of Work, and because success in the modern digitized workplace is primarily based on employees' skill, knowledge, and expertise, it may be time to reconsider making employees real stakeholders who add real value to the organization. Thus, in the new Human Resources paradigm, it might be appropriate to revive these programs in a big way. Thus, it might be time to resurrect the concept of Industrial Democracy.

Employee Stock Ownership Programs

Understanding the value-adding capabilities of all stakeholders, particularly employees, is one of the key building blocks of a successful business in a digitized world. In the knowledge-based organization, it can be said that the leading variable is employee satisfaction. Satisfied employees satisfy customers, and satisfied customers benefit shareholders. So, it can be said that shareholder satisfaction is the lagging variable. The modern organizational value chain starts with satisfied employees and then moves to satisfied customers, and in the end, this results in satisfied owners or shareholders. When an organization's stakeholders see that their personal interests are tied to the company's success, they are more likely to work harder to ensure that the company succeeds. Incentives, like bonuses, can give employees a stake in the outcome. A third option is known as equity sharing, in which each employee has a stake in the business. The right to share in the company's success encourages employees to view the organization in a new light – as if they were owners.

The History of Employee Ownership

Employee Ownership is not a new concept (Business, n.d.). For example, Procter & Gamble and Sears & Roebuck were among the first companies to establish retirement funds for their employees in the mid-1800s. But, according to many who support Employee Ownership today, it aligns the interests of employees and their employers, encouraging corporate success.

The federal government has drafted rules to address the tax implications of Employee Ownership scenarios in response to the increased interest in and implementation of these scenarios. As a result, many strategies and procedures have been devised for establishing and managing employee-owned businesses due to the increased clarity afforded by these regulations.

Employee Ownership Basics

Employee Ownership is a broad concept that refers to the ownership of a firm by its employees. Whether it's all employees or just a select few, this ownership can be either direct or indirect, and it can be partial or entire.

Indirect ownership is when stock is held in a trust or account for employees to benefit from upon exit or retirement. The ownership of a company doesn't need to be evenly distributed in a worker cooperative. Apart from the fact that employees are not forced to join, Employee Ownership differs because only employees can be owners. Employer-owned doesn't necessarily imply that employees oversee all aspects of the business. As in any business, there are managers, supervisors, and executives.

ESOPs, direct purchase plans, stock option plans, ESPPs, restricted stock plans, phantom stock plans, stock appreciation rights, and a 401(k) combined ESOP are all options for providing stock ownership to employees. In contrast to other retirement plans, the ESOP does not require employees to pay a fee upfront. ESOPs allow employees to participate without owning any shares in the company. It is run by a representative of the deceased's estate.

Benefits of Employee Ownership

Employers and employees gain from Employee Ownership agreements. When people have a stake in the success of a project, they are more inclined to work hard and contribute significantly. An incentive to work hard comes from knowing that you're part of the company's profits will grow over time.

Employee involvement, empowerment, and productivity have a significant positive impact on the bottom line for businesses. But, of course, there is a danger that the company may underperform regarding Employee Ownership. Still, this risk also serves as a motivating factor for employees to get more involved.

How Common Is Employee Ownership?

Over 25 million employees in thousands of enterprises in the United States are employee-owners. These companies range in size from small, family-owned businesses to huge, well-known conglomerates like Hy-Vee and New Belgium

Brewing. In recent years, there has been a significant trend toward employee empowerment, and one of the ways businesses are doing so is by giving employees ownership stakes. According to recent trends, employee-owned businesses are becoming more popular, and this trend is projected to continue.

Employee Ownership and the enormous motivation it provides are proving to be a win-win for firms and their employees in today's competitive environment.

And now on to Gain-Sharing.

What Is a Gain-Sharing Plan?

By boosting the employees' financial and emotional investment in the company's performance, Gain-Sharing Plans help to increase profitability. Employees are encouraged to enhance their performance by receiving a financial share of the company's gains due to their efforts. Conventional compensation systems, which are typically viewed as uninspired, could be enhanced or replaced with Gain-Sharing arrangements. The two most common Gain-Sharing Plan Types are the Scanlon Plan and the Rucker Plan.

The Scanlon Plan

In a sense, the Scanlon Plan is the ancestor of all Gain-Sharing arrangements. Incentives are linked to the ratio of production costs to production value, which is a cost-saving employee incentive program. The higher an employee's extra incentives are in a Scanlon plan, the more their production output is worth in relation to their hourly pay. In this example, a windshield repairman for pickup trucks with a traditional compensation plan works 5 hours a day at a $20 hourly rate is paid $100 each day with an average production rate of six trucks per hour. However, if the Scanlon Plan is used, he could earn a bonus of $10 per additional truck repaired each hour. He could increase his production rate to eight trucks an hour, resulting in a bonus of $100 in addition to the standard $100 compensation as an hourly employee. Employees paid hourly only have little incentive to improve their performance. Indeed, a worker trying to manipulate his timesheet may attempt to reduce his performance to display more hours for the same amount of labor. As a result, a Scanlon strategy eliminates the likelihood of such misdeeds. In addition, it serves as an incentive to develop their own productivity.

The Rucker Plan

By tying labor expenditures to a percentage of the total cost of a product, the Rucker plan seeks to lower manufacturing costs. While Scanlon's approach focuses on output amount, this one emphasizes quality over quantity. As a result, it's a good fit for industries where productivity figures aren't subject to significant fluctuations. The ratio of waste and the number of defective components per unit are common Rucker parameters. The goal of a Rucker plan is to maximize efficiency and minimize costs. As a result, Rucker's strategy aims to reward high-quality work while simultaneously reducing manufacturing costs. While most companies who have used Rucker plans have automated or mechanized enough to achieve fairly consistent production statistics, they still rely on their employees to ensure that raw materials are used wisely and that the quality of final products is consistent.

Advantages and Disadvantages of Gain-Sharing Plans

When employees are more engaged in the manufacturing process, and their work is of greater quality, firms reap the benefits of profit-sharing agreements. However, the typical worker may still find it challenging to comprehend how such a system works. It is common for reward programs to focus solely on immediate results, ignoring actions that don't produce immediate returns (Gordon, n.d.).

Activities that are essential to the system or structure, such as brainstorming sessions, are frequently overlooked. As a result, employees may be apprehensive about adopting new methods or concepts since they perceive training sessions as unrewarded efforts.

On the other hand, Gain-Sharing Plans are designed primarily to increase productivity. In some cases, though, excessive productivity is either unnecessary or harmful. According to a recent study, high production figures can harm companies that don't have constant orders (in the form of unsold goods storing charges). Employees who are encouraged to focus on products with better profit margins are more likely to be motivated by Gain-Sharing Plans that encourage strong sales or higher bottom-line profits. Such products are frequently favored by sales and marketing efforts that employees influence. This suggests to customers that the firm is solely interested in providing products with bigger profit margins, which can have a negative impact on the company's image.

Gain-Sharing arrangements, despite their flaws, remain popular and successful incentive programs. Gain-Sharing participants are more likely to put out their best effort and develop a sense of pride in their accomplishments on the job. Indirect benefits include lower staff turnover and less time and money spent on training new employees. Gain-Sharing arrangements also help companies manage their salaries and reduce operating costs when business is slow.

References

Business, T. (n.d.). Employee ownership. Retrieved December 29, 2021 from www.greatgame.com/the-fundamentals/employee-ownership

Gordon, J. (n.d.). Gain sharing plan – explained. Retrieved December 29, 2021 from https://thebusinessprofessor.com/employment-law/gain-sharing-plan-definition

Guzda, Henry, P. (n.d.). Industrial democracy: Made in the U.S.A. Retrieved December 19, 2021 from www.bls.gov/opub/mlr/1984/05/art5full.pdf

Industrial Democracy. (2021, December 29). Retrieved December 29, 2021 from www.encyclopedia.com/social-sciences-and-law/sociology-and-social-reform/sociology-general-terms-and-concepts-71

Patrick Williams, A. (2021, February 7). Ben Franklin had it right with employee ownership. Retrieved December 29, 2021 from www.linkedin.com/pulse/ben-franklin-had-right-employee-ownership-patrick-williams-aif-

Chapter 12

Managing Rewards in The Digital Age

Bashker Biswas

Current and traditional reward systems are based on principles that have been around since the time of Frederick Taylor and Scientific Management. These principles mainly center around the concepts of classification or taxonomy. In other words, things, objects, and even humans of similar characteristics, recognizable attributes, and defining features are slotted or grouped into specific classification categories or groupings. A classification system is just one of the ways people make sense of the intricacies of paying people for the work they do.

Traditional Compensation

In the arena of traditional compensation, classification or slotting has been widely used to group employees for pay purposes around two conceptual pillars. These pillars are internal and external equity.

- **Internal Equity** – established by using a job or position classification system
- **External Equity** – established by surveying benchmark jobs in one's organization with those of other organizations in similar industrial sectors, geographic areas, and other comparable factors

Traditional compensation systems are also typically structured around the following elements:

- Base Pay
- Incentive compensation
- Equity compensation
- Sales compensation
- Expatriate compensation
- Risk benefits
- Retirement benefits
- Perquisites

DOI: 10.4324/9781003122272-12

Base Salary

Fixed Pay, or Basic Pay, refers to the "fixed" portion of a salary. Employees are primarily compensated for their attendance with this pay component (to attract employees). Employees are also paid to do the assigned work by applying the required skills, knowledge, and abilities using typical effort and demonstrating necessary work behaviors.

Put another way, Basic Pay is the amount of money that an employee receives for their work regularly, without any additional incentives. Additional payments that aren't directly related to the work may be included.

To arrive at a starting salary, compensation experts employ a variety of techniques:

- Compensation based on employment status
- Compensation based on skill or competency
- Compensation depending on the market

Compensation books adequately explain these methodologies. In addition, the professional organization WorldatWork conducts seminars and develops various publications describing these methodologies.

Some compensation specialists have attempted to precisely define the distinctions between the Base Pay and Basic Pay. They say Base Pay refers only to the non-incentive wages and salary over 12 months for work performed. Wages and salaries are given out during a 12-month period for work accomplished, including additional compensation not directly connected to labor effort. In contrast to other forms of compensation, such as bonuses, incentives, and other forms of contingent compensation, this one is referred to as "fixed".

Base compensation has other flows (or changes) as well. Cost flows (variations) that have an impact on Base Pay are summarized as follows:

- Changing from part-time to full-time status
- Changing from full-time to part-time status
- Changing from paid leave to unpaid leave
- Changing from a temporary allowance to a temporary adder
- Changing from exempt to nonexempt status in the United States
- Increasing promotions
- Increasing annual performance increments or merit increases
- Reducing salaries
- Bonuses for overtime work
- General raises
- Step increments
- Cost-of-living adjustments
- Workers' compensation (both on and off)

All these factors impact the total amount of money an organization spends on employee salaries and benefits. Recording and analyzing all spending triggers are necessary to understand the true impact of employee-related expenditures. These inflows and outflows must be documented, tracked, and analyzed to anticipate or budget these expenditures. A total gross rate is computed by adding these payments together in the payroll systems in use.

Base salary or basic salary is the fixed part of pay. This pay element is mainly paid to attract and retain employees. Some call this element "the come to work" feature. It is also paid to employees, commensurate with their knowledge, skills, and abilities that they offer to their employers in exchange for the elements of their pay packages. Employees need to demonstrate typical effort and associated relevant work behaviors to receive these pay packages. The Base Pay element of the compensation package is usually the most significant component of the total pay package. In other words, Base Pay is the amount of non-incentive wages or salaries paid over a period for demonstrated work performance. The Base Pay is the main cash component of the total pay package.

In addition to Base Pay, often, there are many added elements to the Basic Pay that are provided for extra effort and time (this is in addition to the regular work hours) put forth by employees in their employment with a specific employer. These added cash elements can consist of the following:

- Overtime pay.
- On-call pay.
- Portal-to-portal pay.
- Hazardous duty pay.
- The Basic Pay and adder form the most significant component of the standard pay package. Also, this is the main cash component.
- Allowances: Allowances are usually temporary adders to the Basic Pay. The customary allowances for housing, transportation, and education are all included. A wide variety of countries make extensive use of allowances. Payments are made in response to specific events or circumstances.
- Pay adders: In the United States, it's not uncommon to see people getting raises simply for doing their jobs. Pay aspects such as overtime, callback, and on-call pay are examples of compensation for labor performed outside of typical working hours. Almost everywhere, there are wage and hour laws that govern these adders.

Incentive Compensation

Incentives or bonuses are monetary rewards given to employees who meet predetermined deadlines. Most businesses use phrases like "incentive targets", "objectives", "measurements", and "ratings" in this context. Incentives relate to incentives made to employees only if certain preset financial or personal goals are achieved.

Incentive compensation motivates employees to meet corporate, group, divisional, or individual objectives within a specific period.

Equity Compensation

In the past, senior executives were the only ones to benefit from employee equity programs. Major accounting adjustments in this pay component have occurred in the past ten years or so. Stock appreciation rights, restricted stock options, and nonqualified stock options are a few of the newer structures for these types of plans. Accounting, tax, and legal considerations play a big role in creating, implementing, and administering these programs. In recent years, there has been a great deal of debate and discussion about CEO pay related to excessive compensation, earnings management, insider trading, ownership culture, stock option pricing and expensing, dilution impacts, and overhang.

Sales Compensation

Ideally, a company's sales compensation plan is based on outcomes, awards are linked to specific accomplishments, and the compensation is adaptable enough to take into account changes in the market. Compensation for salespeople is affected by changes in the company's business model and marketing strategy (EisnerAmper, n.d.).

The following are the three phases necessary to implement an effective sales compensation program:

1 The first step is defining clear, realistic, and challenging sales goals.
2 The second phase accurately measures performance in relation to expectations while keeping track of it. The organization and the sales force benefit from competitive compensation and motivational features that reward accomplishment.
3 The third step is to maintain an eye on the results, make adjustments to the strategy if necessary, and inform the sales staff.

A starting point is a base income or a draw against commissions and commissions linked to short-term goals and annual sales performance. Participation in long-term equity programs, notably for superstars, provides acknowledgment of professional accomplishments.

Expatriate Compensation

Expatriate compensation is made to employees who have been sent to live and work abroad. Payments can be divided into many subcategories within this broad category – for example, housing differential payments, school allowances, tax protection or equalization payments, moving expenditure allowances, foreign-service premiums, and hardship and special area allowances.

Risk Benefits

Payments for illness, disability, and life (really death) conditions are known as risk benefits. Employees receive these benefits instead of direct monetary compensation to help lessen various life risks for themselves and their families.

Retirement Benefits

Retirement benefits are frequent compensation items that companies offer to help employees with their lifestyles when they leave the company. Defined benefit and defined contribution plans are also options for retirement benefits.

Prerequisites

Senior executives typically receive perquisites as part of their remuneration package. The practice is commonplace all across the world. First-class travel, executive aircraft, country club memberships, executive physicals, and financial planning are most common. Direct cash payments or compensation payments in expenditure reimbursements for approved executive benefits are examples.

Current Practices That Do Not Work in The Digital Age

There are many ongoing drawbacks to current payment systems. As jobs become more knowledge-based and complicated in The Digital Age, compensation systems are not in sync with the changes. As such, business leaders are searching for more relevant pay systems. The lack of relevance is demonstrated because employees do not think pay systems lead them to be engaged in their workplaces. Rewards systems often are not integrated with talent management strategies and other HR functions, such as staffing. With elements such as job evaluation methodologies, classification systems have become complicated and not easily understandable by both managers and employees. Also, market-based salary data is not necessarily reliable and valid.

Issues With Job Evaluation Compensation

Internal equity is the main driving force with job analysis and job evaluation systems. Job evaluation systems are complex methods of assessing the internal ranking for a job or position. It is supposedly an objective way of thinking of jobs from an internal equity point of view. Most job evaluation systems use compensable factors to rank the jobs. The methods used to do this job range in complexity, from highly quantitative to very subjective methods. The complex systems give the appearance of objectivity but are usually exposed to many evaluation biases.

The problem with these systems is that many Digital Age jobs cannot be objectively evaluated because of the required fluidity and flexibility of the tasks and duties. Thus, jobs are not jobs anymore; they are flexible roles. Here the work specifics and elements are broadly defined and flexible. Therefore, work outcomes achieved are more important than the evaluation factors used in job evaluation systems.

Job evaluation systems have had a reputation of being "gamed" to force desired rankings instead of a ranking resulting from objective analysis. In addition, job descriptions used to provide the data for the ranking process are often a result of verbal exaggeration and scope inflation.

Job size is the level of the job in terms of the level of responsibilities and the skills required to carry out the role. It is about the job and not the individual doing the job. The major drawback of job evaluation systems is separating the job from the individual. Job evaluation systems do not work for more complex roles where an individual's skills make a big difference in completing the required tasks and work. The job evaluation results are often the biased analysis of individual evaluators, who might or might not have a deep understanding of the work being done.

The evaluators use complex rules of interpretation, which only the evaluating experts understand. These evaluators and compensation specialists are interested in making the process complex and not easily understandable. As a result, job evaluation results are presented as documents of objective fact and obscure a high degree of judgment.

For these reasons, job evaluation systems rarely achieve the intended outcomes and are often discredited by the stakeholders affected by the process results.

But determining the rank or job size is an important element for determining fair pay. A reasonable alternative to the determination of appropriate compensation can be market pay.

Market pay data can be a good substitute for establishing both internal and external job ranking and pay determination but has its issues as well.

Issues With Market Pay

Most companies base their pay systems on market data. To connect internal equity considerations with external market considerations, the concepts of pay grades or pay bands have been widely used.

Jobs of different content and job requirements are slotted into the same pay grade or pay band. Thus, individual employee compensation determination is grouped together and set at the average market pay rates of dissimilar jobs. Therefore, the individual pay determination is now subjected to data averages.

The individual employee's pay is laid aside and set at the average of a group of jobs.

These systems are not transparent to employees. Employees are rarely told where in the salary grade they are placed or even their salary progression potentials. In addition, the market data on which these salary decisions are made is unreliable and is subjected to various subjective decision criteria.

The idea of a Market Rate is especially problematic because it does not consider individual skills and experience. The market value of the highly skilled and experienced individual is greater than for a less skilled individual. Employees will always be prepared to pay more for someone with a strong track record of success. Market data treats all individuals doing the same job as having the same price in the market. The market data averages can be meaningless for the more complex jobs in digital work environments.

So why is there this fixation with Market Rates in making employee pay decisions? It is mainly a substitution element that is being used. Market data makes things easier for employers. Pay decisions are difficult because they involve internal equity, the external market, and individual performance. They also involve the impact of employee relations and engagement and deciding what the business can afford. So employers, instead of focusing on determining what an individual employee should be paid, find the answer in an easier paradigm, the Market Rate for the job. In The Digital Age, the simplistic "Market Rate" pay determination process can be faulty because jobs are becoming varied, and what is achieved depends largely on the extent of the skills of individual employees. In addition, market data does not consider the value of the psychological aspects of the employment relationship. The most important reward paradigm is the psychological connection between the employer and the employee's work in the digital work environment.

Issues With Performance Pay

Nothing causes more controversy and discussion than the question as to whether performance pay really works in the day-to-day grind of a real-life work environment. The conventional wisdom that guides the practice of performance pay is the principle of incentives. This principle is built around the concept that you will receive more productivity if you pay more for what is accomplished. But money as an incentive is only one of the main drivers of more employee contribution. Money is an extrinsic reward; people are equally motivated by various intrinsic rewards. More pay for better performance might lead to a short-term boost in performance, but a precedent is set once paid, making an additional money incentive in the future an expected routine.

So with respect to pay for performance, the key question becomes whether performance-related pay can be used to engage employees and give them a stake in the business's success. In real life, another key question is whether merit pay, pay for performance, and incentive systems have a clear line of sight.

In other words, do employees see the connection between the reward and the reward amount with their efforts and accomplishments? Performance management methods might become demotivating if there isn't a clear line of sight.

The Need for Change

Having described the current state of rewards management in organizations, it is now time to ascertain whether the current Nature of Work is commensurate with traditional pay systems.

The Nature of Work has changed or is changing in many ways. First, we need to note that modern work environments are being dramatically changed for rewards management because of digitization. This has led to dramatic changes to the human element in the work environment. Artificial intelligence and digital applications are making fundamental changes to workforce compositions. The workplace is now more and more in need of a skilled workforce. Now employers need to hire knowledgeable workers – in most cases, highly skilled knowledge workers. Routine, mechanical, and manual labor is slowly being replaced with machines.

A few years ago, on a site visit to the Mini Cooper factory in Oxford, the United Kingdom, the author was astonished to learn that workforce in the factory was downsized from 55,000 workers to 2,500 workers. This is because all aspects of the factory and automobile assembly operations are mostly done by robots now. There were robots all over the place and very few workers. The remaining workers were highly skilled robotic technicians monitoring and troubleshooting problems with the robotic operations. This scenario is playing out in all industrial sectors, from industrial workers to healthcare workers to clerical workers and beyond. Despite these dramatic changes, the need for highly skilled and qualified employees remains very high. In many places, there is a downright scarcity of needed skilled workers.

But for compensation and reward systems purposes, we have to note a few critical and salient nature of workforce changes as highlighted throughout this book:

1   The workforce is becoming highly skilled, and the knowledge and skill requirements for most jobs are increasing by leaps and bounds.
2   Foremost, for most jobs today, digital and computer skills and know-how are a must. However, the jobs people are doing are very different. They are knowledge-based, complicated, and self-managed.
3   The workforce composition is changing dramatically in modern work environments. Again, we find a reduction in regular or career employees. Instead, we see job arrangements like gigged, flexible, contract, and temporary are on the rise.
4   The World of Work has changed dramatically in the past 50 years. The jobs most people do have become complex, varied, and changeable. Modern

thinking as to what motivates employees should encourage employers to rethink how they manage people. Modern knowledge-based employees value intrinsic rewards more and usually seek autonomy in the workplace.

5   It should be noted that currently used expressions such as compensation, rewards, and total compensation need to include both extrinsic and intrinsic rewards. Extrinsic rewards such as cash compensation, such as base salary and bonuses, pension, benefits, and stock incentives, are important, but in the modern workplace, psychological rewards or intrinsic rewards are equally important, more so in The Digital Age.

6   With widespread changes to workplaces introduced because of the effects of the Covid-19 Pandemic, we see the rapid escalation of remote, distant, and hybrid work arrangements. All these changes require us to reinvent, restructure, and reengineer traditional compensation systems to meet the need of the digital workplace. The traditional principles of classifications with its structure of jobs, salary grades, work groupings, pay ranges, annual performance increases, and incentive compensation designs will need to undergo major makeovers.

So, things are changing, but the usual response of Human Resource departments is to leave plans and programs as is and then carry on with what has been done in the past. Their justification is the current practice and programs fit the "best practice" criteria. But now is the time to change the "best practice" paradigm to the "best fit" paradigm. "Best fit" individualized practices and programs can be more appropriate for the rapidly changing Digital Age. Rewards in the changing digital workplace cannot be treated as a mechanical exercise built around the two static pillars of internal and external equity. The nature of employment is changing, and the psychological aspects of the employment relationship have become more important.

The Impact of Digital Technology on Reward Systems

In major firms, the rewards profession must be comfortable acknowledging that they aren't very good at it right now and are, in fact, slapping people in the face with cash. One of the main reasons for this could be the traditional reward model of fixed structures and pay ranges. In addition, larger organizations' tendencies to utilize centralization to increase cost savings do not easily lend themselves to adaptability and flexibility in compensation systems. The good news is that with the improvements in data gathering, data mining, and computing capabilities in The Digital Age, organizations will have the ability to become much more precise in evaluating reward structures. This will encourage judicious application of technology to make employee incentives more engaging and relevant.

Employees are progressively being pushed away from process positions and into creative and caring roles, both of which are difficult to automate. This poses the challenge of how to recognize and reward employee ingenuity. How can rewards be used to help firms foster a culture that encourages individuals to try new things and accept digital change creatively?

It is best to be open about the fact that reward is an art and not a science because pay decisions cannot be made in a dust-free environment of a laboratory. Rather it is buffeted by day-to-day forces of the rough-and-tumble of real life. It is, therefore, preferable to use the "Rate for the Job" model rather than the Market Rate. The "Rate for the Job" model is guided by the Market Rate, where the Market Rate can be determined with a high level of validity. In addition, it should be based on the importance of the job to achieving the company's strategic and operational objectives. It is the amount that the employer determines should be paid for a particular job on the basis that the job is being carried out to meet the required objectives of the company. It should also be applied equitably within the company, but it should not merely seek to replicate the rates offered by other companies. A better approach is to look at market data from a variety of different sources and to form a judgment about what the Rate for the Job should be for the organization.

The "Rate for the Job" model has advantages over pay grades and widely used salary ranges. The "Rate for the Job" model makes it possible to explain clearly and openly to employees how their pay is determined and manage their expectations as to how it will progress in the future. The approach is much better than fitting salaries into salary grades, ranges, and broad pay bands, determined by market data. Explaining the rationale to employees as to why they are positioned where they are in the range becomes an exercise in explaining the logic of a very subjective process. The "Rate for the Job" model helps avoid psychological threats with perceptions of unfairness and uncertainty, making it easier for employers to control costs.

Pay systems should be tied to an organization's talent management strategies in The Digital Age. In most large organizations, different approaches to talent management apply to the workforce. The workforce should be segmented regarding to the different jobs in the organization and the different talent models that apply to them. The reward framework should be designed to fit the talent model related to the job. There are four possible talent models, each pointing to a different approach to designing pay.

1   **Career Model** – long-term career opportunities are available for those who develop within the career path. Pay should be structured within this model so that the framework rewards expertise and progression through the career path.
2   **Market Model** – skills are available in the external labor market, and long-term career opportunities with the employer are limited. A single pay rate should be aligned with the external market in this talent model.
3   **Retention Model** – requires specialist skills for the job, which is not readily available in the external market. Pay should be based on lower starting pay increasing gradually as the employee gains in expertise in the same job.

4   **Contribution Model** – job is flexible and broadly defined, and the employee's capabilities significantly impact results achieved. Pay here is varied by reference to the contribution that the employee makes.

Design of Pay Frameworks

The pay framework should fit the different talent models, and employers with more than one talent model should adopt a segmented approach. However, compensation systems are not set in stone, and each organization must figure out what works best for them. In many instances, the employer's capacity for managing the pay framework should determine the best approach, including their capability to assess skills and performance. The following paragraphs offer some ideas on how to pay to frameworks that could be designed to fit each of the four talent models.

The Career Model

The Career Model simply requires that the pay structure reflect the career path. Care must be taken in determining whether there is a career path and whether it is easy to fall into the trap of designing career paths for every job in the organization.

Career paths can be an illusion, leading to mistakes in reward design. We tend to see only the people who have moved toward the top of the ladder and assume a neat and tidy progression from top to bottom. We do not see all the people who fell or jumped off the ladder before going near the top. To imagine that a career path exists when in fact it does not is a common misconception. Jobs should only be treated as fitting into the career model if employees have a reasonable prospect of progressing from one role to the next; the career model does not apply to jobs toward the top of the career path where realistic opportunities of further promotion may not exist.

There should be a series of clearly defined roles setting out the skills and experience required for each level. This should include a definition of the necessary qualifications, training, and development needed for jobs at each level in the career path. Progression within the path should be based on clearly stated criteria. There must be a commercial necessity for promotion before it can occur.

Pay progression within each job in the career path should also be based on an individual's skills and experience to carry out the job.

The career model only works with enough employees within the career path to give every employee a reasonable opportunity to progress, at least to the established level. Therefore, the model works best for professional groups with large numbers of incumbents and where qualifications and professional experience readily enable employees to be placed at their correct level in the career path.

The Market Model

The Market Model should be based on the spot Rate for the Job, which is determined primarily by the external employment market. For employees who are developing in the job, there should usually be a developing range of pay below the rate for the position. Each employee should be aware of what they need to do to develop to the full Rate for the Job, and there should be a plan to show how they can achieve this.

The Retention Model

The Retention Model is for employers who need to keep employees in the same job for a long duration, typically more than three years. This model works for jobs where the skills are not readily available in the external market, so it is necessary to develop them within the organization. In these circumstances, steady pay can be offered within the same job, subject to the performance of the employee meeting expectations. The traditional Retention Model is achieved through an incremental pay scale, and this is a sound model if:

*   It is affordable in that not all employees end up toward the top of the pay range. This requires that there should be a reasonable number of employees in the organization, so the "churn" of employees enables the cost of those at the top of the pay range to be funded by less expensive employees lower down the range.
*   Progression of the pay ranges is subject to satisfactory performance being achieved. This means that most employees can expect to progress annually, but those not performing to the required standard do not progress.

This model's main selling point is that it's built to reward employees for staying loyal to the company. Employees know that they may not be highly paid early in their role, but if they remain with the employer for several years, they will progress to a good salary level. However, it is not an appropriate model for many modern jobs, but it remains valid for some, especially in the public sector.

The Contribution Model

The last of the talent models is the Contribution Model. This is the model that should be applied where the capabilities of the jobholder have a significant impact on the results achieved in the job. Most Senior Management and professional jobs fall into this model.

Pay should be varied based on the contribution of the individual. The amount by which compensation should vary depends on a fair differential between a jobholder developing into the role and the strongest possible performer in the same job. The variable amount of pay can be achieved in the form of additional base salary, bonus, or nonconsolidated compensation, which can be paid monthly with the salary. Still, it may be withdrawn if performance declines in future years.

Redesigning Executive Compensation

Any company's success hinges on the success of its workforce. Therefore, attracting and retaining personnel are a critical part of any company's success. As a result of increased competition in the marketplace for the finest executive talent and the need to manage scrutiny of such programs from regulators, the public, and shareholders, businesses must find and implement appropriate compensation incentives to attract and retain executives.

Many requirements impact the design of executive compensation programs that have evolved in recent years. These are ranging from changes ushered in by the Dodd-Frank Act to tax code rules for compensation deferral under Section 409A of the Internal Revenue Code as governance and entity-specific rules and regulations. For example, the Tax Cuts and Jobs Act (TCJA) eliminated Section 162's (performance-based) compensation exception. Thus, public firms can no longer deduct CEO salaries in excess of $1 million from their tax returns. Excise taxes are imposed on tax-exempt organizations that pay their leader's excessive wages, among other things, under the TCJA. It's not just about the TCJA causing organizations to rethink their compensation programs; it's also about attracting and keeping vital personnel in The Digital Age while conforming to present standards.

Organizations must consider various aspects in their compensation design decisions to attract and retain future leaders, such as generational shifts in workplace demographics, advancements in technology and mobility, and growth in entrepreneurship for the following reasons:

- **Compensation packages beyond base salary lead to company-wide success.**

Determining the desired compensation package beyond base salary can have a large impact on the financial sustainability of the organization. Therefore, it is important to take into account the types of arrangements that can be made available: (a) short- and long-term incentives; (b) equity-type arrangements (options, restricted stock, units, and others); (c) deferred compensation arrangements; (d) an appropriate level of perquisites; and (e) any severance or change-in-control benefits. An accurate benchmarking analysis can aid firms in determining the industry's most competitive package for the types of executives they want.

- **Technology has made it easier to align pay with performance.**

Information is readily available in The Digital Age, and transparency is increasingly important (including public company requirements to pass the muster of increasing scrutiny on pay disclosures). For performance-based compensation to be a helpful motivator, companies should establish specific, measurable objectives that are realistic and understandable. These objectives should be accompanied by attainable motivational targets that can motivate employees to reach their full potential.

- **Compliance is crucial.**

Once the design principles are set, the terms of the compensation arrangement must be reviewed against all related compliance requirements, including any risk assessments and clawback policies, legal requirements (securities, tax, other laws), accounting, governance, and approval procedures. Then, the program can be memorialized in the documentation and communicated. When compensation arrangement violates compliance requirements, fines, penalties, and hits to the company's reputation can be costly.

The elimination of the performance-based exception to the $1 million deduction limit for a covered executive's compensation under Section 162(m) of the Code could result in renewed efforts in designing performance-based compensation, which could spread to other types of organizations. Instead of structuring performance-based remuneration in a way that fits within the constraints of previous tax rules to preserve a tax deduction, businesses can start with their goals. For performance-based pay paid under a documented binding contract in place on November 2, 2017, which has not been materially amended, some companies can use the TCJA's grandfather rules to extend their exemption from the $1 million deduction limit. They may also find that amending or terminating the contract would be more beneficial to the employer than continuing with an arrangement that does not serve the business.

Assume the company continues to allow deferrals of performance-based plans under programs designed to comply with Section 409A of the Internal Revenue Code. In that instance, the payment design must still adhere to the rules, and it may not quickly depart from previous compensation designs. Undoubtedly, the TCJA will cause organizations to evaluate their executive compensation program designs. Yet, in today's dynamic, mobile work environment, replete with generational shifts, the primary question for any organization undertaking compensation design should be attracting and retaining the desired talent. Utilizing a well-analyzed, compliant, and reviewed compensation program will not only help attract and retain the leaders, but it will also create a sustainable and productive organization for years to come.

References

Biswas, B. (2012). Compensation and benefit design: Applying finance and accounting principles to global human resource management systems. Pearson.

EisnerAmper. (n.d.). Sales compensation. Retrieved December 29, 2021 from www.compensationresources.com/sales-compensation/

PWC. (2015). Creating a reward strategy for a digital age – PWC UK blogs. (n.d.). Retrieved December 29, 2021 from https://pwc.blogs.com/files/creating-a-reward-strategy-for-a-digital-age-2.pdf

Chapter 13

The Human Cloud

Bashker Biswas

There have been many changes to work methods, models, means, and structures brought on by disruptions and transformations in The Digital Age. As more companies around the world begin to explore, utilize, and reconfigure their workforces, the unique concept of the Human Cloud has received a lot of attention.

The Human Cloud

The Human Cloud is an innovative concept that engulfs online/digital labor marketplaces where talent can be matched with those seeking talent. The two parties can utilize the Human Cloud to engage in a work arrangement. In essence, the Human Cloud is a workforce solutions ecosystem. The Human Cloud serves as an online middleman that has aggregated a pool of virtual workers who can be deployed for any interested organization's wide range of services. The number of Human Cloud platforms and intermediaries has grown by leaps and bounds. After the breakout of the pandemic, the Human Cloud has become the technological solution that is the source of many thousands of contracts and freelance workers whom companies can engage virtually, thus avoiding the new challenges of working in physical locations.

So, in essence, the Human Cloud is the facility to meet, greet, communicate, and work from anywhere in the world. Human Cloud platforms allow this virtual engagement.

We'll look at the current condition and evolution of the Human Cloud in this chapter. Then, we will present a comprehensive framework around the related business services and features of Human Cloud platforms. Next, we will present a comprehensive explanation of the concept of a Human Cloud and then take a detailed look at the elements of the Human Cloud.

The Human Cloud is a technical term used to describe online/digital labor and Human Capital acquisition platforms. The Human Cloud platforms help workers find jobs, but they also specialize in managing and optimizing the workforce for the hiring companies. Human Cloud workers, referred in this chapter as Suppliers, are usually contractors, freelancers, consultants, and other

DOI: 10.4324/9781003122272-13

flexible and contingent workforce categories that are asked to perform various tasks or large-scale projects from employers, referred to as Buyers. These individuals prefer flexibility and require a quick and easy way to connect with job openings. As more people in the United States opt to work flexibly and on demand, online staffing platforms are needed to link employees with employers and improve remote worker management.

So, the Human Cloud is a workplace intermediary platform that can enable diverse work arrangements. This includes establishing the work arrangement and also the completion of that arrangement. All of this is performed on a digital platform. In addition, the arrangement often includes payment transactions. These platforms can also support the day-to-day management of the work arrangements.

Human Cloud Service Arrangements

Human Cloud companies can offer different service arrangements. Among the services provided are:

- Facilitating peer-to-peer transactions via the internet or internet-enabled devices
- Recommending Suppliers validated through user-based ratings
- Helping Buyers and Suppliers agree upon working hours and time
- Providing supervision tools to Buyers
- Assisting in payment processing between Buyers and Suppliers

Geographical Flexibility

One of the main advantages of Human Cloud platforms is that it allows geographical flexibility. Work arrangements have the flexibility to be completed from anywhere without the restraints of a physical location. Therefore, it is not surprising that the Human Cloud has quickly become the acceptable conduit for remote work arrangements. As a result, Human Cloud platforms are becoming common for occupations such as software programming, design, content marketing, data validation, transcription, and other knowledge work areas.

The primary reason for the rapid growth of Human Cloud platforms is that companies have greater access to suitable talent by using these platforms. As a result, the Human Cloud platforms are now regarded as the leading Supplier of required talent. Another reason for the growth is the opportunity to reduce costs and at the same time have access to required skills and talent as and when needed.

Management and Administrative Efficiency

By using Human Cloud-based technologies, employers can manage their workforces. Employers can significantly reduce the time currently spent on manual management and administrative processes by utilizing a Human Cloud platform. In addition, Human Cloud platforms facilitate the efficient management of the entire staffing and onboarding process.

When businesses migrate their workforces to a Human Cloud platform, they can break jobs down into individual shifts and assign them to the best performers at the proper time and place, allowing them to optimize operational procedures. The struggle for essential talent is heating up as more professionals take advantage of the flexibility offered by "Gig", contract, and freelance work. In addition, employers who use a cloud-based workforce management tool to manage their employees can make hiring decisions, onboard new employees, and deploy personnel even faster.

Driven by the Four Forces (Digitization, New Public Health Crises, Environmental Sustainability, and Demographic Changes), the Nature of Work is changing across cultures, geographies, and business sectors. These forces and changes are transforming work in many ways. Traditional employment models are being disrupted. Talent management requires creative ways to engage workers, and workers themselves are becoming more comfortable with the increasing digitization of work. Because of these forces, organizations are contemplating the impact of the transformation on the talent supply chain, and more transactional data is becoming available, driving better algorithms and enabling better hiring decisions. As we advance, platform innovation, increased awareness and adoption from stakeholders, and widespread proliferation in access to the internet are all likely to underpin growth in the Human Cloud. This will fuel a further extension of the Human Cloud solutions and platforms to meet the new demands of the global talent marketplace. We'll now look at the different components of Human Cloud platforms.

Elements of the Human Cloud

There are three basic types of Human Cloud platforms in most cases. These are Crowdsourcing, Online Work Services, and Online Staffing platforms. Common Crowdsourcing platforms are Mechanical Turk, Gigwalk, Onespace, and Applause. Online Work Services platforms are Upwork, Talmix, Toptal, UpCounsel, Catalant, and Wonolo. Finally, Online Staffing platforms are Uber, Lyft, Axiom, BTG, Handy, and LiveOps.

1 Crowdsourcing
2 Online Work Services
3 Online Staffing Platforms (Allwork, 2021)

Crowdsourcing

A subsegment of the Human Cloud, Crowdsourcing is an online platform model that enables work assignments to get distributed out and performed (often as disaggregated "microtasks"). It uses a far-flung "crowd" of independent workers who perform (paid or otherwise compensated/incentivized) work at will. Typically, the client of a Crowdsourcing platform is purchasing "an outcome" (as a service output, not a labor relationship). However, Crowdsourcing also includes work arrangements where a "crowd" of workers compete or bid against one another to solve problems or tasks, with the winner(s) selected and compensated based on the merit of their submissions (Allwork, 2021).

The procedure used in the microtask model involves the following steps:

- Project submitted to the platform
- The platform breaks the project into pieces
- Workers complete microtasks at will
- The platform combines completed work and delivers the finished project

The procedure for the contest-based model involves the following steps:

- Challenge is posted on the platform
- Workers submit solutions through the platform
- Winner(s) selected/awarded

Online Work Services

Another element of the Human Cloud is Online Work Services, which is a subset of a Human Cloud platform. This element allows the delivery of specialized services such as customer service, translation, transcribing, writing, editing, and ride-sharing by a group of online workers who utilize the organizing and managing services of a Human Cloud platform provider. The client in these situations is purchasing an outcome, a completed service with no ongoing employment relationship.

Online Staffing Platforms

Online Staffing Platforms are a subset of the Human Cloud that facilitate specific hiring clients and work-seekers to engage each other in mutually agreed-on comprehensive work arrangements. This work arrangement is usually executed virtually without geographical boundaries. In addition, there is usually a legal relationship between the parties in these arrangements, which the platform also facilitates.

There are two types of Online Staffing Platforms. The first type is called the Freelancer Management System. This is a cloud-based workforce management platform. These platforms help parties initiate, manage, and track work arrangements with independent workers. Usually, the parties searching for these independent workers in these platforms do talent sourcing. The second type of Online Staffing platform is called Just-in-Time Staffing (JITS). JITS

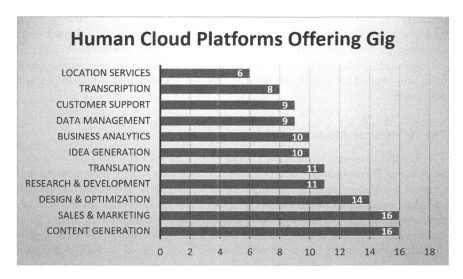

Human Cloud Platforms Offering Gig

Figure 13.1 Human Cloud Platforms (Kaganer et al., 2013)

platforms act as intermediaries who use web/smartphone-enabled technologies and provide staffing for on-site Blue-Collar work. These companies combine technology such as two-sided digital labor marketplace, ratings, and algorithmic recruiting/matching with traditional staffing company services such as screening, interviewing, and other employment services.

Figure 13.1 gives a visual breakdown of the categories of work that are common in Human Cloud platforms.

The Evolution of the Human Cloud

According to staffing industry specialists, the major Human Cloud platforms use four business models to set up Human Cloud platforms.

The Facilitator Model

First, there is the Facilitator Model, which is built to reduce perceived Buyer risks. These platforms have added features to increase Supplier scrutiny. Buyers can look at information about their professional and personal background and the portfolios and the earnings history of the Suppliers. Buyers can also review Supplier skills and data on standardized test results. Buyers can now conduct interviews with Suppliers before making a hiring decision. The workflows have been transparent to the Buyer on the platforms. Some platforms offer project management tools that allow Buyers to create project milestones, review status reports from Suppliers, and link payments to targets and milestones. Some platforms have developed a sophisticated system of remote work management that enables Buyers to monitor Suppliers' online work activity and track time spent on each specific task. Finally, virtual dashboards can allow Buyers to manage teams of Suppliers. This enables Buyers to handle more complex tasks, jobs, and projects. This will allow Buyers to manage virtual workforces more effectively.

The Arbitrator Model

The second category of Human Cloud platforms uses the Arbitrator Model. Sometimes Buyers have to acquire talent to work on highly unstructured and difficult work that might require special expertise, such as specialized research and development work. In these cases, the project's outcome is often uncertain, and the quality of the work is challenging to evaluate. The Human Cloud can tap into a global talent pool and has allowed companies to source highly skilled providers who can work collaboratively on a given project. A Human Cloud model using the Arbitrator Model makes this a more accessible possibility. Buyers can now have an on-demand access ability to source from a pool of skilled Suppliers engaged in a project using various payment protocols. When the talent acquisition is based on targeted outcomes and payments are based on Supplier competition and contests, the perceived risks to the Buyer are much reduced. Sometimes platforms connect Buyers with a global community of creative talent.

An example of a successful Human Cloud platform engagement is when the South Korea-based electronics giant LG Electronics turned to crowdSPRING to carry out a global online competition to design a future mobile phone. More than 400 concepts were submitted for consideration by the LG panel of judges in its 2010 competition.

The Aggregator Model

The Aggregator Model is used by companies when work does not require collaboration in a team. Instead, individuals can perform many simple, repetitive tasks, such as cleaning up an extensive customer contact's database. The Aggregator platform provides Buyers with a single interface to send work to a large number of small Suppliers. These platforms provide an infrastructure to run projects that require the completion of large projects with many repetitive simple tasks and activities at minimal costs and ramp-up time. For example, the famous platform Amazon's Mechanical Turk, or MTurk, has over 500,000 Suppliers. Buyers advertise projects that include a variety of small, repetitive chores that workers are ready to complete for a few cents. These "human intelligence activities", as MTurk refers to them, don't necessitate any special knowledge or skill on the part of vendors. Nonetheless, they require human judgment and are challenging to automate. Translation, audio and video transcription, categorization and tagging, data input, and product or contact search are all common MTurk jobs. For example, since 2009, Zappos, an online store, has employed MTurk to edit customer reviews for spelling and punctuation.

Another Human Cloud aggregator divides projects into categories and then breaks them down into game-like tasks with monetary and nonmonetary rewards for completion and quality. Aggregators have recently started to offer governance services, including microtask definition and quality monitoring. Other aggregators guarantee quality to the Buyer by having more experienced workers review tasks completed by their less experienced counterparts. The automaker Honda, for example, employed an aggregator to complete a project involving tagging objects in images of traffic situations. The automaker used the output to develop an onboard computer functionality to help vehicles avoid road obstacles.

The Governor Model

Finally, the Human Cloud platform can be set up using the Governor Model. The biggest challenge for Human Cloud platforms is completing large complex projects. The Human Cloud needs to be increased in scale to attract large enterprise clients. To fulfill scaled projects using the Governor Model, the platforms use a mix of human project managers to facilitate and manage physically located staff. They also use sophisticated enterprise software for organizing, planning, executing, coordinating, and monitoring individual and team-oriented tasks. Project Governors provide the client layers of services and project governance. This includes collecting project requirements from the client and then carving those tasks into smaller microtasks, flow-charting those tasks into the logical and sequential structure. The Governor also is responsible for Supplier certification and the quality of tasks to be delivered.

In a specific instance of the use of the Governor Model, the Human Cloud platform facilitated breaking down the tasks in a software development project into tasks around conceptualization, requirements specification, design architecture, component production, assembly, certification, and deployment. The tasks were then structured as online competitions. Various Suppliers participated in the competition, and the winning Supplier output then became the input for the next task in the sequence.

In this way, by dividing tasks into microtasks, the Buyers can find highly specialized task specialists, thus assuring a very high-quality output. The platform general manager is usually the overall coordinator of this game plan; thus, the designation, the Governor Model. Using the Governor Model to mitigate risks, the focus shifts from individual Suppliers to the platform. The platform serves as the coordinating point for the Buyer and assumes all project-related risks.

Key Human Capital Concerns and Issues
in the Context of the Human Cloud

Within the context of the Human Cloud, three talent management issues need to be considered.

1   The number of independent Suppliers or service providers
2   The degree of independence these Suppliers will have to complete the assigned tasks
3   The Supplier expertise, which will need to be validated and certified

One of the difficulties within the Human Cloud platforms is managing human talent. When the Human Cloud contracts real innovative tasks using multiple, cross-functional, and cross-disciplinary independent Suppliers to the Buyer, there is a gap in supervision. In addition, the work has to be sequenced effectively within a competition and contest-based mechanism in order for the larger project to be completed with real quality.

The good news is that research indicates independent Suppliers working in various teams that take on challenging tasks and projects are more likely to come up with acceptable solutions than that of single research teams. This suggests that the Human Cloud is more conducive to the crowdsourcing of a large variety of Suppliers with diverse expertise and skills who are tasked, monitored, and managed. In essence, the Human Cloud can be more effective in managing human talent when the projects consist of diverse tasks with complex interdependencies, which requires significant coordination among the various Suppliers.

Another critical Human Capital Management issue within Human Cloud platforms is the ability to source and maintain a constant supply of higher-level skills and expertise. For example, some platforms now boast about having qualified and certified home-call staff capable of managing customer acquisition, customer service, fundraising, and disaster recovery activities for corporate Buyers across various industries. However, this goal is not easy for a Human Cloud platform to achieve and maintain. Sourcing talent is a constant challenge, and the four types of Human Cloud platforms discussed here vary in their ability and norms for Supplier expertise and the range of tasks and jobs they can fulfill for a corporate Buyer. Thus, an ongoing challenge for Human Cloud platforms is to provide continuing professional training in skill enhancements to the Suppliers they have aggregated on their platforms.

MTurk and MobileWorks exemplify that the Aggregator Model requires no unique provider knowledge. In the engagement phase, the Buyer selects one or more Suppliers to complete the task and defines the contract conditions. When it comes to hiring Suppliers, the Buyer must evaluate who is in charge of the selection process and what criteria are used. The Facilitator Model takes a more traditional approach to source, with Suppliers making bids and Buyers conducting their due diligence. Buyers on Elance, for example, evaluate project ideas, assess online resumes, portfolios, and standardized skill test results; research feedback from previous engagements; and, in some circumstances, conduct online interviews to select providers. The Governor Model is similar; however, the Buyer chooses the platform rather than the Supplier. The platform then takes care of the entire Supplier selection process. In both the Facilitator and Governor Model situations, it's critical to pay close attention to the counterparty's competencies. Once chosen, the Supplier or platform takes over responsibility for the project.

The Arbitrator and Aggregator Models are two Human Cloud models that deviate drastically from traditional outsourcing in the Engagement phase. Suppliers can often self-select work on a posted project in these setups. Suppliers are enticed to participate if the reward offered is commensurate with the perceived effort required. On InnoCentive, for example, "grand challenges" – incredibly complicated scientific problems needing top-level expertise – can pay up to $1 million, yet a simple "human intelligence task" on Amazon MTurk, such as data entry, may pay as little as 10 cents. Nonfinancial considerations, such as reputation or education, may also play a role. crowdSPRING's creative designers prefer "open" projects. The Buyer's input on submitted designs is visible to all, rather than "pro" projects, where all communication between the customer and the creative is kept confidential. During this phase of operation, the Buyer concentrates on executing the sourcing endeavor since Suppliers have been identified and conditions have been agreed upon.

In the Facilitator and Arbitrator Models, traditional dyadic Buyer-Supplier coordination requires the Buyer to be prepared to maintain close, continuing relationships with the Supplier or Suppliers to give feedback and oversight. As a worker executive pointed out, Buyers sometimes believe they can just say, "Here is what I want", and then return later to see it completed. That is never a good idea. The result will be poor, and purchasers will be dissatisfied unless both sides commit to spending time interacting and communicating. With its concentration on simultaneous microtask processing, the Aggregator paradigm requires less ongoing coordination. Consider gathering classified product instances from Amazon MTurk employees and archiving them in a product database. In this situation, most coordination is done implicitly – through highly defined activities – and the Buyer-Supplier relationship is kept at arm's length with little continuous engagement. Workflow coordination is available through several Aggregator platforms and third-party companies.

Smartling, a New York-based firm that provides translation services for websites and mobile apps through its platform, has created workflow activities that speed up the translation process and cut down overall job time. However, the Governor Model's intricate interdependencies among tasks and providers necessitate extensive coordination, which is the platform's job, not the Buyer's.

TopCoder and LiveOps use a sophisticated proprietary Supplier governance layer to allow cooperation. More complex jobs may require the engagement of human "platform managers", who collect project requirements from the Buyer at a high level and accept total responsibility for selections at lower levels, restricting the Buyer's involvement to an as-needed basis.

Keeping Quality in Check

Except for the Governor Model, the Buyer is responsible for quality control in all models. The customer evaluates a single project deliverable delivered by the contracted Supplier on a Facilitator platform. In order to accomplish this, the Buyer must have in-house expertise. For example, when a Supplier recruited on Elance produces a translated document, the Buyer must have the ability to analyze and rate the translation's quality.

The Aggregator approach introduces a new difficulty: scalability. The Buyer must evaluate the quality of several jobs accomplished by a group of Suppliers in this situation. While some of the jobs, such as product categorization or data entry, are simple, ensuring the quality of thousands of them is tough. Some platforms include tools to help Buyers with quality monitoring. For example, Amazon MTurk uses a reputation system to rank Suppliers over time. Others, such as CrowdFlower, a microtask crowdsourcing platform, allow customers to mix "test" activities into their workload and reject Suppliers that fail the tests.

The Arbitrator Model uses redundant project deliverables produced by rival vendors to decrease risks and simplify quality monitoring for the Buyer. Having various options makes it easier for the Buyer to select the best delivery that meets their needs. This could be particularly beneficial in instances where quality is more subjective. Take, for instance, the frequent task of creating a logo. Comparing numerous designs supplied by different designers assists the Buyer in determining which logo best expresses the company's concept. The Governor Model delegates quality control to the platform through various methods, including tiered peer review and Supplier testing.

Project Failure and Intellectual Property Leakage Concerns

Another popular strategy is to certify Suppliers. For example, the *USA Today* newspaper enlisted the help of software testing marketplace uTest to test new mobile apps on various hardware and software configurations. uTest certifies its testers by comparing new testers to existing testers by having them "play in a sandbox" or conduct equivalent tasks on a copy of the code being tested. Risk management project failure (noncompletion) and intellectual property (IP) leakage are the two biggest dangers of a Human Cloud venture for the Buyer.

Arbitrator and Aggregator are two models with a lower probability of project failure than the others. This is due to the built-in redundancy. Since there are numerous redundant providers for the task scope, one failing Supplier has little to no influence. However, traditional project failure concerns exist in the other models. For example, Supplier nonperformance directly causes a delay in the Facilitator Model. While the Buyer can respond with financial penalties and negative criticism, these options are of little use in time-sensitive projects. A preferable strategy is to rely on rigorous due diligence during the initiative's Engagement Phase and close supervision during its Operational Phase. Under the Governor Model, project failure is similar. Nonetheless, the platform, not the end Supplier, is the responsible counterparty here, boosting the leverage of threatening penalties and legal methods against a failing source.

The dangers associated with intellectual property vary significantly among the various models. The Buyer essentially depends on a virtual, remote, and frequently foreign provider. The Aggregator Model, with jobs often consisting of dull, repetitive microtasks, poses the least danger to IP among the four platform models. Vendors say that if the tasks are sufficiently atomized, Suppliers won't be able to guess what the broader project is about, reducing IP risk dramatically.

The Arbitrator Model poses the largest IP issue. On the one hand, typical Arbitrator jobs demand highly qualified Suppliers, such as industrial design or scientific difficulties; on the other hand, the competition model presupposes that several (sometimes numerous) vendors have access to all project-related information. The Buyer's IP risks are increased by combining these two elements. Arbitrators manage IP-related risks in a variety of ways. By default, all new Suppliers must execute a legal agreement that complies with IP requirements. IP transfer from the winning Supplier to the Buyer is also facilitated via sites like InnoCentive and crowdSPRING, which often do so without disclosing the Buyer's identity.

On the front end of prevention, Supplier education is critical. One crowd-SPRING executive stated that their biggest task is to educate the community, especially all the new creatives that join every day. It's also tough to protect IP using the Facilitator approach. Supplier nondisclosure and noncompete agreements are popular, but they can be difficult to enforce, especially with Suppliers from underdeveloped nations. The IP risk is passed to the platform under the Governor Model, which can be held accountable if the contract is broken. Many Governor platforms have made significant investments in developing IP protections. For example, TopCoder can keep all competitions within the game plan private and do background checks on all coders who participate. Of course, the Buyer will incur an additional expense as a result of this.

In all four models, managing the Human Cloud will necessitate a thorough knowledge of outsourcing best practices and collaborative project management. The person in charge will also need to know how to break down procedures and tasks and organize and manage input from a large number of small, diverse, geographically dispersed Suppliers, many of whom will have various cultural backgrounds. In addition, they will require a firm grasp on nonmonetary motivations such as reputation management, learning, and community involvement.

What Will Happen Next?

Larger Buyers prefer to do business with large Suppliers. Outsourcing and off-shoring, the two prior sourcing waves, took off only when the Supplier marketplace had grown enough to match the scale. New Human Cloud models now provide creative ways to overcome the coordination and control challenges that arise with scale – with a large number of micro Suppliers. We've already seen signs that several significant organizations worldwide are starting to use these platforms, primarily in the IT space, but adoption is steadily spreading to other areas as well.

Unlike previous sourcing waves, the Human Cloud will disproportionately favor small customers, the global sourcing industry's mostly ignored long tail. Human Cloud platforms increase these purchasers' reach because they frequently lack the resources and skills to outsource abroad.

The Human Cloud should prove to be a leveler for small enterprises, allowing organizations like Rief Media to compete against giant corporations that previously benefited from economies of scale. The broader sourcing market is shifting as well. Much like cloud computing is transforming the software business, the Human Cloud will redefine the outsourcing environment. As some companies use crowdsourcing internally, we expect traditional outsourcing providers to enter the Human Cloud space in the coming years.

Furthermore, as Human Cloud platforms erode their traditional strengths in providing local short-term labor, traditional labor market middlemen are beginning to recognize the threat of disintermediation. As a result, Human Cloud platforms are expected to evolve in three ways in the future years: task decomposition, real-time work, and social governance. First, Human Cloud platforms will create easy visual tools to assist project managers in breaking down a project into smaller tasks. Second, managers will quickly construct workflows that combine internal chores with those performed outside by a Human Cloud causing the business process outsourcing industry to be disrupted. Third, new forms of cloud sourcing will be enabled by advancements in real-time crowdsourcing, in which workers are paid a retainer to stay on call for task requests.

Finally, social governance systems will continue to evolve, allowing the best workers to oversee, train, and approve the work of others. Due to all three orientations working together, we anticipate migrating many tasks from the Governor Model to the Aggregator Model. The Human Cloud is currently a minor component of the global sourcing environment, but it is proliferating as it continues to evolve. Prominent outsourcing and offshoring vendors are already experimenting with Human Clouds and likely will embed them in the services they provide. Pure-play Human Cloud platforms have already gathered millions of experts worldwide. They now need to find new consumers for their services. We feel it will only be a matter of time before they can make the connection.

References

Allwork. (2021, October 27). What is the human cloud? Retrieved December 29, 2021 from www.allworknow.com/what-is-the-human-cloud/

Kaganer, E., Carmel, E., Hirschheim, R., & Timothy, O. (2013). Managing the human cloud. *MIT Sloan Management Review* 54: 23.

Chapter 14

The Obsolete Labor Laws

Bashker Biswas

There are many areas of current labor legislation that need updating or even a significant redo based on the many changes in the modern workplace to adapt to the unique needs in The Digital Age. Foremost of these current laws that need attention are in areas of unionization, collective bargaining, working conditions, and pay and benefits.

The First Angle Enhancing Labor Unions

In the area of unionization, there are mainly two angles to the proposed argument. The first angle is presented by those who want changes to further enhance union organizing and representation.

Collective Bargaining

Collective bargaining legislation has been the guiding light for labor and management relations since the passage of the Wagner Act. Despite the many hurdles along the way, the legislation surrounding labor relations has promoted industrial peace resulting in unprecedented economic growth for nations around the world. But now that the World of Work is changing, so do labor relations need to change, albeit from two different angles.

The Obsolete Laws

Workers communicated mostly during shift breaks in industrial hallways and at the end of the shift in beer parlors in the 1930s, when the Wagner Act was enacted (the statute that ultimately provided American workers the ability to organize and join unions and engage in collective bargaining). The times are different now because the only contact point for most workers is via email, Instagram, or Facebook groups. So, today workers who are talking about organizing need more protection because now workers cannot guarantee that their communications will be kept private. It might be even more onerous for

DOI: 10.4324/9781003122272-14

workers to organize when they have no idea who might be reading their emails or secretly spying on their activities in social media groups.

A recent Harvard Law School Report states that labor rules need to be overhauled to meet the requirements of workers in The Digital Age. This report was compiled from inputs provided by a wide array of experts such as labor leaders, scholars, and activists (Gurley, 2020).

The report focused on union-management relations and organizing efforts by legal unions. In the era of social media, communications during organizing campaigns have now shifted from beer parlors to Facebook and other similar digital media. Thus, organizing laws and regulations need to be changed to reflect the changing communication protocols. In addition, rules should be put into place to prevent employer interference in employee communications, just like the currently enacted laws have provisions to prevent employer disruptions aimed at legitimate union communications.

> If workers are organizing on Facebook or through other digital means, it should be unlawful for the employer to lurk on their pages – just like employers aren't allowed to look through the windows of the union halls in the old days.
>
> (Gurley, 2020).

In light of the changing times, the Harvard report recommendations include ideas such as employee representation on corporate boards and establishment of rights for "Gig Workers" and contractors, much of which we addressed in Chapters 6 and 12. Now it has become imperative to establish the digital rights of workers.

> "When [legislators] looked out at the economy in 1935, they saw factories where people worked similar shifts at similar jobs", Benjamin Sachs, an author of the report and a professor of labor at Harvard Law School, told Motherboard. "But the modern workplace is fissured. Now we have gig workers and temp workers and franchised workers and freelancers. Empowering workers in the modern economy is different".
>
> (Gurley, 2020)

> "There is no actual water cooler anymore", Sharon Block, another author of the report, and director of Harvard's Law School's Labor and Workplace program, told Motherboard. "We recommend that employers should have to create digital meeting spaces, virtual water coolers, where there's a safe space for workers to talk with each other about their collective interests".
>
> (Gurley, 2020)

As more people work remotely, often hundreds or thousands of miles away from their coworkers, guaranteeing workers' digital rights can be a critical step toward regaining labor power. The paper's authors propose that when a quarter of a company's employees indicate support for a union, union organizers be given access to company email systems and that alternative digital places for workers to organize without being watched are created.

According to Block, a former member of the National Labor Review Board (NLRB), "In the old days, you had employers writing down the license plate numbers of cars driving to the location of a union meeting. The modern analog is employers on Facebook groups, trying to figure out who's there and using that information to the detriment of workers" (Gurley, 2020).

According to the research, workers should sign digital cards during the card checking processes, and digital spaces should be available for them to do so. A card check allows workers to form unions when a majority sign authorization cards.

With the rapid increase of online business, old methods of striking and picketing are no longer feasible. New concepts like cyber picket lines are being considered. Strikers now cannot march in front of a physical store or facility to discourage shoppers from that establishment; one cannot picket in front of Amazon because there is no physical Amazon store. Concepts like digital picketing are cropping up. So, with this concept, every time a customer goes to buy something from an online store, they might see a button say, "to cross the picket-line, click here". While many of these ideas and concepts seem unrealistic, many are arguing that maintaining a balance in political and economic power in the United States is unlikely to happen without a whole overhaul of the country's labor laws. Now, there is a great deal of political and economic inequality, which could lead to a destabilization of democracies across the world. This can be largely attributed to a lack of updated labor laws, which eventually takes away employee empowerment.

The Second Angle: Update Union Wins or Eliminate Them

The second angle is espoused by those who suggest that because of the many changes in work systems, structures, and the very Nature of Work, unions' continuation and influence are not conducive to how work is performed in The Digital Age. Many parties strongly believe other aspects of union-related issues need updating. Put differently, many voices in the political arena and the industry firmly believe that the time has come to change the very structure of unionization in the modern workplace.

Industrial-Era Labor Laws Are Less Attractive to Workers

Labor regulations in the United States do not satisfy the needs of modern American workers. Union members are not eligible for individual raises, and employers cannot give nonunion employees a formal voice in the workplace. These limits were put in place by Congress in the 1930s for a predominantly industrial economy that no longer exists. We now live in a digital world. Congress must now reform America's labor laws to meet the challenges of the twenty-first century. According to some analysts, the decline in union membership implies that American labor regulations are out of pace with the modern economy. Traditional labor unions no longer have the same attraction as they once had. Outdated restrictive labor laws now seem to hold both employers and employees impotent to make meaningful arrangements (Sherk, 2013; Sherk, & Jolevski, 2014).

For example, union wage rates are legally created with both a minimum and a maximum rate, which is then codified in the bargained agreement. Without the union's authorization, a unionized company may not pay employees more than the union-negotiated rate. While unions are happy to accept group raises, individual performance compensation is often resisted. Unions insist that employers base promotions and raises on various subjective factors rather than actual performance.

There have been cases where companies gave individual raises to employees. These raises were on top of the union's pay. In these cases, the unions protested, saying that the pay increases violated their collective bargaining agreements. They took issue with certain entry-level workers being paid more than senior union members. The union brought charges. Federal district courts ordered the firms to reverse the wage raises in several areas. Union members are fewer than half as likely as nonunion employees to get performance pay nationwide.

This prevents union members from joining a one-size-fits-all approach when all employees brought essentially the same talents to the bargaining table. However, the Nature of Work is evolving. Employers have automated many repetitious jobs. Employers are flattening hierarchical organizational structures at the same time.

Merging of Management and Worker Roles

In many self-managed work situations, management and worker roles are merging. The lines between management and labor are becoming increasingly blurred. Employers are increasingly expecting people to make their own decisions and take the initiative on the job. Employers want to recognize individual accomplishments, and employees want to be recognized for them, but collective bargaining agreements make it impossible to do so. Nonunion employees are likewise denied a voice on the job under federal labor regulations. Employee involvement (EI) programs and workgroups, where workers and supervisors can meet to address workplace concerns, are popular among employees and employers. This is Industrial Democracy, in its true sense, operating in the workplace. There are many examples of effective EI programs that advance worker interests. For instance:

- In Flint, Michigan, Webcor Packaging (1997), a manufacturing company, created a plant council made up of five workers who were elected and three managers who were appointed. They were tasked with finding ways to improve work rules, wages, and benefits. Each of them asked those around them for suggestions and then made those recommendations to the Management Team.

- In Elkhart, Indiana, workers at Electromation fought against a proposed change to the bonus the company wanted to offer for good attendance. Instead of enforcing the new incentive structure, the managers met with randomly selected workers and created a committee to find creative solutions to workplace issues. The Management Team promised to implement these recommendations if they weren't cost-prohibitive.

The U.S. Congress and the RAISE Act

The U.S. Congress should bring labor law into the twenty-first century. Congress should repeal legal provisions that discourage employee involvement programs. Congress should also remove the union's ability to prevent individual performance raises (S. 1633 (116th): Raise Act, n.d.).

The U.S. Congress has made steps to make these proactive modifications to restrictive legislation. Here is an example:

In 2012, Senator Marco Rubio (R – FL) and Representative Todd Rokita (R – IN) sponsored the Rewarding Achievement and Incentivizing Successful Employees (RAISE) Act. This act proposes that employers keep union rates as a wage floor while ensuring that they never establish a ceiling on what employees can earn. This bill states that neither the exclusive representation of employees in a bargaining unit by a labor organization nor the terms of a collective bargaining contract or agreement entered into after the passage of this bill can prevent an employer from paying an employee higher wages, pay, or another compensation than the contract or agreement allows. The RAISE Act is a two-page measure that would amend the National Labor Relations Act (NLRA) to allow employers to pay salaries above those specified by collective bargaining agreements. Employers might give merit-based pay hikes to individual employees under this move, regardless of the salary scales under the workplace's collective bargaining agreement.

"There is nothing more American than rewarding hard work", Rubio said. "Union bosses should not be able to arbitrarily block a performance-based raise earned by a hard-working employee. The RAISE Act would bring greater fairness and opportunity to the modern workplace by giving American workers the freedom to earn more money for a job well done" (U.S. Senator for Florida, Marco Rubio, 2019).

U.S. Representative Dusty Johnson, a new sponsor for the 115th Congress, reintroduced the RAISE Act in June 2019, replacing longtime sponsor, former Rep. Todd Rokita. Senator Marco Rubio has repeatedly introduced the Senate version of the bill since 2012.

"Great workers make businesses successful. When employers want to share profits with their hardest-working employees, regulations and union requirements shouldn't be allowed to stand in the way", Johnson said. "The RAISE Act will provide employers flexibility to give hard-working employees a raise. Hard work should be rewarded, not discouraged" (U.S. Senator for Florida, Marco Rubio, 2019).

Neither chamber has approved the legislation in previous Congresses.

Reforms like these would make federal labor rules more relevant to workers in today's economy. Employee speech should not be restricted in the workplace, and employees should not be discouraged from making progress via hard labor.

Updating Working Conditions Legislation

On April 29, 2019, the U.S. Department of Labor (DOL) issued an opinion letter clarifying its position on how "Gig Workers" should be classified. The letter will come as a relief to many who work in the Gig Economy. Based on the facts provided and taking into consideration the specifics of the company that solicited the letter, their workers would be appropriately classified as "independent contractors" and not as "employees" under the Fair Labor Standards Act (FLSA).

It could be said that the DOL's opinion letter laid out a worst-case scenario for workers and an excellent benefit for companies. But the DOL's position on "Gig Economy" classification may not matter all that much for many workers. This is because, in jurisdictions with more stringent worker categorization criteria for their wage and hour laws, "Gig Workers" may still be considered as "employees" under those laws, even if the FLSA does not apply. As a result, employers in those states must follow state wage and hour regulations regardless of the DOL's position on worker categories, which means they must pay minimum wages, work maximum hours, and comply with overtime rules.

AB5 in California

The state of California necessitates further vigilance. This examination is warranted due to California's vast population. The state changed its worker classification test from the more forgiving "ABC" test to the less forgiving "ABC" test. The California Supreme Court adopted a test in *Dynamex Operations West v. Superior Court* that requires "hiring entities" to show (California Lawyers for the Arts, 2020):

A   The person is independent of the hiring organization in connection with the performance of the work, both under the contract for the performance of the work and in fact

B   The person performs work that is outside the hiring entity's business

C   The person is routinely doing work in an independently established trade, occupation, or business that is the same as the work being requested and performed (EDD State of California, n.d.)

A corporation can only lawfully designate its employees as independent contractors if all three parts of the ABC test are met.

In California, the ABC test appears to be here to stay with the state's Department of Industrial Relations issuing an opinion stating that the test applies to claims originating under California wage orders. The ABC test is very different from the prior approach employed in California, which is replicated in the DOL opinion letter and is used in several other states. California courts used to consider the following elements when determining the totality of the circumstances (Steven F. Pockrass Indianapolis Author, 2021):

- Maintaining control over work specifics
- The degree to which workers are a regular and integrated component of the corporate activity
- The work's long-term viability
- Whether the workers have a specific trade or profession
- Whether the workers present themselves as businesspeople
- Whether the laborers are hired for normal labor
- Investing more than only personal service and hand tools by the workforce
- Whether the workers have a profit or loss potential
- Whether or not employees have the option of purchasing income protection insurance

Similarly, the DOL's opinion letter focuses on six factors:

1   The nature and extent of the potential employer's control
2   The worker's relationship with the potential employer's permanency
3   The worker's investment in facilities, equipment, or helpers
4   The level of skill, initiative, judgment, or foresight required for the worker's services
5   The worker's profit or loss opportunities
6   The degree to which the worker's services are incorporated into the operations of the potential employer

Many states use a test similar to or identical to the one used by the DOL. Other states, such as Connecticut, New Jersey, and Massachusetts, have all adopted the ABC test for identifying an employee under state wage and hour regulations as California has. Workers who would otherwise be categorized as independent contractors under the DOL's interpretation of the FLSA can and will be classified as employees in those states. To avoid misclassification, businesses must take the time to assess classification decisions and the possibility of conflicting interpretations under state and federal law.

Labor Law Implications for the Post-Covid Work Environment

Then there are labor law issues that have to be dealt with in the post-Covid work environment. Finally, as states, cities, and counties take steps to reopen and recover from the Covid-19 Pandemic, businesses are facing an unclear future with many questions still needing answers.

Employers must comply with applicable regulations despite the unanswered questions while establishing a strategy to reopen and recover. Employers must find ways to comply with federal and state wage and hour rules while designing and implementing reopening programs, from the everyday challenges of classifying personnel to the more complicated issues of testing (National Law Review, 2020). When concerns with Covid-19 began, many employers adjusted their employee compositions to cope with economic uncertainties. Employers will and are certainly confronting more adjustments to the structure of their firms and work habits as they reopen and rehire staff. Nevertheless, many think that there will be a New Normal as the Covid-19 Pandemic ends.

As exempt, salaried employees are brought back to work, employers must ensure they retain their exempt status. This includes complying with minimum salary requirements and ensuring that the job duties comply with exempt test definitions. If this is not done, employers may face the risk liability for misclassification, which includes the financial liability of unpaid overtime.

If employers bring exempt employees back on a part-time basis, they need to consider that the FLSA requires that exempt employees working part of a workweek based on employer requirements still need to be paid their entire salary for that week. So, suppose an employer has the idea of bringing back an exempt employee for four out of five workdays and automatically takes a reduction in salary action to account for the shorter workweek. In that case, the employer needs to communicate to the employee beforehand that the salary is reduced. If the employer fails to communicate this, the failure to do so may affect the employee's exempt status.

Legal issues need to be addressed if exempt employees are brought back from furlough but are paid a lower rate. In these cases, employers should ensure that the salary meets federal and state minimum salary levels. The employee's responsibilities haven't altered significantly enough to make them nonexempt. The correct explanation for the pay cut is revealed (e.g., the reductions are due to the pandemic, and they correlate to a decreased schedule). Employers must also ensure that they follow state rules governing how salary decreases should be communicated to employees. Particular attention should be paid when exempt personnel, even those performing nonexempt responsibilities to offset staff shortages, spend most of their time on exempt-type duties.

When employers reclassify previously exempt employees to nonexempt because of a change in business needs caused by the Covid-19 Pandemic, they should be careful when they reverse the decision and return these employees to exempt status. Attention should be paid to notice requirements given to employees when changing their classification. In addition, employers should evaluate the company's financial circumstances and changing economy before reclassification to ensure that the exempt classification is expected to remain. Plans to reopen may include schedule changes, including staggered shifts, a continued or new focus on remote work arrangements, or overall change in hours. Employers must consider how this may affect all exempt and nonexempt alike.

When adopting these changes, employers must note that exempt, salaried employees must normally get their full compensation every week they work, with a few exceptions. As a result, if a salaried employee is told not to work for a week, the employer must make sure that this is followed or face liability – this means that the exempt person cannot answer emails, respond to texts, or do anything else. Similarly, suppose less work is available but must still be completed each week. In that case, employers cannot withhold an exempt employee's salary due to fewer hours from week to week, as mentioned earlier. Instead, the employer must plan ahead of time for the reduced hours and create a "new" compensation that will be paid every week as they work.

On the other hand, exempt employees cannot be paid hourly, daily, or on another basis, because this would void their exemption. Therefore, employers should consider whether changes in workload or responsibilities necessitate reclassifying exempt personnel. For example, new schedules may affect the number of hours worked by nonexempt personnel. Regardless, nonexempt employees must be paid the minimum wage set by state and federal law for all hours worked.

Moreover, as companies weigh the costs and benefits of teleworking, they must ensure that nonexempt employees keep correct time records and are compensated for all hours worked. According to the law, employers should compel nonexempt employees to keep accurate records of their rest and food breaks and take them. Furthermore, companies may consider demanding that all overtime be preapproved to ensure that overtime is tracked and not put the company under financial duress.

While some firms have chosen to reopen, the lingering psychological fear and real medical vulnerabilities brought on from the Covid-19 Pandemic may make some employees feel insecure going to work. Employers should examine whether they may appropriately compel these employees to use vacation or other paid time off benefits during this time, in addition to assessing whether permitting them to stay home is a reasonable accommodation under the Americans with Disabilities Act (Flett, 2017). In addition, using vacation or other paid time off may help companies figure out how to pay exempt employees their required compensation even though they do not work full weeks. Before accessing a work site or returning to work, many businesses introduce testing, such as temperature checks. Employers must consider whether employees must be paid for this time when electing to implement temperature tests, similar to security screenings necessary before entering the workplace. Whether or not screenings are considered paid time is determined by the company's location. Paying employees for time spent through screening will always be the riskier strategy, regardless of where a company is based. As a result, companies should investigate ways to reduce screening time and comply with local and state mandates requiring screens.

These challenges and more will continue to be present as more firms enter The Digital Age and implement many of the recommendations from this book. As today's workforce sees their strength and have confidence in speaking up, labor laws need to ensure that both workers and employers are provided the right structures and limits for both to be successful.

References

A Robust Public Debate: Realizing Free Speech in Workplace Representation Elections. (n.d.). Retrieved December 29, 2021 from www.thefreelibrary.com/A+robust+public+d ebate%3a+realizing+free+speech+in+workplace . . . -a0105916030

California Lawyers for the Arts. (2020, February). Life after AB5: A toolkit – California lawyers for the arts. Retrieved December 29, 2021 from California Lawyers https://calawyersforthearts.org/resources/Documents/AB5%20ToolKit_February%202020.pdf

EDD State of California. (n.d.). Employment status: ABC Test. Retrieved February 18, 2022 from https://edd.ca.gov/Payroll_Taxes/ab-5.htm

Flett, K. (2017, September 17). Working from home as a reasonable accommodation under the ADA: Credeur v. state of Louisiana. (n.d.). Retrieved December 29, 2021 from https://beyondthefineprint.com/2017/09/working-from-home-as-a-reasonable-accommodation-under-the-ada-credeur-v-state-of-louisiana/

Foley & Larnder LLP. (2019, May 13). Despite DOL 'gig economy' opinion letter, state wage and hour laws that provide greater protections for workers still trump Fair Labor Standards Act. Retrieved December 29, 2021 from www.jdsupra.com/legalnews/despite-dol-gig-economy-opinion-letter-65400/

Gurley, L. K. (2020, January 27). Technology has made labor laws obsolete, experts say. Retrieved December 29, 2021 from www.vice.com/en/article/5dm3vx/technology-has-made-us-labor-law-obsolete-experts-say

National Law Review. (2020, May 6). Returning to work after covid-19 means more wage & hour concerns. Retrieved December 29, 2021 from www.natlawreview.com/article/returning-to-work-after-covid-19-means-more-wage-hour-concerns

NLRB v. Webcor Packaging, 96–5423 (United States Court of Appeals, 6th Circuit July 11, 1997.

S. 1633 (116th): Raise Act. (n.d.). Retrieved December 29, 2021 from www.govtrack.us/congress/bills/116/s1633/summary

Sherk, J. (2013, January 23). Labor unions: Declining membership shows labor laws need modernizing. Retrieved December 29, 2021 from www.heritage.org/jobs-and-labor/report/labor-unions-declining-membership-shows-labor-laws-need-modernizing

Sherk, J. & Jolevski, F. (2014, January 28). Labor unions: Stagnant membership shows need for labor law modernization. Retrieved February 18, 2022 from www.heritage.org/jobs-and-labor/report/labor-unions-stagnant-membership-shows-need-labor-law-modernization

Steven F. Pockrass Indianapolis Author. (2021, January 8). DOL publishes final rule for determining who is an independent contractor. Retrieved December 29, 2021 from https://ogletree.com/insights/dol-publishes-final-rule-for-determining-who-is-an-independent-contractor/

U.S. Senator for Florida, Marco Rubio. (2019, May 23). Senators Rubio, Barrasso, Cornyn and Representative Johnson reintroduce Bill allowing employers to award performance-based raises to unionized workers. Retrieved February 18, 2022 from www.rubio.senate.gov/public/index.cfm/2019/5/senators-rubio-barrasso-cornyn-and-representative-johnson-reintroduce-bill-allowing-employers-to-awared-performance-based-raises-to-unionized-workers

Chapter 15

People Analytics and Measurements

Bashker Biswas

This is the era of data analytics. Almost every area of organizational decision-making and analysis is being based on data analytics. Concepts, subject matter thoughts, and ideas with associated software applications and function-specific data analytical tools are widely used.

Current Trends in Data Analytics

There is a plethora of educational opportunities that focus on data science. Analysts and decision-makers are urged to develop hands-on skills using professional data scientists' tools, languages, and libraries. Various data science skills, techniques, and tools are used to complete projects and generate organizational analysis and decision-making guidance. Analysts import and clean data sets, analyze and visualize data, and then build and evaluate machine learning models and data pipelines. People and business functions are being urged to think and work as data scientists. Therefore, data science is one of the hottest professions these days. The demand for data scientists and analysts who can analyze data and communicate results to guide data-driven decisions has never been greater.

This is the new era of data-driven excellence. Some say that an area that was once only under the purview of technically savvy professionals has evolved into a significant organizational cultural phenomenon. This modern analytical environment connects a more comprehensive and diverse set of business professionals to a wider variety of data. It empowers them with data tools that enhance business relevance and technical sophistication.

Companies indicate that their data management capabilities integrate extremely well with their organization's analytics strategies. Organizations are using augmented analytics such as machine learning. They use analytical tools such as regression analysis and modeling, decision trees, and multilayer neural networks. Organizations are developing strong data governance policies supported by a technology platform as a toolset. Businesses and organizations say that their use of modern data analytics results in annual revenue. They also indicate that data analytics leads to double-digit annual workforce productivity growth.

DOI: 10.4324/9781003122272-15

The most significant barrier to extracting value from data and analytics has been organizational. Many companies struggle to introduce data-driven insights into day-to-day operations and business processes. Also, companies are faced with a massive hurdle in introducing rigorous data analysis because of the shortage of the right talent, not only data scientists but also data translators whose skills are an optimal mix of data-savvy and industry and functional expertise.

Data for all business functions has become a critical corporate asset. This data aggregation comes from various sources such as the internet, smartphones, sensors, payment systems, cameras, and many other sources. While data itself will become increasingly commoditized, value is added by possessing scarce data and the staff who have the skills to aggregate data in unique ways and provide valuable analytics. It is also hoped that massive data integration capabilities can break up organizational and technical silos, leading to new insights and models. Data can enable faster and more evidence-based decision-making.

Data and analytics are already shaking up multiple industries, and the effects will only become emphasized as more organizations embrace a data analytic corporate culture. Even bigger impacts will be felt when deep learning develops and matures. This is positioned to give machines the capabilities to think, problem-solve, and understand the language of data analysis. So, organizations that can utilize these capabilities effectively will create significant value and differentiate themselves. Those who don't will, therefore, be at a significant disadvantage.

Human Resource Analytics

Within the context of the rapidly advancing environment of data analytics, it is becoming very important for the Human Resource Management (HRM) function to adopt this major cultural and operational shift. Therefore, in this chapter, we will take a deep dive into the subject of HR Data Analytics. But note, Human Resource Analytics is not a new concept. It has been around for a while.

What Is HR Analytics?

Human Resource Analytics (HR Analytics) is the area in analytics that deals with people measurements and applying the analytical process to Human Capital within an organization to improve employee performance and employee retention.

Data about your employees at work is not collected by HR Analytics. Instead, its fundamental purpose is to provide insight into each HRM process, collect vital data, and then make informed and effective decisions about improving the processes based on that data.

The History of HR Analytics

But, first, let us look at the history of HR Analytics and Measurements.

In the 1960s, when computing was still done on mainframe computers, there slowly grew a discipline called a personnel system. This function mainly existed for mainframe computer companies. And that is IBM and the BUNCH – Burroughs, Univac, NCR, Control Data, and Honeywell.

The personnel departments of these companies usually had a Personnel Research Department, and a subsection of this department was the Personnel Systems Department. The charter of the Personnel Department was to cover both the hard and the soft subjects (more about this later on this chapter) research for the Personnel Research Department. The department consisted of HR subject matter experts, Systems Analysts, and Programmers. Programming then mainly was done using Fortran and COBOL programming languages. The Personnel Systems Department's primary function was developing and maintaining the Personnel Records database. In addition, the Personnel Systems Department was tasked to design and develop relevant, appropriate, and required computer-generated management reports, which allowed decision-makers to manage various aspects of the personnel function effectively.

Reports were generated for Benefits and Pension administration, and key data-based reports were developed to analyze turnover statistics, recruitment effectiveness, and training and development outcomes. This was when HR Analytics was first introduced. Not surprising that HR Analytics and Measurement found its beginning in the mainframe computer industry. This was much before Google introduced this discipline.

As part of the effort, there were one-of-a-kind analysts whose job included mathematical and statistical modeling in Human Resource planning, specifically compensation and benefits planning. These analysts were categorized as advanced systems research design and development. This type of work was not traditional industrial psychological research, often seen as the "soft" side of HRM. These analysts did tasks from the least complex to the most complex. Here is the task hierarchy:

- Maintenance of Systems Already Implemented
- Implementation of Developed Systems
- Development of Approved Systems
- Design of New Systems
- Feasibility Research on New Systems
- Creative Systems Problem-Solving

These analysts assisted in developing computer-oriented reports and systems for HR functions, including Human Resource Development, Staffing, International Personnel, and so on. These analysts also coordinated data-based activities in the area of Human Resource planning and reporting. They further assisted in consolidating staffing-level statistics and payroll data analysis. Their work led to the implementation of increased exception reporting. In addition, it led to the development of comprehensive turnover analysis systems to detect specific, significant changes and causes. Finally, they studied current reports and evaluated them to identify changes that would make them more effective.

The Saratoga Institute Initiative

The Saratoga Institute Initiative was a pioneering effort in HR Analytics. Saratoga Institute programs and methods are based on more than 35 years of expertise in Human Capital research and were founded in 1977 by Dr. Jac Fitz-enz. Saratoga is a thought leader in the Human Capital business and the publisher of the world's largest database of Human Capital knowledge.

The Saratoga Institute is a PricewaterhouseCoopers (PwC) Human Resource Services offering, providing a unique approach to studying Human Capital Management through its Workforce Diagnostic system. They collect and report data intelligence on key workforce, HR, and financial data, including HR staff and structure, compensation and benefits, staffing, hiring, retention, and separations. This database helps organizations understand the implications of any organization's survey results. The organization's data can be compared to competitors' data, and targets for improvement can be developed. Saratoga Institute also assists organizations in conducting employee surveys, which helps gain insights directly from the workforce. Questions such as why employees leave the organization or whether the HR programs align with what the employees want can be answered.

HR Analytics and Measurements Explained

Human Resources managers can answer the following questions regarding their organization's HR system using HR Analytics (Question Pro, 2021):

- Do you have a high turnover rate among your employees?
- Do you know which of your staff will be leaving your company in the next 12 months?
- How much of an employee's departure is viewed as a travesty?

The first question is simple for most HR executives to answer for their company. However, it is challenging to answer the other two questions for most, especially if you lack specific data. To answer the other two questions, executives need to combine different data and analyze it thoroughly as if they were a professional data analyst. Furthermore, they can make better decisions by analyzing other Human Capital questions and be able to forecast so much more using this data. Active HR Analytics starts the moment a company begins to use data acquired from its employees to assess their challenges.

Employees are essential to the success of any company, and it is obvious that this is the case. For every company to be successful, it must attract the right people, manage talent acquisitions, and utilize its resources to the most. Every manager should be familiar with these five HR metrics:

1 **Employee Churn** – Using data from the past, churn is defined as the percentage of employees who have left the company since the beginning of their employment. Analyzing your workforce's churn is done through employee churn analytics. Predicting the future and reducing staff churn are two benefits of employee churn analytics. Therefore, employee turnover analytics rely on both current and past attrition data.

2 **Capability** – Any company's performance is unquestionably influenced by its personnel's amount of competence and capabilities. Using capability analytics, organizations can identify the fundamental competencies that the team should possess. A company's workforce competencies can then be compared to these benchmarks to see if there are any discrepancies.

3 **Organizational Culture** – It's not only difficult to change culture, but it's also infamous for being pinpointed. The culture of a company or business is typically made up of unstated norms, procedures, and patterns of human behavior. Using organizational culture analytics is a way to understand the workplace culture better. It is easier to track changes as well. Keeping tabs on cultural shifts is a valuable tool to see the early indicators of a toxic work environment.

4 **Capacity** – It's true; capacity affects revenue. A workforce's operational efficiency can be measured using capacity analytics. For example, it's hard to tell whether meetings and conversations are taking time away from productive work in a company specializing in clothing design or whether employees are simply too lax about their responsibilities. This type of behavioral analysis is a form of capacity analysis, which identifies how much room an individual has for development.

5 **Leadership** – It's better to have no leadership than to have bad leadership. Employee turnover is a direct result of ineffective leadership. Such organizations have a tough time keeping employees, which hampers their ability to function fully. Analyzing and dissecting a variety of facets of a leader's performance in the workplace reveal everything from the excellent to the poor to the ugly. It's possible to collect data through qualitative and quantitative methods like surveys, polls, focus groups, or ethnographic studies employing a combination of the two methodologies.

Since its inception, HR Analytics has progressed significantly. Organizations may now track various metrics to assure the accuracy of their people, talent, and workforce analytics. HR Analytics enables HR managers to make data-driven decisions to attract, manage, and retain a successful workforce by applying statistics, modeling, and evaluating employee-related elements to improve business outcomes. As a result, HR Analytics has numerous advantages, including increased return on investment, higher retention rates, and improved company operations.

The Benefits of HR Analytics

Thanks to technical improvements, HR Analytics has come a long way from when it was first introduced. HR professionals can now do so much more with their data-driven metrics, thanks to the evolution of HR Analytics. They may go from merely evaluating goals and Key Performance Indicators (KPIs) to data-gathering. Let's look at some of the latest HR metrics that are now available to HR practitioners.

Latest HR Metrics

Turnover Forecasts

One of the numerous benefits of HR Analytics today is accurately predicting the chances of any employee leaving. This HR metric is predictive and can save you a lot of money on your recruitment efforts.

Employee Engagement

Employee Engagement has become a critical HR metric for businesses as more companies recognize their employees' impacts on their bottom line. The Employee Engagement measurement allows companies to see how involved their employees are in various initiatives, to see how much they believe in the organization and identify with the corporate image or brand, and to discover action items for employers and employees to align with the company's strategic plan. Improved retention and lower turnover rates are two advantages of this new HR metric. There are numerous advantages to HR Analytics nowadays. One of these advantages is that personnel are hired based on their abilities rather than their educational backgrounds. Many businesses have discovered that having a degree does not always imply that an applicant is a better fit for a job opening. In some circumstances, experience is far more valuable than education. Thanks to the advent of HR Analytics, businesses can now ensure that they're hiring the best people for any open positions based on their performance rather than their educational background alone.

Diversity Hiring Rate

Even though our world is getting more diverse, many firms are having problems hiring diverse people. Thanks to the advancement of HR Analytics, businesses may now increase their Diversity Hire Rate and realize the benefits of that diversity. The growth of HR Analytics is still in progress, from obtaining data but not doing anything with it to calculating the possibility of an employee sticking with your organization for a long time. Despite this, it continues to improve HR practices across the board. You won't be able to reap the vast benefits of HR Analytics today until you have correct HR metrics in place at your company.

Strategic Management Metrics

HR Analytics helps your firm become more strategic; data enables you to deal with present difficulties and plan for the future more effectively. Some of the specific advantages of HR Analytics can be summarized as follows:

- **Improve Your Hiring Process** – The acquisition of new employees is an essential part of your HR strategy, and it is a year-round endeavor. Your talent acquisition (TA) team is always on the go, whether it's recruiting for a new department, expanding an existing one, or creating an entirely new position. An organization can only hope everything goes smoothly when it hires a new employee after finding the perfect individual. How many people apply, and when do they drop out? What are your favorite job boards? How many candidates do you need to contact to close a job opportunity? These are just a few questions you would want to use analytics to answer. Use this information to get a clearer idea of what's causing delays and fill any gaps.
- **Reduce Attrition** – Retaining employees is becoming increasingly complex, especially among the Millennial workforce. To stop the rate of attrition, conduct exit interviews and gather data, analyze these reasons and patterns, and then develop a solution.
- **Improve Employee Experience** – There must be regular meetings between management, HR representatives, and employees to determine what aspects positively and negatively affect employee experiences.

This is a crucial first step in enhancing the working environment for employees. In many firms, the employee experience begins with the employment process. Therefore, the first meeting you have with a candidate is equally as important as any other HR-related activity when deciding whether or not to hire them.

- **Gain Employee Trust** – You can see what's going on in the company and what the employees think about it, thanks to HR Analytics. It's easier to correct what's reportedly faulty and improve future operations when you're armed with data. You can see what's working and what isn't working. Employees notice when processes are enhanced, and new ones are introduced. They are confident that the Management Team will consider their input. It is essential to achieve high levels of staff involvement and productivity to achieve long-term employee satisfaction and retention.

HR Analytics does not require expensive software, an enormous crew, and lengthy procedures. As a starting point, you can have one-on-one dialogues with employees, record their comments, add management to the conversation, involve various functions in the planning process, establish a strategy, and commit to it. In order to ensure that all employees are aware of the employee experience and can improve, the data must be available to everyone. Drive initiatives, solve problems, and bring about positive changes in your organization using the data you've collected.

Employee Engagement, employee retention, health and well-being, productivity, and work culture can all be improved by using HR Analytics (Question Pro, n.d.).

Improve Your Talent Processes With HR Analytics

In addition to pre-hiring, hiring, and annual performance assessments, talent processes are far more extensive than this. Training, recreational activities, and therapy are just a few of the options to explore. A few processes, such as regular one-on-ones, skip-level meetings, and employee focus groups, should be typical in any organization. It is critical for HR to keep an eye on their talent processes and detect any issues or bottlenecks. It's great to meet with staff, but this may not always be practical. The idea of doing employee surveys is a great one: get their feedback and ideas, work on them, and let them know they're being considered.

Exit Surveys

Exit surveys are another type of employee survey that may be used. This is an excellent method to learn what your employees think about your company's perks and experience, as well as what changes they'd like to see for those who remain employed.

HR Analytics Software

To keep track of your staff, HR Analytics software is crucial.

It aids with collecting and maintaining data across several office locations, departments, and roles, among other things.

The following are some of the most significant advantages of using HR Analytics software:

- **Ease of Use** – Long training sessions or certificates are not required for these user-friendly technologies or platforms.
- **Dashboard** – Dashboards show all of the relevant information in one place. You may look at historical and current data across a wide range of parameters, including tenure, roles, reporting, and so on. Managers can make better judgments with the help of this information.

- **Upgrades** – These tools and software are regularly upgraded in terms of usability, security, reporting, and other factors.
- **Branding** – These platforms can be customized to reflect your brand colors, needs, and requirements to reinforce organizational culture initiatives.

An HR Analytics Example: Analyzing the Financial Impact of Employee Engagement

Human Resource professionals have to map and collect all necessary data to get started with HR Analytics. Consider, for example, the hypothetical case where an organization wishes to determine the financial impact of Employee Engagement.

To make conclusions based on these statistical inputs, you will require statistics on Employee Engagement and your company's financial performance. So, an organization makes sure to deploy an Employee Engagement Survey once every year. This is an excellent place to start if you want to discover how engaged your employees are at work. The output of this collective data can be used to examine critical working areas. In addition, the ability to effectively forecast the future is nearly impossible to ignore when a wealth of data is available. And it doesn't end there; you can make forecasts in several aspects of your firm, such as which new employee will be the best producer or how much money should be allocated for staff training.

HR Analytics Dashboard

The HR metrics dashboard is essential for Human Resource strategy and planning. It's a tool that helps people make better decisions at work, particularly in the Human Resources department and for other stakeholders. Let's start with the basics before going any further.

The top three functions of an HR dashboard help leaders to:

1 **Monitor Human Capital** – Regular reporting allows HR to keep track of the organization's actions by tracking key workforce KPIs. As a result, new trends can be predicted, and emerging issues can be addressed before negatively influencing the company.
2 **Help HR Performance** – Managers can use reports to learn about any significant changes or developments in their teams. For example, consider the accounting department, which has a high rate of personnel turnover. Managers will be more likely to prioritize employee retention and weigh the risks of replacing a departing employee.
3 **Tackle Problem Areas** – The metrics dashboard offers a great way to tackle problem areas with greater transparency. If the system is transparent and well known, HR will be able to pay more attention to a particular

area that needs improvement. Because HR Analytics are online, the HR metrics dashboard aids in providing this transparency.

Predictive HR Analytics Trends

Here are some of the most important HR Analytics trends for 2022 and beyond:

- **Artificial Intelligence (AI) and Automation in Hiring** – Recruitment will alter dramatically as AI and automation become more prevalent in HR.

Candidates are being screened and contacted via chat and voice assistants. It will also tell the difference between legitimate applications and bogus ones with enhanced filtering capabilities.

Programs for onboarding and training will be increasingly virtual and interactive in the future. Progress in AI, natural language processing (NLP), and machine learning (ML) are the primary reasons behind this.

- **Performance Management** – Performance is reviewed to help managers and teams stay productive and aligned toward achieving organizational goals. By getting more detailed analytics provided by the HR Analytics tools, leaders will improve their recruitment, succession planning, and career pathing.
- **Predictive Reporting** – Rich workforce analytics will help identify attrition risks and preemptively take measures to arrest that. It will help determine the strengths and weaknesses of employees, which will help in designing better and efficient teams.

HR Measurements

HR metrics are data elements or measures used to evaluate the operating effectiveness of HR policies and programs and can serve as operating benchmarks. The term "Workforce Analytics" refers to the computational analysis conducted on current workforce metrics and then uses that data to make value-adding predictions.

Therefore, the development of key HR metrics and the Workforce Analytics performed on that data can guide the creation of great HR measures that lead to organizational effectiveness. In turn, these HR measures can create better overall organizational results. HR departments that utilize these metrics to enhance their effectiveness can demonstrate the value of their policies and programs to executive management (Fica, 2020). Thus, HR metrics and measurements are valuable to the HR department because they build an effective, data-driven people strategy and regularly develop and distribute HR analytical reports (Fica, 2020).

It is one of the most critical HR KPIs to gauge the success of the recruitment process. Key metrics of the recruitment process include the Time-to-Hire Rate and the Cost-per-Hire Rate.

The Time-to-Hire Rate is the average number of days a job is posted until the applicant accepts the offer. The Time-to-Hire Rate can be measured by adding the time (number of days that it took to hire the candidate) for each candidate and dividing it by the number of new hires hired during a specified period. Tracking the Time-to-Hire Rate is important since it can shorten the recruiting process, improve recruiting efficiency, and help in developing a better applicant experience (Strikwerda, 2020).

The Cost-per-Hire Rate identifies how much it costs to hire a new employee. For example, the costs could include the recruiter's time, the listing of the job posting on a third-party site, and time spent interviewing. The Cost-per-Hire Rate can be measured by adding internal and external hiring costs and then dividing that total by the number of employees during a specific period. Analyzing the Cost-per-Hire Rate can be important since it can lead to analyzing different techniques in sourcing, identifying, and then working with the best candidates. It can also find areas where recruitment cost savings can be generated.

A vital HR metric is the HR-to-Employee Ratio. This metric is calculated by dividing the HR department staff by full-time employees and then multiplying by 100 to derive a ratio. If the ratio is high, this could mean that employees are over-specialized or the HR department is not operating with digital efficiency. On the other hand, if this ratio is lower, then the HR department may be understaffed.

Yet another important HR metric is the Total Employee Turnover Rate. The Total Employee Turnover Rate is measured by the number of terminations per year divided by the average number of total employees multiplied by 100 to derive a percentage. Measuring the Total Employee Turnover Rate can assist with understanding the effectiveness of the organization's retention strategies. In addition, this analysis can take corrective actions or plan new initiatives to improve employee relations.

Another HR metric is the Absenteeism Rate. The Absenteeism Rate calculates the average number of days employees are absent, excluding paid time off, in a specific period and dividing by the number of employees. Measuring the Absenteeism Rate indicates how many hours employees invest in the organization.

Other important HR metrics measure Employee Satisfaction and Employee Engagement. Measuring Employee Satisfaction and Employee Engagement assists HR departments and management understand how employees feel about working in a specific organization. The more contented and productive a company's workforce is, the greater its chances of success. Although one of the most challenging measures to collect is Employee Engagement. Surveys can be done utilizing semantic differential scales on valid and accurate questions using relevant psychometric procedures. Measuring these results will provide the measure of Employee Engagement and Satisfaction.

Employee Performance metrics can be developed and tracked by conducting performance self-assessments, peer reviews, and management assessments.

These appraisals can include a 360-degree feedback element to obtain performance improvement and corrective actions (Fica, 2020).

Training and development effectiveness measures are yet another important measure. Measuring training and development effectiveness is a key HR activity. Another measure used to measure training effectiveness is Training Costs per Employee. Accounting for training costs as a separate controllable line item can assist HR departments in making better decisions on developing personnel with continuous learning programs.

Human Resource Metrics Data Comparison

Collecting and analyzing comparative data on Human Resource metrics can be used for benchmarking an organization's metrics with a comparator group. Benchmarking is a method for measuring the effectiveness of processes and systems to enhance organizational performance. HR can utilize benchmarking data to compare their organization against a specific comparator group within the same market segment in a particular industry. For example, comparing the organization's Cost-per-Hire Rate with a similar organization can lead to quite a few analytical questions. Those metrics that stake up well to the benchmark data can help encourage the continuance of those practices that led to the favorable comparison. For example, in terms of recruiting costs, the data from benchmarking may illustrate that current recruiting costs are in line with the industry data.

When comparing with benchmarking data, it is recommended that the comparison results aid decision-making but not exclusively on this data. Therefore, blanket adherence to benchmark data is not recommended. "Best practice" does not necessarily lead to "best fit".

Nowadays, the HR department has many sources of HR metrics benchmarking data. Various data aggregators are increasing their benchmarking services by collecting data from clients. Data is collected on compensation practices, turnover rates, absenteeism, time-to-fill open positions, and how HR functions are staffed (Zielinski, 2018).

One of these reputable sources is Visier. Visier is regarded as a leader in people analytics. Fortune 500 companies have credited Visier for improving their employee retention, Employee Engagement, Diversity Hiring Rate, and more. Visier utilizes data to link workforce analytics to strategic business results, conducting "what-if" analysis and other significant trends in HR Analytics. Visier also utilizes benchmarking to obtain better visibility into the demographics of the workforce, creating strategies to attract great candidates and retain them (Visier, 2021).

Another very important source of HR metrics is PwC's Saratoga Institute offering (mentioned before in this chapter). PwC's Saratoga Institute is acknowledged as the world's leader in workforce measurements. PwC is known for its partnership with hundreds of senior leaders and HR depart-ments from many organizations and industries worldwide. This collaboration involves facilitating a thorough, evidence-based approach to workforce-related decision-making. In terms of analytics, PwC's Saratoga Institute HRIS Workflow integration platform can connect directly into an organization's HRIS to pull raw data. The data is then used to calculate the organization's metrics and merge them into comparator databases producing client-specific metric comparisons which can deliver insight and strategic analysis. In terms of collecting comparative data, PwC can also analyze an organization's macro employee performance against comparator groups based on headcount and revenue in the same or other industries. PwC can also tailor data analytics for peer group comparisons, as well as customize and align an organization's HR/talent benchmarks to the organization's strategic goals (Price Water-house Cooper, n.d.).

In the following table, other relevant HR metrics and measurements are identified and defined:

Hr Metric Or Measurement	Definition (Formula)
Revenue per Employee	Sales Divided by Employees
Span of Control	Employees Divided by Managers
HR Staffing (%)	Employees Divided by HR Professionals, Multiplied by 100
Budgeted Benefit Burden Rate (%)	Benefit Burden for Employees divided by Benefits Budgeted, Multiplied by 100
Compensation and Benefits Cost Revenue	Compensation Costs plus Benefits Costs Divided by Revenue
Average Benefits per Employee	Cost of Benefits Divided by Employee
Recruiting Cost per Employee (Cost per Hire Rate)	Recruiting Costs Divided by Employee
Training Cost per Employee	Training Costs Divided by Employee
Employee Productivity	Productivity (Output) Divided by Employee
Cost-of-Materials, Labor, and Overhead Ratios	Costs Divided by Sales for Each Category
Labor Cost Percentage of Revenue (%)	Labor Cost Divided by Sales, Multiplied by 100
Time to Fill Vacancies	Days with Vacancy Divided by Role
Compensation Impact of Replacement Hires	Salary of Departing Employee minus Salary of New Hire
Pipeline Utilization	Internal Promotions Divided by Outside Hires
First Year of Service Turnover Rate (%)	Measures Hiring Manager Satisfaction, Performance Rating, and New Hire Turnover
Labor Cost Revenue Percent (%)	Assesses the Investment in Labor Costs to Generate Each Dollar of Revenue

As seen in this chapter, HR Analytics is a data-driven method to improve people-related decisions to advance individual and organizational success.

Using cutting-edge firms as a case study, this new curriculum examines various methods for attracting and retaining top people.

Even though organizations have traditionally relied on their employees to be successful, many company executives still depend on important personnel choices on intuition, experience, advice, and guesswork. On the other hand, today's bosses can help their employees make better decisions based on data and rigorous analysis that leads to higher organizational productivity.

References

Fica, T. (2020, January 16). The key HR metrics you should be measuring. Retrieved February 18, 2022 from www.bamboohr.com/blog/key-hr-metrics

HR Advice. (2021, February 24). HR analytics–the treasure hidden behind of effective HR managers. Retrieved December 29, 2021 from https://medium.leaveboard.com/hr-analytics-d8589e91f8b3

Price Waterhouse Cooper. (n.d.). Saratoga: Metrics that can answer the questions about your workforce of the future. Retrieved February 18, 2022 from www.pwc.com/us/en/products/saratoga.html

Question Pro. (2021, July 15). HR analytics: Definition, example, HR metrics dashboard and predictive HR analytics. Retrieved December 29, 2021 from www.questionpro.com/blog/hr-analytics-and-trends/

Question Pro. (n.d.) Workforce analytics: An overview. Retrieved December 29, 2021 from www.questionpro.com/workforce/workforce-analytics.html

Strikwerda, L. (2020, March 18). Shorten time-to-hire by removing these 5 bottlenecks. Retrieved February 18, 2022 from https://learn.g2.com/time-to-hire-metric

Visier. (2021). HR trends 2021: People strategies for an uncertain future. *Visier*. Retrieved from https://hello.visier.com/hr-trends-2021/

Zielinski, D. (2018, February 20). Rise of new consumer-like technologies shake up corporate learning market. Retrieved February 18, 2022 from www.shrm.org/resourcesandtools/hr-topics/technology/pages/rise-of-new-consumer-like-technologies-shakes-up-corporate-learning-market.aspx

Chapter 16

The Human Asset Lifecycle Model (HALM)©

Bashker Biswas

This book made a case for two propositions.

The first proposition is that the very Nature of Work is changing worldwide. This phenomenon has been evolving over more than three decades, and now it has hyper-accelerated because of the Covid-19 Pandemic. The transformation of the Nature of Work has been mainly ushered in by the digitization of work in all areas of the working world. But, since March 2020, the Covid-19 Pandemic and each new variant have also introduced a health security dimension to the already digitally changing Nature of Work.

The second proposition we have presented in this book is that because the Nature of Work is changing, the people dimensions of work also need change. The relationships of how humans will function, operate, and interact will also need to change. And these are the arguments, analyses, and solutions we have presented in the book.

The Case for Change

This then leads to the proposition that an organization's role, functional orientations, and strategic directions of people specialists (currently designated as Human Resource Management Professionals) will also need to change.

An effective structure needs to be developed for the Human Resource function and its programs and policies in our New World. There is a New Normal to how jobs are being designed. There is a New Normal to how human talent is acquired. There is a New Normal on how work is performed. There is a New Normal in employment relationships and contracts. There is a New Normal for working and employment conditions. And, there is a New Normal on how workers feel appreciated.

A critical review of the principles and assumptions of the current formulations and structures of Human Resource Management needs to be conducted. The need to change should focus on the obsolescence of the functional approach and replace it with a structure for ongoing Human Capital or Resources Management in The Digital Age. Thus, radically different employer-employee contracts and relationships need to be put in place with an emphasis on valuing the people.

DOI: 10.4324/9781003122272-16

In the March 28–April 3 issue of the *Economist* in an article titled, "The Importance of People", it said that the Covid-19 Pandemic brought into focus the changing role of the "People", or Human Resource Management function. This laid the stage for a changed Human Resource Management paradigm brought upon by externally and internally induced forces of change. For the right HR leader, this is the "Perfect Opportunity" (The Economist, 2020).

This book has laid out the game plan for this "Perfect Opportunity".

Companies need to recognize and explore the changing job and work trends as we have in this book. Major questions need to be asked and answered. New structures, processes, and systems need to be discussed, analyzed, and proposed that create a thriving environment for all management and workers.

Organizations need to recognize the history and evolution of the current Employment Contract. In reviewing our proposed conceptual structure of these workforce relationships, they should create and reinforce a new Employment Contract appropriate for their unique digital workplace.

Business leaders need to recognize that in The Digital Age, the very nature of how work is performed is changing. Many of the traditional employment categories are becoming obsolete. The designations of Blue-Collar and White-Collar work may not be appropriate anymore. The newer concepts of work categories, such as contingent work, flexible work, and so on, should be crafted and utilized toward maximizing productivity.

Companies need to recognize that the very Nature of Work has changed, and now people work in newer ways such as remotely, on specific "Gigs", in a collaborative manner, and in shared roles. The way employers or managers relate to workers might need to be revisited. The boss-subordinate relationship is changing toward a more shared relationship. Technology may even take over many of the administrative activities of managers, so an emphasis should be placed on investing in the human element that will still be needed to do the things automation cannot.

Organizations need to recognize that a new form of freelance worker is thriving and meeting the needs of consumers everywhere. These "Gig Workers" are becoming a major component of many modern work environments. The workers are neither guaranteed steady work nor regular compensation and benefits, nor do they want them. Yet, they are an integral part of modern workforces. Companies need to ask how they may best utilize their workers and integrate them into their overall organizational culture.

Business leaders need to recognize that since the onset of the Covid-19 Pandemic, remote work has led to higher productivity and employee effectiveness. As the Covid-19 Pandemic comes to an end, it is most likely that this type of work will become more prevalent and regular in modern work environments. Many of their newer remote workers won't even live in the same state. Therefore, companies need to address the unique needs of remote workers and modify the unique Human Resource processes that best serve them.

Companies need to recognize and study the opportunities that these digital communities have in collaborative efforts. This challenge will be important for Human Resource professionals attempting to build high-performing work teams in digital environments because we know that cultures that support teamwork are powerful. Human Resource challenges lie in building a culture of social cohesion in a workforce with disparate compositions. Companies need to reconsider how to build power corporate cultures that include these virtual teams using the required levels of group intelligence, speed, problem-solving, and learning that only a culture supported by technology can deliver.

Organizations need to recognize and examine individual and team behavior in the workplace and their impact on work performance. Leaders need to examine subject areas such as motivation, leadership, communication, and teamwork in the context of our New World.

Business leaders need to recognize the impact our productivity continues to have on the environment and place the custodianship of Green Initiatives into the Human Resource department. A Green Human Resource approach looks at all the functions and activities of the company's effort within the context of sustainability and earth-friendly practices and leads them toward real societal change. HR specialists are best positioned to lead these efforts successfully.

Companies need to recognize and find ways to place employees as owners to enhance the organization's value to key stakeholders such as customers and shareholder owners in turn. Human Resource departments can implement programs to extend employee ownership to increase their perceptions of partnership that leads to higher outcomes.

Organizations need to recognize the shortcomings of current compensation systems by tracing the foundations and evolutions that created them. Instead, companies should modify their current rewards and formulate new rewards that are more meaningful in today's digital workplace. They should consider our new philosophy of paying the person or person-based pay instead.

Business leaders need to recognize and leverage the benefits of using the Human Cloud platforms that enable work arrangements and work completions to be established and executed through a digital/online platform. They can control work being done through digital media channels including crowd-sourcing, online work services, and online staffing and onboarding platforms easily by using these platforms.

Companies need to recognize that many of the current labor laws have little to no impact in the changing digital workplace. Leaders should study the evolution and environmental factors governing the passing of the current laws and how past work environments led to their passage. Then, they can begin working with their local, state, and federal representatives to help pass new protections for their workforce and to ensure a level-playing ground among their competitors. This will help to avoid the clashes of labor and management of the past.

Organizations need to recognize that the whole area of people data analytics and measurements is undergoing significant changes. The inadequacies of current accounting rules and regulations regarding the proper accounting of Human Capital monetary outlay should be noted. Companies should implement Human Resource accounting concepts to analyze their people-related costs. HR leaders can use new sensors, and "big data" optimizes work in various organizational units while improving the effectiveness of different Human Resource policies.

The Era of Human Asset Capital Management

In recent times, Human Capital has become a central concept in labor economics and macroeconomics, economic growth theory, development economics, the economics of education, and the theory and practice of HR Management and strategic planning.

Investments in knowledge, training, and redeploying employee skills can be compared to investments in more efficient machines to improve labor productivity. Resources spent in education, training, and other forms of Human Capital investments can be analyzed, measured, and understood similarly to how economists, accountants, and financiers understand investments in physical capital like factories and equipment.

The American Accounting Association has defined Human Capital accounting as the process of identifying and measuring data from Human Resources and communicating this information to interested parties. Firms increasingly recognize the worth of their firm's Human Capital. Therefore, the accounting profession is faced with the challenge of providing a framework for measuring and accounting Human Capital Resources and then providing that information within financial reporting systems.

But the vagaries of accurate measurement of Human Capital continue to plague the advocates of Human Capital Management. So, there are still challenges to be addressed if the Human Capital framework is to be truly embraced. One such roadblock is how current accounting standards measure and account for Human Capital investments.

The Human Element of Labor: Costs or Expenses?

Is the human element of labor outlays cost or expense? What is the difference? Where can one find Human Resource expenditures in the current accounting structure and system? Are the current classifications within the accounting framework appropriate? What changes can one anticipate in the current expense/cost classification resulting from the differences in how work is currently done and how it will be done in the future? These and other questions need to be answered if we consider the labor element as Human Capital on par with financial capital.

The words "cost" and "expense" are used interchangeably in accounting. But a cost incurred can be an asset or expense in the current accounting standards.

Especially in transactions like acquiring a physical asset, the cost classification can become an important decision. For example, when a physical asset is acquired, there could be many costs involved, such as purchase price, freight costs, and installation costs. So, the accountant must decide which cost to include as an asset and which costs should be expensed immediately. Those costs that are expensed immediately can be called revenue expenditures. And costs that are not expensed immediately but are included in asset accounts are referred to as capital expenditures.

An expense is, in actuality, a cost that is expended in producing the revenue for the business. In other words, expenses are those monetary outlays that flow through to determine the profit or loss, whereas costs that have not been used up remain a cost and are reported in the balance sheet as an asset with the current value.

Consider the following as an example of how the rhetoric of the value of Human Capital is not in sync with current accounting thinking on how to account for the value of Human Capital.

Let's consider monetary outlays for research scientists within a firm – a key Human Capital investment. Suppose a firm buys a laboratory machine for the research lab. The cost of this machine might be $20,000 with an additional $5,000 expensed for installing the machine. As of the date the firm acquires this machine, the current accounting system will increase an asset account by debiting that account with the total purchase cost of the machine plus all costs necessary to make the machine ready to use. And then, the accountant would periodically record a debit entry to a depreciation expense account spread over the machine's useful life, using an acceptable depreciation schedule. This expense would then be recorded to determine profit or loss, matching it against the current period's revenue.

Whereas, if the same firm were to hire a research scientist during the same period, the costs that the firm incurred to hire that scientist, namely salary, benefits, recruitment advertising, search fees (which can be pretty significant), interviewing costs, and other hiring costs, will all be currently expensed and reported in the income statement. This can lead to a distortion in income measurement because the research scientist's service will, in reality, extend over more than one year. Human assets certainly add value to a firm for more than a mere one year. But currently, the accounting rules require that all of the Human Resource cost outlays be expensed during the current period. This is because the individual contribution of the scientist is indeed an asset. But the accounting measurement system does not consider it as such.

Total compensation-related outlays for these scientists are all considered expenses for the current period. But in accounting systems, the cost outlays for physical products (the machines the scientists use) are considered assets and are only expensed over a period of time – their useful life. The scientist's useful life to the organization is only limited to one year, thus depreciating the scientist's intrinsic value over only one year.

The issue of reporting intangibles also needs to be discussed in connection with recording Human Capital outlays. Under current accounting standards, intellectual property that an employee brings and utilizes within the employment setting is not considered a recognizable asset. The current accounting system only records certain other intangibles, such as copyrights, patents, and trademarks, as assets. The irony is that the intangibles are the employees' outputs with specifically valuable intellectual property. In the era of knowledge work, this is a major roadblock to truly valuing the Human Capital of a firm.

In many cases, there can be a big difference in book value versus the market value of the assets. For example, in a recent year, Google (now Alphabet) had stockholder's equity value of $22.7 billion in their financial books. In contrast, Google's market value during the same period as determined by multiplying Google's market price of its shares by the number of outstanding shares was about $179 billion. Naturally, such a vast difference undermines financial reporting. However, it can be assumed that most of this significant difference is because of not recognized intangibles. And one of the most significant intangibles to the value of Google is its Human Capital assets.

Thus, one can safely say that there is a lack of clarity within the current accounting standards framework as to how and where Human Capital monetary outlays are classified in accounting systems.

Many academics and industrial subject matter experts have developed Human Capital measurement processes and formulae. As a result, various valid measurement frameworks have been created. Moreover, these measurement techniques have been structured to meet the current accounting standards that establish the criteria as to whether something is considered an "asset" in the accounting systems of a firm. But the author contends that a fundamental change in conceptual thinking needs to occur in the mindsets of the accounting standard-setting bodies, that is, International Financial Reporting Standards and U.S. General Accepted Accounting Principles. These rulemaking bodies have to look at Human Capital expenditures as capital costs and not operating expenses, in line with the other factors of production.

Human Capital is the key strategic factor that drives the return on all tangible capital investments. Human Resources will continue to become a critical part of an organization's intangible assets in the knowledge economy. Firms, therefore, must adapt their financial practices to account for intangibles giving due consideration to Human Capital assets.

A Fleeting Intangible Asset

Currently, knowledge workers only plan on staying with an employer for just a few years because their intrinsic value is not captured under the current accounting standards. Unless a firm can retain a knowledge worker, that person becomes a very fleeting intangible asset. An improved Human Capital accounting system will account for the fact that retaining the best workers and turning over nonperformers enhance the firm's value.

Our good news and bad news predictions for the future underscore the necessity of embracing the realities of intangibles. The good news is that we have much better technology at our fingertips than we did 25 years ago. And the bad news is, technology is changing so quickly that we have difficulty keeping up with it. Therefore, firms must be smarter when it comes to managing their intangibles, especially Human Capital intangibles.

The Human Asset Lifecycle Model (HALM)©

Thus, as we end this book, here we present a whole new Human Capital Management process model:

The Human Asset Lifecycle Model (HALM)© encapsulates and integrates most of the changed Human Capital initiatives discussed in the book. The model groups the required new or revised Human Capital activities, programs, and initiatives into a logical sequence with a strategic human asset management paradigm. Strategic Chief Human Resource Officers can use this strategic Human Resource model as the road map for Human Capital Management in the New World. HALM organizes the whole Human Capital Management function into a process model, giving it a new look. The thinking is based on

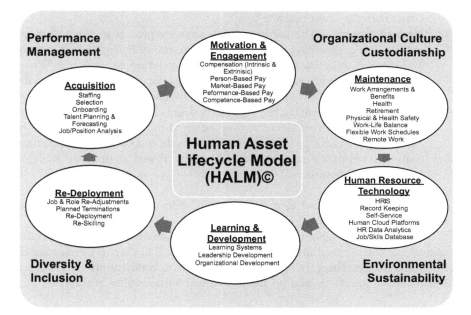

Figure 16.1 Human Asset Lifecycle Model (HALM)©

modern business management principles such as process management and the networked and connected organization.

1   **Acquisition** – It starts with the strategic acquisition of human assets. Gone are the days of mere recruiting and staffing. Instead, we need to change the paradigm in the new Human Capital mindset and talk about the effectively planned acquisition of human assets.

2   **Motivation and Engagement** – We move on to the unique dimension involved in managing human assets, which is motivating the acquired assets. The various programs needed to keep the assets motivated and engaged fall within this process link.

3   **Maintenance** – Then comes the maintenance of the human asset. The programs and initiatives within this link all need to be designed and developed with all the new thinking discussed in this book that is related to the changing Nature of Work.

4   **Human Resource Technology** – Next, we move on to the whole new area of Human Resource technology that must be deployed to stay in sync with the digitized workplace. All modern Human Capital digital technologies that are the best fit for the organization must be considered.

5   **Learning and Development** – Then we move on to learning and development. Continuous learning must be a critical strategic pillar in the new digitized workplace. Therefore, constant learning and development must be considered, developed, and implemented, considering the "best fit" rather than the "best practice".

6   **Redeployment** – The last link in this strategic process is asset redeployment. Gone are the days, as this book has continuously maintained, merely looking at human asset expenditures as an operating expenditure. When human assets are in excess of current business needs, those assets cannot be eliminated for short-term profit. These shortsighted actions have long-term costs both internal to the organization and externally and existentially. Therefore, careful consideration must be given to redeploying temporarily excess human assets into other areas both inside and outside the organization. This requires a mindset reset. However, creative options are available and should be considered.

As HALM is illustrated as a cycle process, once Redeployment has been made, the lifecycle starts all over again.

Most important, these main links in the HALM need to operate within the critical workplace environments of our New World. These are (1) Performance Management Systems, (2) Organizational Culture Custodianship, (3) Diversity and Inclusion initiatives, and (4) Environmental Sustainability initiatives.

Closing Remarks

We have advocated the need for a mindset change in human asset management. No more can we merely look at the human element as resources. This resource mentality is an inside-out view of managing human assets. Because of the many current external forces affecting the human side of the enterprise in the new digitized workplace, now is the best time to look at human asset management from the outside in. Our New World continues to change, and top business leaders will be those who understand the past, examine their present, and make the necessary changes in their organizations for the future!

References

Coyle, D. (2018). *The culture code: The secrets of highly successful groups.* New York: Bantam.
The Economist. (2020). *The importance of people: The coronavirus crisis thrusts corporate HR chiefs into the spotlight.* London: The Economist.

Index

Printed in the United States
by Baker & Taylor Publisher Services